Trust and Security
in Collaborative Computing

SERIES IN COMPUTER AND NETWORK SECURITY

Series Editors: *Yi Pan (Georgia State Univ., USA) and*
Yang Xiao (Univ. of Alabama, USA)

COMPUTER AND NETWORK SECURITY

Vol. 2

Trust and Security
in Collaborative Computing

Xukai Zou
Indiana University-Purdue University Indianapolis, USA

Yuan-Shun Dai
University of Tennessee, USA

Yi Pan
Georgia State University, USA

 World Scientific

NEW JERSEY · LONDON · SINGAPORE · BEIJING · SHANGHAI · HONG KONG · TAIPEI · CHENNAI

Published by

World Scientific Publishing Co. Pte. Ltd.

5 Toh Tuck Link, Singapore 596224

USA office: 27 Warren Street, Suite 401-402, Hackensack, NJ 07601

UK office: 57 Shelton Street, Covent Garden, London WC2H 9HE

British Library Cataloguing-in-Publication Data
A catalogue record for this book is available from the British Library.

ISBN-13 978-981-270-368-2
ISBN-10 981-270-368-3

Printed in Singapore.

This book is dedicated to Xukai's wife Suqin and Yuanshun's wife Jiafeng. Yi Pan would like to thank Sherry, Marissa and Anna for their love, support and encouragement during the preparation of the book.

Preface

Information and communication technologies, along with society's drive for collaboration in the modern world, make "collaborative computing" and its applications possible and even necessary. Trust in such an environment will eventually determine its success and popularity due to people's desire for privacy, integrity and reliability. Today's Internet and existing networks are not trust-oriented in design and might be compromised by many untrustworthy factors, such as hackers, viruses, spam, faults, and system failures. Compared to the two-party interaction model (i.e., the client-server service model), collaborative computing environments are group-oriented, involve a large number of users and shared resources, and are complex, dynamic, distributed, and heterogeneous. These factors offer a good environment for hostile elements to lurk. Besides the previously mentioned untrustworthy factors, collaborative computing environments suffer from dangerous attacks by malicious internal members. Those problems restrain full utilization of the computer systems in collaborative computing. The trusted and secure collaborative computing is one of the objectives for the next generation of the Internet, which is trustworthy and security-oriented. This monograph summarizes the authors' and other researchers' efforts to develop such a trusted environment that possesses high security and reliability for the collaborative computing. The important modules composing the trusted and secure computing environment are elaborated, including Secure Group Communication, Access Control, Dependability, Key Management, Intrusion Detection, and Trace Back. The theories and technologies in this book are illustrated with examples to help readers easily understand. One of the examples in collaborative computing is Grid computing that is popular today. The monograph also discusses security and reliability in grid computing. One typical collaborative computing application is medical practice and healthcare research based on medical information systems. A real project for developing a nationwide medical information system with high dependability and security is described.

X. Zou, Y. Dai and Y. Pan

Acknowledgments

The authors would like to thank many people for their help during the writing and publishing of the book. We thank the colleagues from World Scientific Inc. for their support and guidance to the book. We also thank the help on editing some content from our students Leah Cardaci, Ashhar Madni and our lead network engineer Scott Orr, on drawing some figures from our students Manish Madhusoodan and Xiang Ran, and on proof-reading from Lori M. Bruns, Associate Faculty in the English Department at IUPUI.

This work was partially supported by the U.S. NSF grant CCR-0311577 and IUPUI RSFG (Research Support Funding Grant).

Contents

List of Figures

List of Tables

Chapter 1

Introduction

1.1 Overview of Trusted Collaborative Computing

Information and communication technologies, along with society's drive for collaboration in the modern world, make "collaborative computing" (CC) and its applications possible and necessary. Typical CC applications include, but are not limited to, multi-party military actions, tele-conferencing, tele-medicine, interactive and collaborative decision making, grid-computing, information distribution, and pay per view services. Trust in such an environment can eventually determine its success and popularity due to the corporate and human's desire for confidentiality and integrity of their personal and/or shared information. The current Internet is not security-oriented by design. Security patches and more powerful computing/storage resources available to hackers may result in more security vulnerabilities. Compared to the two-party interaction model (such as the client-server service model), CC environments are group-oriented, involve a large number of entities and shared resources, are complex, dynamic, distributed, and heterogeneous and may possibly even include hostile elements. Systems experience failures due to internal faults and external attacks from hostile entities. In addition, there is the problem of insider threats, by which attacks are from malicious parties inside the organizations or members of CC groups. Consequently, building a Trusted Collaborative Computing (TCC) environment is very difficult and requires a long term persevering endeavor.

The theme of TCC is to make CC environments and applications highly secure and dependable and be able to not only protect systems against components failures but also defend against external attacks, even the attacks from internal malicious users. TCC will be able to not only migrate traditional CC applications from untrustworthy environments to a secure and reliable platform, but also provide security guarantee/services for new emerging CC applications. From the technical point of view, TCC would encompass both security and reliability and seek the seamless integration of advanced security and reliability technologies.

TCC environments are characterized by collaborative tasks which require multiple entities to work together and share their resources. The first key issue in this environment is that multiple participating entities must communicate securely among one another. IP multicast provides efficient transmission of messages to a group of users; however, the open nature of IP multicast makes it unable to provide strong confidentiality. Thus, secure group-oriented communication is the first fundamental function for TCC. Another key requirement is related to resource sharing and data exchange. Access to shared resources/data must be finely controlled; otherwise attackers and malicious users can access resources to which they are not entitled to access, abuse, tamper, and even damage the resources. Thus selective data sharing, at different granularity levels and along with access control, becomes another fundamental function. These two classes of fundamental functions should be sufficiently flexible in supporting various possible forms of interactive access relations between the parties and the resources in the system. Consequently, we can identify four fundamental security requirements for TCC: secure group communication (SGC), secure dynamic conferencing (SDC), differential access control (DIF-AC), and hierarchical access control (HAC). Cryptography is a powerful tool to support all these functions.

As is well known, key management is the most important yet difficult issue in such context. How to generate, distribute, update, and revoke keys in large and dynamic environments is an important challenge. This book covers and classifies typical key management schemes for these security functions.

Intrusion is a very serious security problem in computing and communication systems. Intruding attacks, such as Denial of Services (DoS), are easily launched but very difficult to defend. Such attacks exist in CC environments without doubt, moreover, they are more serious in CC environments because the attacks can be launched by internal malicious users and/or the collusion among internal users and/or external attackers. Knowing intrusion attacks and becoming familiar with intrusion detection and defense technologies are crucial for designing and implementing TCC environments. This book presents a comprehensive survey and classification about intruding attacks, detection and response mechanisms, and trace back technologies.

Reliability is a coherent requirement and feature of TCC. A fault or failure from any part/component of TCC environments would degrade the performance of the systems and affect multiple party collaboration and interaction; furthermore, it may have serious consequences. For example, it could be potentially disastrous if a patient's records fail to be loaded due to system failures and they are unavailable in the event of a life-threatening emergency. Grid computing is a recently developed technology for complex systems with large-scale resource sharing, wide-area communication, and multi-institutional collaboration. It could become a potential platform hosting TCC framework and applications. Therefore, this book will discuss advanced reliability technologies in the context of grid computing environments. Moreover, it also contributes one chapter on the security issues in grid computing.

The medical information system (MIS) is a typical collaborative computing application in which physicians, nurses, professors, researchers, health insurance personnel, etc. share patient information (including text, images, multimedia data) and collaboratively conduct critical tasks via the networked system. On one hand, people would be willing to step into the MIS age only when their privacy and integrity can be protected and guaranteed within MIS systems. On the other hand, only secure and reliable MIS systems would provide safe and solid medical and health care services to people. This book devotes one chapter to discuss trusted and seamless MIS systems, including why security and reliability technologies are necessary and how they can be integrated with the existing MIS systems to make the systems highly secure and dependable.

In the rest of this chapter, we present basic concepts and preliminaries used in the remainder of the book. These include: one-way functions, (one-way) hash function, the Chinese Remainder Theorem (CRT), the Discrete Logarithm Problem (DLP), and secret sharing. Included are also universal generating function, graph theory, and Bayesian approach, fault-tree analysis, binary decision diagram, and reliability block diagram.

1.2 Basic Concepts in Terms of Security

Definition 1.1. A function $F = f(x)$ is called a one-way function if it is easy to compute F given x however it is computationally difficult to compute a preimage x given F.

Definition 1.2. A function $F = f(x)$ is called a (cryptographic) hash function if it is a mapping: $\{0,1\}^* \to \{0,1\}^n$ (i.e., from a bit-string of arbitrary length to a bit-string of fixed length) and satisfies the following three properties [Stinson (1995)]:

(1) One-way, that is, given $F \in \{0,1\}^n$, it is difficult to find an $x \in \{0,1\}^*$ such that $F = f(x)$.

(2) Matching resistant, that is: given $x \in \{0,1\}^*$, it is difficult to find a $x' \in \{0,1\}^*$ such that $f(x') = f(x)$

(3) Collision resistant, that is, it is difficult to find $x, x' \in \{0,1\}^*$ such that $f(x') = f(x)$.

It is worthy to mention that in many situations, the one-way function is utilized in the form of $F = f(x, y)$. It has two inputs x, y and the two inputs can form a binary string by some operations such as concatenation, exclusive-OR, etc.

The most important feature of a cryptosystem or secure group communication scheme is its strength in preventing opponents (attackers) from breaking the system. There are two basic mechanisms to discuss the security of a cryptosystem: *computational security* and *unconditional security* [Stinson (1995)].

Definition 1.3. A cryptosystem is defined to be computationally secure if the best algorithm for breaking it requires at least N operations, where N is some specified, very large number. On the other hand, a cryptosystem is defined to be unconditionally secure if it cannot be broken by attackers, even if the attackers collude and have infinite computational resources [Stinson (1995)].

Unconditional security implies that when an opponent does not know the secret key k, then k appears to him as a random element in the key space; that is, the opponent has no way of distinguishing the key k from any other element in the key space. As for computational security, in general, a computationally secure cryptosystem utilizes one-way functions. A prominent example is a public-key based system, which is always computationally secure, but never unconditionally secure. On the contrary, secret-key based systems generally belong to the category of unconditional security.

Another approach used to discuss the security of secure group communications and hierarchical access control, is that of *k-resilient security*.

Definition 1.4. A scheme (system) is said to have *k-resilient security* if it is secure against the collusion of any subset of up-to k opponents but cannot defend against the collusion of some $k + 1$ or more opponents.

For k-resilient security, the value k is a system security parameter and can be set/selected during the system setup. In general, the larger the k is, the more secure a system will be. In contrast, the system will become more inefficient in terms of both space and time complexity.

The Discrete Logarithm Problem (DLP) is the basis of many cryptographic primitives including the ElGamal public-key cryptosystem [ElGamal (1985); Stinson (1995)], the Diffie-Hellman key exchange protocol, and the ElGamal signature scheme [ElGamal (1985); Stinson (1995)]. The following is its definition [Stinson (1995)].

Definition 1.5. Let G be a cyclic group of very large finite order n, which without loss of generality we denote multiplicatively. Let $\alpha \in G$ be a generator of G, thus, for any element $\beta \in G$, there is a unique positive integer a, $0 \leq a \leq n - 1$ such that $\beta = \alpha^a$. The related Discrete Logarithm Problem (DLP) can be stated as follows: Given the group G, the generator α and an element $\beta \in G$, determine the unique $a \in [0, n - 1]$ such that $\beta = \alpha^a$. We denote the integer a by $log_\alpha \beta$.

We wish to point out that the intractability (or otherwise) of DLP is not intrinsically a group-theoretic property, but rather depends on the representation of the particular cyclic group G. Note for example that every cyclic group of order n is isomorphic to the additive group $\mathbb{Z}_n$ under addition modulo n. However, if α is a generator of $\mathbb{Z}_n$ then gcd $(\alpha, n) = 1$, and if β is an arbitrary element of $\mathbb{Z}_n$, the discrete logarithm problem now becomes $a\alpha = \beta$. However, since gcd $(\alpha, n) = 1$, α has a multiplicative inverse, say γ, in the ring $(\mathbb{Z}_n, +, \cdot)$, which can be efficiently computed by means of the Euclidean algorithm. We then have that $a = \beta\gamma \bmod n$, and the DLP has a trivial solution, independently of n.

In general, DLP is intractable in the cyclic multiplicative group $\mathbb{F}^*$ of a finite field $\mathbb{F} = \mathbb{F}_q = GF(q)$ of order $q = p^m$. DLP is also generally intractable in very large cyclic components of a chosen elliptic curve $\mathcal{E}$ over a finite field $\mathbb{F}_q$. In both the finite field and elliptic curve case the order of the cyclic group must be such that certain well known attacks cannot be mounted.

In the case where we work with a field $\mathbb{Z}_p$ of prime order p, The DLP is described in a simpler way as follows:

Definition 1.6. Let p be a large prime and $\alpha \in \mathbb{Z}_p$ a primitive element (i.e., generator) of $\mathbb{Z}_p^*$. The question is: given any $\beta \in \mathbb{Z}_p^*$, find the unique integer a, $0 \leq a \leq p - 2$ such that $\alpha^a \equiv \beta (\text{mod } p)$. As before we denote the integer a by $log_\alpha\beta$.

In the latter case also, care should be exercised in the choice of p so that certain known attacks will not compromise the DLP. It is rather clear that for secure choices of the parameters, the DLP problem induces, in fact, a one-way function. Thus, any system or protocol based on DLP is *computationally secure*.

The Chinese Remainder Theorem (CRT) is used as a theoretical foundation and practical tool in many cryptosystems as well as schemes for secure group communications, such as the Secure Lock [Chiou and W.T.Chen (1989)]. We review the CRT below (See also [Stinson (1995)].)

Theorem 1.1. *Suppose* $N_1, \ldots, N_r$ *are pairwise relatively prime positive integers, i.e.,* $gcd(N_i, N_j) = 1$ *if* $i \neq j$, *and let* $N = N_1 \cdot N_2 \cdots N_r$. *For any given integers* $a_1, \ldots, a_r$, *consider the following system of congruences:*

$$x \equiv a_1 \ (\text{mod } N_1)$$
$$x \equiv a_2 \ (\text{mod } N_2)$$
$$\vdots$$
$$x \equiv a_r \ (\text{mod } N_r).$$

Then the system has a unique solution modulo N, namely :

$$x \equiv \sum_{i=1}^{r} a_i n_i y_i \ (\text{mod } N)$$

where $n_i = N/N_i$ *and* $y_i = n_i^{-1} \ (\text{mod } N_i)$ *(i.e.* y_i *is the multiplicative inverse of n_i modulo N_i). On the other hand, given any $x \in \mathbb{Z}_N$, $a_1, \ldots, a_r$ can be uniquely computed as* $a_i \equiv x \bmod N_i$.

There are two kinds of cryptosystems: *secret-key* (or *symmetric*) *cryptosystems* and *public-key* (or *asymmetric*) *cryptosystems*.

In a secret-key cryptosystem, the sender and receiver share a common secret key k, belonging to a very large set of possible keys, the *key space* $\mathcal{K}$. Each key $k \in \mathcal{K}$ uniquely determines functions e_k (the *encryption transformation*) and d_k (the *decryption transformation*). The bijections e_k and d_k are inverses of each other under composition of functions, and each can easily be derived from the other. Therefore secret-key cryptosystems are also called *symmetric cryptosystems*. The domain $\mathcal{P}$ and co-domain $\mathcal{C}$ of e_k are very large sets, and in many applications, $\mathcal{P} = \mathcal{C}$, in which case e_k and d_k are permutations on the *message space* $\mathcal{M} = \mathcal{P} = \mathcal{C}$.

In *public-key* cryptosystems, two transformations e_A (*encryption*) and d_A (*decryption*) are determined by each communicant A. These transformations are bijections and inverses of each other as in the case of secret-key cryptosystems above. However, in this case it is computationally infeasible to determine d_A given e_A, and equally infeasible to determine e_A from d_A. The transformation e_A is made public, while d_A is kept secret, known only by A. When participant B wishes to send a secure message x to A, he/she looks up e_A from a public directory, computes $y = e_A(x)$ and sends y to A. To recover the message, A computes $d_A(y) = d_A(e_A(x)) = x$.

RSA is one of the most widely-used public-key cryptosystems. RSA is based on the fact that no efficient algorithms are known (except on a quantum computer) to find the factorization of a large integer as the product of prime factors. In contrast, the problem of determining whether a given integer is prime (or composite) can be solved efficiently by both probabilistic algorithms [Koblitz (1994); Menezes *et al.* (1996)], and recently by a deterministic algorithm [Agrawal *et al.* (2002)]. In particular, if $n = pq$ is the product of two primes, the multiplicative group of units $\mathbb{Z}_n^*$, of the ring $\mathbb{Z}_n$, has order $\phi(n) = (p-1)(q-1)$, where $\phi(.)$ denotes Euler's ϕ function. It is now easy to see that knowledge of $\phi(n)$ is equivalent to knowing the factorization of n. If $x \in \mathbb{Z}_n^*$ then $x^{\phi(n)} \equiv 1 \bmod n$, (Fermat's little theorem), and RSA is based on this fact.

Because the RSA cryptosystem involves arithmetic with very large integers, the encryption and decryption operations are rather slow and the system is used mostly in a large number of key management and other cryptographic protocols rather than for message encryption. It is important to note that from a theoretical point of view RSA can be seen as a system based on the fact that the order of the underlying group ($\mathbb{Z}_n^*$) is not publicly known.

The formal definition of RSA is as follows.

Definition 1.7. Let $n = pq$ where p and q are large primes. Let the ciphertext space and the plaintext space be both $\mathbb{Z}_n$, and define
$$\mathcal{K} = \{(n, p, q, a, b) : ab \equiv 1 \bmod \phi(n)\}.$$
For $K = (n, p, q, a, b)$, define
$$\text{the encryption rule as } e_K(x) = x^b \bmod n$$
and

the decryption rule as $d_K(y) = y^a \bmod n$

$(x, y \in \mathbb{Z}_n)$. The values n, b comprise the public key, and the values p, q, a form the private key.

It is rather interesting to note that $x^{ab} \equiv x \bmod n$ for all $x \in \mathbb{Z}_n$ rather than just the units of $\mathbb{Z}_n$.

One of the most difficult problems in secret-key cryptosystems is to establish a secret key between two communicants. In 1976, Diffie and Hellman proposed an elegant protocol, based on DLP , for two parties to achieve a shared secret key over an insecure channel. This is the well known *Diffie-Hellman key exchange* protocol [Diffie and Hellman (1976)]. We give its formal definition as follows.

Definition 1.8. Suppose p is a large prime and g is a generator of $\mathbb{Z}_p^*$ such that the DLP problem in $\mathbb{Z}_p^*$ is intractable. Parameters p and g are publicly known to members m_1 and m_2. Member m_1 selects a random number $a_1 \in [1, p-2]$, computes[1] $b_1 = g^{a_1} \bmod p$, and sends b_1 to m_2 over the insecure channel. Similarly, m_2 selects a random number $a_2 \in [1, p-2]$, computes $b_2 = g^{a_2} \bmod p$, and sends b_2 to m_1. As a result, each of m_1, m_2 is able to compute the shared secret key $SK = b_2^{a_1} = g^{a_1 a_2} = b_1^{a_2} \bmod p$.

However any individual other than m_1 or m_2 cannot compute SK even if he/she knows the public parameters p, g and has intercepted the public components b_1 and b_2. For $i \in \{1, 2\}$, a_i is called the *Diffie-Hellman private share* or simply *private share* of m_i, and b_i the *Diffie-Hellman disguised public share* or simply *public share* of m_i. We call the derived secret key $SK = g^{a_1 a_2}$ a DH key.

Secret sharing schemes are secure schemes which recover a *secret* (the key) from an appropriate number of *shares* belonging to particular privileged subsets S_i of participants. Combining the shares of all the members of such a privileged subset S_i yields complete knowledge of the secret, but combining shares of members of any proper subset $T \subset S_i$ yields absolutely no information about the secret. An elegant implementation of secret sharing is Shamir's (k, n) Threshold scheme [Shamir (1979a)], described below.

This scheme is based on the polynomial interpolation. Given k points $(x_1, y_1), \ldots, (x_k, y_k)$ with distinct x_i in a two-dimension plane, there is one and only one polynomial $q(x)$ of degree k-1 such that $q(x_i) = y_i$ for all i.

---

[1] In a Diffie-Hellman based system, any operation will be performed by mod p. We often omit the mod p for simplicity.

To divide the secret data D into n pieces D_i $(i = 1, \cdots, n)$, we pick a random k-1 degree polynomial, $q(x) = a_0 + a_1 x + a_2 x^2 + \cdots + a_{k-1} x^{k-1}$ in which $a_0 = D$, and evaluate: $D_1 = q(1), \ldots, D_i = q(i), \ldots, D_n = q(n)$.

Given any subset of k of these D_i values (together with their identifying indices), we can find the coefficients of $q(x)$ by interpolation, and then evaluate $D = q(0)$. Knowledge of k-1 of these values is not enough to compute D. The formal definition is as follows.

Definition 1.9. Given any secret D to share (suppose D is an integer), we pick a prime p which is larger than both D and n, where n is the number of users. The coefficients $a_0, \ldots, a_{k-1}$ in $q(x)$ are randomly chosen from a uniform distribution over the integers in $[0,p)$, and the values $D_1, \ldots, D_n$ are computed $D_1 = q(1), \ldots, D_i = q(i), \ldots, D_n = q(n)$ modulo p. Finally, each user U_i is given its share D_i.

This (k, n) threshold scheme has some interesting properties:

- The size of each share does not exceed that of the original secret.
- When k is kept fixed, D_i pieces can be dynamically added or removed without affecting the other D_i pieces.
- It is easy to change the D_i pieces without changing the original secret D - all we need is a new polynomial $q(x)$ with the same a_0. This method would enhance the security because the pieces exposed by security breaches cannot be accumulated unless all of them are values of the same version of the $q(x)$ polynomial.
- A hierarchical scheme can be obtained in which the number of pieces needed to determine D depends on an individual's importance. For example, a person of the higher importance can be given two or more shares.

1.3   Basic Concepts in Terms of Reliability

Reliability is the analysis of failures, their causes and consequences. It is the most important characteristic of product quality, as things must work satisfactorily before considering other quality attributes. Usually, specific performance measures can be embedded into reliability analysis by the fact that if the performance is below a certain level, a failure can be said to have occurred.

The commonly used definition of reliability is the following.

Definition 1.10. *Reliability* is the probability that the system will perform its intended function under specified working condition for a specified period of time.

Mathematically, the reliability function $R(t)$ is the probability that a system will be successfully operating without failure in the interval from time 0 to time t:

$$R(t) = P(T > t), \quad t \geq 0 \tag{1.1}$$

where T is a random variable representing the failure time or time-to-failure.

The failure probability, or unreliability, is then

$$F(t) = 1 - R(t) = P(T \leq t)$$

which is known as the distribution function of T.

If the time-to-failure random variable T has a density function $f(t)$, then

$$R(t) = \int\limits_{t}^{\infty} f(x)dx$$

The density function can be mathematically described as $\lim\limits_{\Delta t \to 0} P(t < T \leq t + \Delta t)$. This can be interpreted as the probability that the failure time T will occur between time t and the next interval of operation, $t + \Delta t$. The three functions, $R(t)$, $F(t)$ and $f(t)$ are closely related to one another. If any of them is known, all the others can be determined.

Usually we are interested in the expected time to next failure, and this is termed mean time to failure.

Definition 1.11. The *mean time to failure (MTTF)* is defined as the expected value of the lifetime before a failure occurs.

Suppose that the reliability function for a system is given by $R(t)$, the MTTF can be computed as

$$MTTF = \int\limits_{0}^{\infty} t \cdot f(t)dt = \int\limits_{0}^{\infty} R(t)dt \tag{1.2}$$

Example 1.1. If the lifetime distribution function follows an exponential distribution with parameter λ, that is, $F(t) = 1 - \exp(-\lambda t)$, the MTTF is

$$MTTF = \int_0^\infty R(t)dt = \int_0^\infty \exp(-\lambda t)dt = \frac{1}{\lambda} \qquad (1.3)$$

This is an important result as for exponential distribution. MTTF is related to a single model parameter in this case. Hence, if MTTF is known, the distribution is specified.

The failure rate function, or hazard function, is very important in reliability analysis because it specifies the rate of the system aging. The definition of failure rate function is given here.

Definition 1.12. The *failure rate function* $\lambda(t)$ is defined as

$$\lambda(t) = \lim_{\Delta t \to 0} \frac{R(t) - R(t + \Delta t)}{\Delta t R(t)} = \frac{f(t)}{R(t)} \qquad (1.4)$$

The quantity $\lambda(t)dt$ represents the probability that a device of age t will fail in the small interval from time t to $t + dt$. The importance of the failure rate function is that it indicates the changing rate in the aging behavior over the life of a population of components. For example, two designs may provide the same reliability at a specific point in time, but the failure rate curves can be very different.

Example 1.2. If the failure distribution function follows an exponential distribution with parameter λ, then the failure rate function is

$$\lambda(t) = \frac{f(t)}{R(t)} = \frac{\lambda \cdot \exp(-\lambda t)}{\exp(-\lambda t)} = \lambda \qquad (1.5)$$

This means that the failure rate function of the exponential distribution is a constant. In this case, the system does not have any aging property. This assumption is usually valid for software systems. However, for hardware systems, the failure rate could have other shapes.

When a system fails to perform satisfactorily, repair is normally carried out to locate and correct the fault. The system is restored to operational effectiveness by making an adjustment or by replacing a component.

Definition 1.13. *Maintainability* is defined as the probability that a failed system will be restored to a functioning state within a given period of time when maintenance is performed according to prescribed procedures and resources.

Generally, maintainability is the probability of isolating and repairing a fault in a system within a given time. Maintenance personnel have to work with system designers to ensure that the system product can be maintained cost effectively.

Let T denote the time to repair or the total downtime. If the repair time T has a density function $g(t)$, then the maintainability, $V(t)$, is defined as the probability that the failed system will be back in service by time t, i.e.,

$$V(t) = P(T \leq t) = \int_0^t g(x)dx$$

An important measure often used in maintenance studies is the mean time to repair (MTTR) or the mean downtime. MTTR is the expected value of the repair time.

System repair time usually consists of two separate intervals: passive repair time and active repair time. Passive repair time is mainly determined by the time taken by service engineers in preparation, such as traveling to the customer site. In many cases, the cost of travel time could exceed the cost of the actual repair. Active repair time is directly affected by the system design. The active repair time can be reduced significantly by designing the system in such a way that faults may be quickly detected and isolated. As more complex systems are designed, it becomes more difficult to isolate the faults.

Another important reliability related concept is system availability. This is a measure that takes both reliability and maintainability into account.

Definition 1.14. The *availability* function of a system, denoted by $A(t)$, is defined as the probability that the system is available at time t.

Different from the reliability that focuses on a period of time when the system is free of failures, availability concerns a time point in which the system does not stay at the failed state. Mathematically,

$A(t) =$Pr(System is up or available at time instant t)

The availability function, which is a complex function of time, has a simple steady-state or asymptotic expression. In fact, usually we are mainly concerned with systems running for a long time. The steady-state or asymptotic availability is given by

$$A = \lim_{t \to \infty} A(t) = \frac{\text{System up time}}{\text{System up time} + \text{System down time}}$$
$$= \frac{\text{MTTF}}{\text{MTTF} + \text{MTTR}}$$

The mean time between failures (MTBF) is another important measure in repairable systems. This implies that the system has failed and has been repaired. Like MTTF and MTTR, MTBF is an expected value of the random variable time between failures. Mathematically, MTBF=MTTR+ MTTF.

Example 1.3. If a system has a lifetime distribution function $F(t) = 1 - \exp(-\lambda t)$ and a maintainability function $V(t) = 1 - \exp(-\mu t)$, then MTTF=$1/\lambda$ and MTTR=$1/\mu$. The MTBF is the sum of MTTF and MTTR and the steady-state availability is

$$A = \frac{MTTF}{MTTR+MTTF} = \frac{1/\lambda}{1/\lambda+1/\mu} = \frac{\mu}{\lambda+\mu}$$

1.4 Abbreviations and Notations

Abbreviations:
ACP – Access Control Polynomial
CA – Central Authenticator
CPRS – Computerized Patient Record System
DLKM – Dual-Level Key Management
DoS – Denial of Service
DDoS – Distributed Denial of Service
DIDS – Distributed Intrusion Detection System
GC – Group Controller
GSI – Globus Security Infrastrcuture
HAC – Hierarchical Access Control
HIDS – Host based Intrusion Detection System
IDS – Intrusion Detection System
KMS – Key Management Server
LCM – Least Common Multiple
MANET – Mobile Ad hoc NETworks
MTST –Minimal Task Spanning Tree
NIDS – Network based Intrusion Detection System
RMS – Resource Management System
PKI – Public Key Infrastructure
SOS – Secure Overlay Service
VISTA – Veterans Health Information Systems and Technology Architecture
VO – Virtual Organization

Notations:
SID_i Every valid user/machine is assigned a permanent secret key SID_i

z A random integer which is changed and made public every time
$A(x)$ Access control polynomial (ACP)
$P(x)$ Public polynomial sent to users for key distribution, $P(x) = A(x)+K$
P The system prime used for modular computation
U_i A group member in a certain group
v_j A certain vertex in an access hierarchy
$\hat{k}_i$ A secret node key
k_i A private node key
$f(x, y)$ or $h(x)$ The public one-way hash function
ID_i A unique public identity assigned to each vertex in an access hierarchy
m The number of users in a certain node
n The number of vertices in an access hierarchy
$e_{i,j}$ The public edge value on the edge from v_i to v_j.
% Modular operation

1.5   Outline

This book consists of seven chapters, which are listed and described, as follows:

Chapter 1. This chapter presents an introductory overview of TCC. The chapter begins by introducing central problems of TCC, such as security and dependability in CC environments. It proceeds to introduce preliminaries for TCC and notations used in the rest of the book. Finally, an outline of the subsequent chapters of the book is presented.

Chapter 2. This chapter discusses the first one of the main security requirements/functions in TCC environments: secure group communication (SGC) and interaction. The primary issue for SGC is group key management. This chapter gives a comprehensive overview over the state-of-art group key management schemes. The chapter also contains a discussion on secure dynamic conferences (SDC).

Chapter 3. This chapter discusses another important security requirement and function in TCC environments: data sharing/exchange and access control. The chapter mainly focuses on cryptography based hierarchical access control (CHAC) techniques.

Chapter 4. In this chapter, we discuss and classify intrusion attacks, their corresponding detection and response technologies. In particular, we discuss typical traceback techniques and introduce a new DoS/DDoS defendant architecture, called Secure Overlay Services (SoS) and proposed by Dr. Keromytis's research group.

Chapter 5. As a representative of collaborative computing, grid computing is a newly developed technology for complex systems with large-scale resource sharing, wide-area communication, and multi-institutional collaboration. Although the developmental tools and infrastructures for the grid have been widely studied, grid reliability analysis and modeling are not easy because of its largeness, complexity and stiffness. This chapter introduces the Grid computing technology, analyzes different types of failures in the grid system and their influence on its reliability and performance. The chapter then presents models for star-topology grid considering data dependence and tree-structure grid considering failure correlation. Evaluation tools and algorithms are developed, based on Universal Generating function, Graph theory, and Bayesian approach.

Chapter 6. Grid computing environments are typical CC paradigms that users offer and share their resources. In this omnipresent environment, security becomes a critical factor to its success. This chapter introduces the Grid Security problem, its challenges and requirements. Moreover, we present a dual level key management scheme which can offer secure grid communication and fine-grained access control to shared grid resources. In the remainder of the chapter, some examples of typical grid services present how grid services are supported by this scheme.

Chapter 7. Medical Information Systems (MIS) help medical practice and health care significantly. Security and dependability are two increasingly important factors for MIS nowadays. On one hand, people would be willing to step into the MIS age only when their privacy and integrity can be protected and guaranteed within MIS systems. On the other hand, only secure and reliable MIS systems would provide safe and solid medical and health care service to people. In this chapter, we discuss why the security and reliability technologies presented in the previous chapters are necessary and how they can be integrated with the existing MIS systems. We also present a Middleware architecture which has been implemented and integrated with the existing VISTA (Veterans Health Information Systems and Technology Architecture) and CPRS (Computerized Patient Record System) in the U.S. Department of Veterans Affairs seamlessly, and does not modify/replace any current components.

Chapter 2

Secure Group Communication (SGC)

As indicated in Chapter 1, the first issue in TCC environments is that multiple participating entities communicate securely among them for collaborative tasks, which requires secure group communication. This chapter discusses this first important issue for TCC.

2.1 Overview of Secure Group Communication (SGC)

Secure Group Communication (SGC) refers to a scenario where a group of users (also called members) can communicate amongst one another in a way that outsiders are unable to glean any information despite having access to the messages exchanged.

Traditional two party communication systems are built on client-server architecture that uses the *unicast* technology for communication. In unicasting, each packet is individually routed and sent to the receiver, which works well for two party communication. Many group communication systems are built by extending traditional client-server architecture. However this extension is not efficient, since it depends on unicast, and hence requires the sender to send packets equal in number to the number of receivers. This approach is certainly inefficient and non-scalable for supporting group communication with a large number of users.

Technology like multicast or broadcast offers great possibility for building an ideal SGC system. Multicast technology requires the sender to send just one copy of any packet. Multicast enabled routers on the network make copies of the sent packet and forward them to the multiple receivers located at different segments of the network topology. But multicasting is like radio station transmission - anyone can listen to it, which jeopardizes the confidentiality of the messages sent. Encryption solves the problem of confidentiality and secures the group communication, but it creates the problem of distributing the encryption/decryption key(s) to the group members securely and efficiently.

CC environments are distributed and inherently dynamic in nature. Members can join or leave the group at any time. Moreover, multiple group members may join, leave, or be evicted simultaneously. Group key management is often complicated due to high group dynamics.

Some basic terms/operations associated with dynamics in SGC are briefly discussed in the following section.

Group initialization (setup). The group is *formed* by legitimate members and the initial group key is distributed to the members.

Member join. During group communication, a user *joins* the group to become a member of the group and participate in present and future group communications.

Member leave. During group communication, a group member *leaves* or is evicted from the group and will no longer be able to comprehend (decrypt) the group communication messages.

Bulk operation. Multiple members *join*, multiple members *leave*, multiple members join and others leave the group simultaneously. In some situations, when a member requests joining or leaving the group, the joining or leaving operation is not conducted immediately, but is postponed for some time. The purpose of postponing operations is to accumulate more joining and leaving requests so that these multiple requests can be processed in bulk. This can also be considered as a *bursty* or *aggregate* operation. The objective of bursty operations is to increase performance.

Periodic rekeying. The group key is changed periodically, independently of members joining or leaving.

Group splitting (partition). In certain applications, a group may be divided into two or more independent subgroups. Another scenario for group splitting is necessitated by a physical network partition. The group is then partitioned into multiple temporary subgroups.

Group merge. Two groups may fuse into a larger group in some SGC applications. Moreover, previously split groups due to an earlier network partition may need to merge again without member interaction.

From the security point of view, secure group key management is trying to guarantee that only current group members can possess the current group key. This means that outsiders, old group members, and future members should not be able to obtain the current group key. Therefore, there are at least two security requirements in SGC:

Backward secrecy. When a member joins a group, the group key needs to be changed so that the new member cannot obtain the old group keys to decrypt previous messages (in case he/she has intercepted and stored such earlier messages).

Forward secrecy. Whenever a member leaves a group, the group key needs to be changed so that the ex-member does not possess the current group key, otherwise he/she would be able to decrypt future group messages.

Group key management refers to the technique to deal with generation, distribution, updating and revocation of group keys. There are different terms (mechanisms) for group key management. Several main terms are listed as follows.

Key Distribution. refers to one class of group key management, by which a new group key is selected and distributed (by the group controller or a member) to all group members during the initialization or update stages.

Key Agreement. refers to one class of group key management methods, by which the shared secret key is agreed upon by all group members and contains the shares of all members.

Authenticated Key Exchange (AKE). refers to the protocols that allow a group of members to establish a common group key in such a way that the authenticity of the members is guaranteed.

Self Healing. refers to the ability of a member to recover a missed broadcast session key from previous and/or subsequent broadcasts without interacting with the group controller.

2.2   Typical Group Key Management Schemes for SGC

As discussed in the previous section, the secrecy and privacy of the group communication is achieved by encrypting the group messages by a secret key, which is known only by the members of the group. The secret key, also known as *group key* is accessible only to the group members and hence, only the group members can decrypt the messages. Obviously, the mechanism for sharing such a secret group key amongst the members of the group has to be secure and efficient. Therefore, the first and often most important problem facing SGC is that of *key management*.

Based on the mechanisms employed by the group members to establish the shared group key, group key management schemes can be typically classified into four categories [Zou *et al.* (2004b)]: (1) centralized key distribution, e.g. key graph and one-way function chain (OFC) [Canetti *et al.* (1999b)]; (2) decentralized key management, e.g. Iolus [Mittra (1997a)]; (3) distributed/contributory group key agreement, e.g. DISEC [Dondeti *et al.* (2000)]; and (4) distributed group key distribution, e.g. optimized group key rekeying [Rodeh *et al.* (2000)]. We discuss these four types of group key management in this section.

2.2.1   Centralized Group Key Distribution

2.2.1.1   Key Tree (Logical Key Hierarchy)

In July, 1997 Wallner et al. [Wallner *et al.* (1998)] proposed a tree based group key management scheme named *Logical Key Hierarchy* (LKH). Wong et al. [Wong *et al.* (1998)] proposed a generalized key tree scheme called *key graph*. Caronni et al. [Caronni *et al.* (1998)] and Noubir [Noubir (1998)] published ideas similar to LKH, followed by many researchers proposing improvements and enhancements to LKH. LKH is a really good centralized solution to the problem of key management in SGC. In LKH, the Group Controller (GC) is responsible for maintaining the multicast group. The GC manages a virtual tree in the form of a binary tree, called the *key tree* or LKH (see Figure 2.1).

The members of the group are placed at leaf nodes of the tree. Every node in the key tree is assigned a cryptographic key. The key at the root is called the *Traffic Encryption Key* (TEK) and is used as the group key for securing group communication. All other keys are called the *Key Encryption Keys* (KEKs). Members are placed at the leaf nodes and every member gets the key at his/her leaf node. The key at every other node is encrypted by its children's keys and multicast. Thus, every member gets the keys along the path, from its leaf to the root. The key at the root node (TEK) is shared by all members. For example consider member U_7, he/she will have keys k_7, k_{6-7}, k_{4-7} and k_{0-7}(TEK).

When a member U_l leaves the group, all the keys that U_l knows (i.e. the keys from the root to the parent of U_l) need to be changed. Similarly, when a member U joins, the GC decides its position in the tree and it is required to change all the keys from the parent of the joining member to the root. In either case of a leave or a join, the GC changes required keys in a bottom

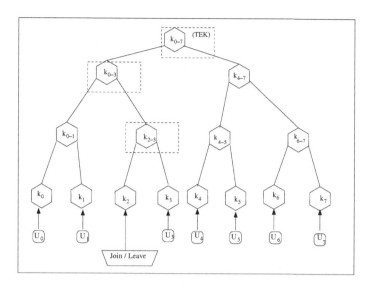

Fig. 2.1 A typical LKH with an example of a member change (join/leave).

up manner. Every key that is changed is encrypted by its children's keys (some of which are new changed keys) and broadcast to all the members. Figure 2.1 shows an example of a member change and its effect on the key tree.

If there is no free node available in case a member joins, the GC expands the tree. The GC generates a new root and the old root becomes a child of the new root. The number of keys which need to be changed for a join or a leave is $O(log_2(n))$ and the number of encryptions is $O(2log_2(n))$ where n is the number of members in the multicast group.

The key tree can be generalized to a $d - ary$ tree ($d \geq 2$) [Wong *et al.* (1998, 2000)]. In a $d - ary$ key tree, each internal node can have up to d children. The members are placed at the leaf nodes just as in LKH (see Figure 2.2). Each member has the keys of all nodes in the path from its leaf to the root. The root key is shared by all the members and is the group key. For a $d - ary$ key tree, the height of the tree reduces with a larger d, for the same number of members.

Batch rekeying is defined as performing one key tree update for multiple joining and/or multiple leaving users. It is also called bulk operation. Batch rekeying will enhance the performace for key update and reduce the key update frequency. In particular, the key tree based batch rekeying will be more efficient when more members are involved in batch rekeying because

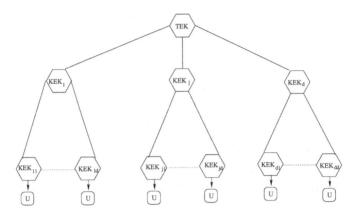

Fig. 2.2   A typical $d - ary$ key tree.

the more members there are, the more chances they will have to share keys, and the shared keys are updated just once in each batch operation. There have been some schemes proposed by batch rekeying based on the key tree scheme [Lee *et al.* (2002); Li *et al.* (2001); Pegueroles and Rico-Novella (2003); Setia *et al.* (2000); Zhang *et al.* (2001)]. Most recently, the authors in [Ng *et al.* (2007)] propose a balanced batch rekeying scheme. The scheme consists of three algorithms: two merging algorithms and one balanced batch rekeying algorithm. The two merging algorithms mainly deal with batch join operations and the balanced batch rekeying algorithm, which repeatedly calls (one of the) two merging algorithms, mainly deals with the batch leaving operations. The main feature of all three algorithms is to minimize the height difference in the key tree without adding extra communication costs. We briefly summarize its three algorithms below.

Let ST_A and ST_B be two subtrees which will be merged and d be the degree of the key tree. Let H_{min}, H_{max}, $H_{min\_ST\_X}$ and $H_{max\_ST\_X}$ be the minimum height of a leaf node in a key tree, the maximum height of a leaf node in a key tree, H_{min} of a subtree ST_X, and H_{max} of a subtree ST_X. Let $H_{insert} = H_{min\_ST\_A} - H_{max\_ST\_B}$.

The **balanced batch rekeying algorithm** is described in Figure 2.3.

MergeAlgorithm 1 is called when $H_{max\_ST\_A} - H_{min\_ST\_B} > 1$ and $H_{max\_ST\_A} - H_{max\_ST\_B} \geq 1$ and is described in Figure 2.4.

MergeAlgorithm 2 is called when $H_{max\_ST\_A} - H_{min\_ST\_B} \leq 1$ and $H_{max\_ST\_A} - H_{max\_ST\_B} \leq 1$ and is described in Figure 2.5.

After the key tree has been reorganized, the GC needs to inform the members of their new locations so that the members can identify their

Algorithm 2.1.

/* **Balanced Batch Rekeying Algorithm** */

Find and mark all key nodes needing to be updated.

/*They are on the paths from each leaving member to the root */

Remove all marked key nodes.

/*So, two types elements left: remaining subtrees&joining members */

Classify all siblings of the leaving members as joining members.

/*Because all KEYs the leaving members store cannot be used */

Group the joining members into subtrees, each with d members.

/*Except the last one having 1 to $d-1$ members */

Repeatly mearge two minimum subtrees until one subtree left.

/*either **MergeAlgithm 1** or **MergeAlgorithm 2** is called */

Form the update and rekey messages and multicast to members.

Fig. 2.3 Balanced batch rekeying.

Algorithm 2.2.

/* **Algorithm 1 for merging** ST_A **and** ST_B */

Compute $H_{insert}=H_{min\_ST\_A} - H_{max\_ST\_B}$.

For $d > 2$, search for an empty child node in ST_A at level H_{insert} or $H_{insert} - 1$.

/*if $H_{insert} = 0$, levels 0 and 1 are searched */

If such a node exists, insert ST_B as the child of the node. Done.

Mark a proper node at level H_{insert} or 1 if $H_{insert} = 0$.

/*The marked proper node is the one with the greatest number of leaf nodes at level $H_{min\_ST\_A}$ and denoted as $N_{insert\_ST\_A}$ */

If $d > 2$, search the root of ST_B for an empty node.

If such a node exists, insert $N_{insert\_ST\_A}$ as the child of ST_B and insert ST_B at the old location of $N_{insert\_ST\_A}$. Done.

Create a new node at the old location of $N_{insert\_ST\_A}$ and insert $N_{insert\_ST\_A}$ and ST_B as the children of the new node.

Fig. 2.4 Merging algorithm 1.

Algorithm 2.3.
    /* **Algorithm 2 for merging** ST_A **and** ST_B */
For $d > 2$, search for the root of ST_A for an empty child node.
If it exists, insert ST_B at the empty child node. Done.
Create a new key node at the root and inserts ST_A and ST_B
as its children.

Fig. 2.5   Merging algorithm 2.

new keys. In order to do so, the GC will multicast an update message
consisting of the smallest node ID s of the usable key tree and the new
node ID s'. Using s', the members can compute the new keys s_0 via the
function: $f(s_0) = d^l(s' - s) + s_0$, where l denotes the level of the usable key
tree.

2.2.1.2   *Other Proposed Schemes*

In 1997, Hamey and Muckenhim proposed *Group Key management Protocol
(GKMP)* [Hamey and Muckenhim (1997a,b)], which is considered as the
first solution to the problem of key management for SGC. GKMP assumes
the presence of a central trusted authority, termed as the group controller
(GC). Also, it is assumed that there exists a secure channel between the GC
and every member of the group (public key cryptosystems could be used
to implement these secure channels). The GC selects a group key (k_G) and
distributes it to the members through the secure channels. When a new
member joins, the GC selects a new group key k_N and encrypts it with
the old group key, i.e. $k' = \{k_N\}_{k_G}$ and broadcasts k' to the group. The
new member gets the new key k_N through the secure channel he/she shares
with the GC. In case of a member leave, the GC selects a new group key
k_N and sends it to the remaining members of the group, over the secure
channels, one key at a time using unicast messages. Clearly, the naive
solution proposed in GKMP is not scalable. GKMP is also inefficient due
to the use of unicast based secure channels very frequently.

The *Core based tree* approach [Bakkardie (1996)] assumes a *group initiator* (GI). The GI designates a number of routers as *cores* or *core routers* and
the tree that connects all the cores is called a *core tree*. Several branches
emanate from the core tree. These branches are made up of other non-core

routers forming the shortest path between the router to which a member host is directly attached and one of the core routers. The GI provides each core with membership control information in the form of a member inclusion list or a member exclusion list. A member wishing to join a group, sends the join request to one of the cores. On approval from the core, the path connecting the member to the core tree forms a new part of the group multicast tree. The GI may act as a *Key Distribution Center* (KDC), which generates two keys: the *Data Encryption Key* (DEK) and the *Key Encryption Key* (KEK). The KDC sends these two keys to the new member through a secure channel. To update the DEK on member join, the KDC multicasts to the group the new DEK encrypted with KEK. CBT assumes that a member once removed, would not receive any further multicast messages and hence would not harm the group. This assumption is not valid in a global multicast environment. In addition, good core replacement is a difficult problem.

Sherman et al. [Sherman and McGrew (2003)] proposed the *One-way Function Tree* (OFT) scheme. The OFT scheme assumes the presence of a secure channel between the GC and every group member. The scheme also uses a logical key tree (as in LKH) maintained by the GC with group members placed at the leaf nodes. Every node x in the OFT key tree has 3 values associated with it 1) the node secret S_x, 2) the blinded node secret $B_x = f(S_x)$ and 3) the node key $K_x = g(S_x)$, here $f()$ and $g()$ are one way functions known by the GC and the nodes. The GC randomly generates the node secrets for the leaf nodes and calculates the node keys and the blinded node secrets. For all the internal nodes, the node secret is $S_x = B_{x_l} \oplus B_{x_r}$, where x_r and x_l are the right and left children nodes of node x respectively. The GC calculates node secrets, blinded node secrets and node keys in a bottom up manner.

For every node x, the GC encrypts the blinded node secret B_x by $K_{\hat{x}}$ and broadcasts it, where $K_{\hat{x}}$ is the node key of sibling $\hat{x}$ of node x. Every leaf node gets its secrets by a unicast message from the GC. Any member x can calculate its own node key as $K_x = g(S_x)$ and the blinded node secret as $B_x = f(S_x)$. x can calculate the blinded key of its sibling from the broadcast from the GC. Using its own blinded key and the sibling's blinded key, x can get the parent node p's node secret. Using parent's secret x can get secrets of parent of p. Continuing this way, a member x gets all the keys from its node to the root and also the root key which is the group key.

In case of a member join or leave, the GC changes the node secret of the sibling of the node at which change took place. The GC also recomputes all the secrets for the path from leaf where change took place to the root and rebroadcasts the encrypted blinded node secrets. Thus, upon receiving the rekeying broadcasts, all the members can reconstruct the tree and get the keys along the path from their leaf to the root. The main advantage of OFT over LKH is that the number of broadcast messages is halved from $2log(n)$ to $log(n)$. Canetti et al. [Canetti *et al.* (1999a)] proposed the *One-way Function Chain* (OFC) scheme, which is a variation of the OFT scheme.

2.2.2 *De-centralized Group Key Management*

The decentralized group key management approach involves splitting a large group into small subgroups. This is done with the view of distributing the work load of key management to different levels in the system and avoiding concentration of work at one single place. We have seen that the central entity (the group controller or the key distribution center) in the centralized schemes often becomes a single point of failure and a performance bottleneck. The de-centralized approach tries to avoid these problems and helps achieve better performance and fault tolerance. A typical de-centralized scheme, known as the Iolus protocol, follows, along with brief reviews of other schemes proposed in literature.

2.2.2.1 *Iolus*

In 1997, Mittra proposed *Iolus* [Mittra (1997b)]. In Iolus, a framework with a hierarchy of agents is used to divide a large group into a number of subgroups. The basic idea is to avoid the membership change in one subgroup to affect the keys in any other subgroup.

A group is decomposed into a number of several subgroups located at different levels of a tree. A *Group Security Agent* (GSA) manages each subgroup. The GSA of the top-level group (root subgroup) is called the *Group Security Controller* (GSC). The other GSAs are called *Group Security Intermediaries* (GSI). Each subgroup has independent keys and there is no common group key shared by all members. The GSI is a bridge between its parent subgroup and its own subgroup, and possesses both subgroup keys. The members encrypt the messages using the subgroup key and send it to the GSI. On receiving the message, the GSI decrypts it, re-encrypts the message with the key of the adjacent subgroup and retransmits the message to the adjacent group. An example is illustrated in Figure 2.6. Let us assume a member of the subgroup 3 (say u_3) wishes to send a message

M to the entire group. u_3 encrypts the message using K_3 and broadcasts it ($y_3 = \{M\}_{K_3}$). All members of subgroup 3 decrypt y_3 using K_3 and obtain M. GSI_3 now broadcasts $y_1 = \{M\}_{K_1}$. All members of subgroup 1, including GSI_4 are able to recover M from y_1 as they all know K_1. Now GSI_4 broadcasts $y_4 = \{M\}_{K_4}$ to members of subgroup 4. GSI_1 broadcasts $y_0 = \{M\}_{K_0}$ to subgroup 0 and hence, all members of subgroup 0, including the GSC and GSI_2 are able to decrypt y_0 to obtain M. GSA_2 uses the same procedure to securely send the message to the remaining subgroups (subgroups 2 and 3).

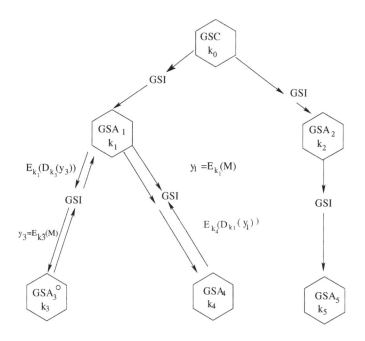

Fig. 2.6   The Iolus scheme.

Iolus handles membership join/leave in an efficient way, such that only the keys of the subgroup where the change occurs are affected. When a member joins or leaves a subgroup SG, the GSA of the subgroup selects a new subgroup key and sends the key to the members in the new SG. As a result, the subgroup keys of other subgroups remain unaffected by the membership change in SG.

2.2.2.2   *Other Proposed Schemes*

In Iolus, since all information (keys, messages) is exposed to all GSAs, the correct functioning of the protocol requires the assumption that the GSAs are all trusted. Usually the GSAs are third party entities and hence, cannot be trusted completely. The Dual Encryption Protocol (DEP), proposed in 1999 by Dondetti et al. [Dondeti *et al.* (1999)], overcomes this problem. DEP also uses a hierarchical subgrouping of members with a *SubGroup Manager* (SGM) managing each subgroup. However, the SGMs are not required to be trusted in DEP. The SGM acts as an intermediary and possesses the key of its own subgroup and also the key of its parent subgroup. The group members are divided into another kind of subsets, called *key-subgroups*, which are independent from the subgroups. Corresponding to the subgroups and key-subgroups, there are three kinds of keys: (i) A Data Encryption Key (DEK) shared by the entire group and used for encrypting data messages. (ii) Key Encryption Key (KEK), one for each key-subgroup. These are used to encrypt the DEK. (iii) Local Subgroup Key (LSK), one for each subgroup S, and it is used for encrypting the above encrypted DEK. The DEK is thus encrypted twice, once by a KEK and then by a LSK. Hence, the protocol is known as *Dual Encryption Protocol*. The DEP protocol provides a scalable multicasting approach for secure group communication. However, the scheme can only be used for one-to-many communications. Moreover, if a leaving member shares its KEK with a participant SGM, it can lead to a collusion attack.

Rafaeli and Hutchison proposed *Hydra* [Rafaeli and Hutchison (2002)],a decentralized architecture for group communication. The Hydra architecture consists of two levels, namely, the top level, comprised of the *Hydra Servers* (HSs) and the bottom level, consisting of the members. Correspondingly, there are two secure multicast groups. The first one is called *HS-group* and is used by the top level HSs to agree upon a common group key. The second one is known as *Hydra-group*, and is used by the HSs to distribute the common agreed key to respective subgroup members. Each subgroup has a subgroup key and it is used to protect the common group key within a subgroup. It is shared between the HS managing the subgroup and the subgroup members.

In 1999, Briscoe proposed a new scheme called MARKS [Briscoe (1999)]. The protocol suggests a method for separately controlling individual secure sessions between multiple senders and receivers. The mechanism involves the division of the time period to be protected into small portions of time and using a different encryption key for each slice of time. A *Binary Hash Tree* (BHT) is created from a single root seed and the leaves form the encryption keys. The internal nodes are also known as seeds. Users who wish to communicate receive the seeds required to generate the required keys. The keys in the proposed scheme change with time, and hence cannot be used in applications where dynamic membership change occurs.

In 2000, Setia et al. proposed Kronos [Setia *et al.* (2000)], a scalable group-rekeying approach for secure multicast. Kronos is based on the idea of periodic group re-keying, i.e. a new group key is generated after a certain period of time instead of every instant when a member joins or leaves. Kronos does not employ the central controller for generation of keys and hence is fault-tolerant. However, achieving clock synchronization in distributed environments can be hard. Additionally, the security of the group can be compromised as the scheme uses a previous key to obtain a new key.

2.2.3 (Distributed) Contributory Group Key Agreement

2.2.3.1 *Tree based Group Diffie-Hellman Key Agreement*

Tree based Group Diffie-Hellman key agreement (TGDH) [Kim *et al.* (2000a, 2004c)] extends the two party Diffie-Hellman key exchange scheme to a tree structure for multi-party communications. Let p be a large prime and g a primitive element in Z_p. In TGDH, all members maintain an identical virtual binary key tree which may or may not be balanced. The nodes in the key tree are denoted by $\langle l, v \rangle$, where l is the level in the tree and v indicates the sequential index of the node at level l. We will have $0 \leq v \leq 2^l - 1$ since level l holds at most 2^l nodes. The root node is labeled as $\langle 0, 0 \rangle$, and the two children of a parent node $\langle l, v \rangle$ are labeled as $\langle l+1, 2v \rangle$ and $\langle l + 1, 2v + 1 \rangle$, respectively. Every node $\langle l, v \rangle$ except for the root node is associated with a secret key $k_{\langle l,v \rangle}$ and a blinded key $bk_{\langle l,v \rangle} = f(k_{\langle l,v \rangle})$, where $f(x) = g^x \bmod p$. The key $k_{\langle l,v \rangle}$ of a parent node is the Diffie-Hellman key of its two children, i.e., $k_{\langle l,v \rangle} = g^{k_{\langle l+1,2v \rangle} k_{\langle l+1,2v+1 \rangle}} \bmod p = f(k_{\langle l+1,2v \rangle} k_{\langle l+1,2v+1 \rangle})$, thus, the secret key $k_{\langle l,v \rangle}$ of a node can be formed from the secret key of one of its two children and the blinded key of the other child by using the Diffie-Hellman key exchange protocol. Every blinded key $bk_{\langle l,v \rangle}$ is publicly broadcast by some member(s) to the group. All group members are hosted on leaf nodes respectively. Every member U_i selects its own Diffie-Hellman private share a_i, and computes the corresponding Diffie-Hellman disguised public share b_i. Suppose a leaf node $\langle l, v \rangle$ hosts member U_i, then the secret key $k_{\langle l,v \rangle}$ for the node is a_i, and the blinded key $bk_{\langle l,v \rangle} = g^{k_{\langle l,v \rangle}}$) is b_i. Member U_i can compute all secret keys from its leaf node $\langle l, v \rangle$ to the root node $\langle 0, 0 \rangle$, and of course, U_i will receive all blinded keys in the key tree. The root node has secret key $k_{\langle 0,0 \rangle}$, and there is no need for $bk_{\langle 0,0 \rangle}$. The group data encryption key (DEK) is obtained by passing $k_{\langle 0,0 \rangle}$ through a one-way function.

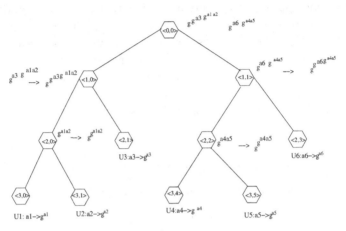

Fig. 2.7   Tree based Group Diffie-Hellman key agreement. The notation $k \to g^k$ means that members compute the secret key k, then compute the blinded key.

Figure 2.7 illustrates a key tree with six members. As shown in the figure, node $\langle 3, 1 \rangle$ hosts member U_2 and is associated with U_2's private share a_2 and public share $b_2 = g^{a_2}$. Member U_2 can compute $k_{\langle 2,0 \rangle} = g^{k_{\langle 3,0 \rangle} k_{\langle 3,1 \rangle}} = g^{a_1 a_2} \bmod p$ after receiving $b_1 = g^{a_1}$. Next, U_2 computes and broadcasts $bk_{\langle 2,0 \rangle} = g^{g^{a_1 a_2}}$. Next, U_2 proceeds to compute $k_{\langle 1,0 \rangle} = g^{k_{\langle 2,0 \rangle} k_{\langle 2,1 \rangle}} \bmod p = g^{a_3 g^{a_1 a_2}} \bmod p$, after receiving $bk_{\langle 2,1 \rangle} = g^{a_3}$ from U_3. Further, U_2 computes and broadcasts $bk_{\langle 1,0 \rangle} = g^{k_{\langle 1,0 \rangle}} \bmod p = g^{g^{a_3 g^{a_1 a_2}}} \bmod p$. Finally U_2 computes $k_{\langle 0,0 \rangle} = g^{g^{a_3 g^{a_1 a_2}} g^{a_6 g^{a_4 a_5}}} \bmod p$ after receiving $bk_{\langle 1,1 \rangle}$. It is clear now that the root key $k_{\langle 0,0 \rangle}$ contains the Diffie-Hellman private shares of all members. Thus, the group key is obtained by a uniform contribution of all group members.

As indicated in the above example (for U_2), the initial computation of the root key is performed in multiple rounds by all members. In general, each member U hosted on leaf node w, computes recursively the secret key of each node v_i, ascending along the path from w to the root, using the secret key of v_i's child on the path, and the blinded key of the other child of v_i.

Summaries of the join and leave operations follow. A *sponsor* is a member defined as follows: (i) The *sponsor* of a *subtree* is the member hosted on the rightmost leaf in the subtree, and (ii) The *sponsor* of a *leaf node v* is the member hosted on the rightmost leaf node (other than itself) of the lowest subtree to which v belongs.

When a new member U requests to join the group, U begins by broadcasting its public share. Next, all pre-existing members determine the insertion location for U on the tree, and determine U's sponsor. Each member updates the key tree by adding a new (leaf) node for U, a new internal node, and removes all secret keys and blinded keys from the sponsor's leaf node to the root node. Then, the sponsor generates its new private share, computes all secret and blinded keys from its leaf node to the root, and broadcasts all new blinded keys. Every member computes the new root key after receiving the new blinded keys. It can be seen that the root key is computed in one round. Similarly, the root key can be computed in one round for a single leave. Generally, for multiple leaves there will be multiple sponsors. The sponsors need to collaborate to compute secret and blinded keys in multiple rounds in a way similar to the initial setting up phase, limited by $O(log_2(n))$. After all sponsors compute and broadcast all blinded keys, every member can compute the root key. Similarly, multiple joins (and merging) can be performed in multiple rounds. A network partition can be treated as *"multiple leaves"* from the point of view of any subgroup resulting from the partition.

2.2.3.2 *Other Proposed Schemes*

Most of the proposed schemes for distributed key management extend the two party Diffie-Hellman key exchange protocol for a group of n users. The first attempt to extend the Diffie-Hellman key exchange for group settings was made by Ingermarsson et al. [Ingemarsson *et al.* (1982)] and is called the *ING protocol*. The protocol requires the n members to be positioned cyclically at the nodes of an n-gon, such that $u_i = u_j$ when $i = j$ mod n. The ING protocol requires $n - 1$ rounds and the rounds need to be synchronized with respect to the members. The ING protocol does not scale well in cases where there are a large number of members in a group. Additionally the communication overhead increases with the increase in the number of members.

In 1994, Burmester and Desmedt proposed a group key agreement scheme, called the *BD protocol* [Burmester and Desmedt (1994)]. The BD protocol is very efficient and requires only two rounds to achieve the common group key. The group key generated in the protocol is $K_G = g^{r_0 r_1 + r_1 r_2 + \cdots + r_{n-1} r_0}$, where r_i is the secret share of a member U_i. The main advantage of the BD protocol is that it requires very low computational overhead. However, the communication cost is high ($2n$ broadcasts are required).

Another extension of the DH protocol was provided by Steiner at. al, who proposed a series of protocols, namely GDH.1, GDH.2 and GDH.3. The group key achieved in the protocols is of the form $g^{r_0 r_1 \cdots r_{n-1}}$, where the symbols have their usual meaning.

In 1998, Becker and Wille [Becker and Wille (1998)] proposed a group key agreement protocol based on the Diffie-Hellman key exchange, called the *Octopus protocol*. The protocol blends the concepts of de-centralized key management and contributory key agreement. The large group (comprising of n members) is split into four subgroups (each having $n/4$ members). Every subgroup has a leading member who is responsible for collecting the secret shares from all the subgroup members and is also responsible for computing upon a common group key along with other subgroup leaders.

In [Dondeti *et al.* (2000)], Dondeti et al. proposed a distributed group key agreement scheme known as the DIstributed Scalable sEcure Communication (DISEC) protocol. DISEC and TGDH, discussed in the previous section, use the same mechanism to form the group key (root key): stepwise and iterative two-party key agreement following a binary tree structure. The difference is that DISEC uses a generic one-way function to compute blinded keys but TGDH uses specific g^x and DISEC uses a generic *mix* function to compute parent node keys but TGDH uses Diffie-Hellman key exchange $(g^x)^y$. Moreover, DISEC and OFT, discussed in Section 2.2.1, also share the similar idea for binary tree: computing node blinded keys and parent node keys using a one-way function. However, unlike OFT, DISEC does not require a central GC and is distributed in nature.

2.2.4 *Distributed Group Key Distribution*

The centralized and de-centralized schemes suffer from the problem of having the GC (or subgroup controllers) as a performance bottleneck and a single point of failure. Distributed schemes attempt to fix these problems, but are insufficient. Also, the contributory key agreement schemes are vulnerable to the Man-in-the-Middle attack. Authentication of members is a problem in contributory schemes. This section presents a new class of group key management scheme: distributed group key distribution (DGKD) [Adusumilli *et al.* (2005)], which overcomes these problems.

2.2.4.1 *DGKD*

The DGKD scheme assumes existence of a virtual tree structure as in previous schemes. But the major difference is that every leaf node has the public key of the member present at that leaf while the internal nodes have secret keys (see Figure 2.8). Every member manages this virtual tree independently and updates it upon membership changes. The DGKD scheme eliminates the need of a trusted central authority and introduces the concept of sponsors and co-distributors. All group members have the same capability and are equally trusted. Also, they have equal responsibility, i.e. any group member could be a potential sponsor of other members or a co-distributor (depending on the relative locations of the member and the joining/leaving members in the tree). If a sponsor node fails, a new sponsor for the joining/leaving member is chosen by other members, making the scheme robust.

A sponsor is a group member and the sponsor of a subtree is defined as the member hosted on the rightmost leaf in the subtree (note: "rightmost" can be equally replaced with "leftmost"). Every node has a sponsor which is responsible for maintaining the node key. Figure 2.8 shows a DGKD tree and the nodes' sponsors. The sponsors can be determined efficiently. A co-distributor of a sponsor is the sponsor of a node on another path whose key is not known to the original sponsor.

Whenever there is a member change (either join or leave), the sponsor initiates the key change and rekeying process. The rekeying process consists of 2 rounds. In the first round, the sponsor sends the changed keys to co-distributors, by encrypting the new keys with the public keys of the co-distributors. In the next round, the co-distributors distribute the changed keys to their respective members in a parallel manner.

The example shown in Figure 2.9 explains the above principle. Suppose current members are $U_0, U_1, U_2, U_3, U_4, U_6, U_7$. When a new member joins, all members can determine its position in the tree (here as U_5) and also determine that U_4 is the sponsor of U_5. So U_4 initiates the rekeying process as follows: 1) generates new keys k'_{4-5}, k'_{4-7}, and k'_{0-7}. 2) after determining the co-distributors U_3 and U_7, encrypts as follows and broad-

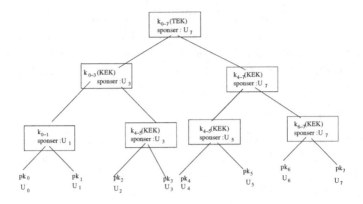

Fig. 2.8   A tree showing sponsor for each node.

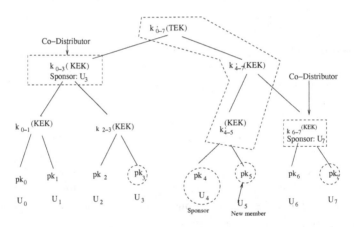

Fig. 2.9   A new member joins (becomes U_5), U_4 is sponsor and U_3 and U_7 are co-distributors.

casts: $\{k'_{4-7}, k'_{0-7}\}_{pk_7}$, and $\{k'_{0-7}\}_{pk_3}$. 3) U_3 will decrypt k'_{0-7} and encrypt it as $\{k'_{0-7}\}_{k_{0-3}}$ and U_7 will decrypt k'_{4-7} and k'_{0-7} and encrypt them as $\{k'_{4-7}\}_{k_{6-7}}$ and $\{k'_{0-7}\}_{k_{4-7}}$. 4) U_4 also encrypts and sends the keys to U_5 as $\{k'_{4-5}, k'_{4-7}, k'_{0-7}\}_{pk_5}$. As a result, all the members will get the new keys.

The DGKD scheme gives various algorithms for deciding a sponsor (co-distributors) and handling join and leave operations. It is worthy to mention that the DGKD scheme also addresses the issue of member authentication due to the use of public keys.

2.3 Enhanced Group Key Management for SGC

The schemes presented in the previous sections are basic format for group key management. In this section, we will discuss some enhanced formats for group key management. These include group key management for SGC in wireless and mobile ad hoc networks, authenticated group key management, block-free group key management, self-healing group key management, and secure dynamic conferencing.

2.3.1 *SGC for Wireless and Mobile Ad Hoc Networks*

The recent developments in wireless network over the past few years have revolutionized the way people use computers and networks. More and more people are starting to use mobile handhold devices to exchange information over the Internet. There are many possible scenarios in which secure group communication would be required in such wireless networks. There could be a group of people at a convention who wish to form an ad hoc network on the fly to communicate amongst one another. Such communication needs to be held in private such that only the specified members are able to comprehend the messages and no one else.

Wireless networks are easy to deploy and have desirable characteristics such as flexibility, robustness, and inherent support for scalability and mobility. However, the advantages attributed to such wireless networks come with an associated cost of complicating endpoint management and security. The wireless networks use a common shared access medium and hence, are more vulnerable to attacks from intruders. Anyone can tune his/her wireless device to a specific radio frequency to capture all communication occurring on that frequency. The problem is further complicated due to the fact that the mobile devices used for such communication are power constrained. Hence, it is difficult to directly adopt the SGC techniques for wired networks to wireless networks as the former techniques have inherent latency and are computationally expensive.

Since wireless networks can have different structures, it is best to match the key management protocol with the structure of the network for group communication. An example could be a LAN with an access point. The access point is a central trusted authority and hence, a centralized key management protocol could be used. On the other hand, for mobile ad hoc networks (MANET), it is best to have a distributed key agreement protocol as there is no central trusted entity. In the following section, a novel key agreement protocol for wireless ad hoc networks is presented.

2.3.1.1 *CRTDH*

The CRTDH scheme [Balachandran *et al.* (2005)] uses the Chinese Remainder Theorem (see Theorem 1.1) and Diffie-Hellman key exchange (see Definition 1.8) to achieve distributed key agreement for secure group communication in wireless ad hoc networks. Assuming a group of n users, $\{U_1, U_2, ..., U_n\}$ has to be formed, the following operations are performed by each member U_i (where $i = 1, ..., n$) to obtain the shared group key.

U_i selects the Diffie-Hellman (DH) private share x_i and broadcasts the public share $y_i = g^{x_i} \bmod p$. U_i then receives the public shares from all other members in the group and computes the DH key shared with each of them as $m_{ij} = y_j^{x_i} \bmod p$, where $j = 1, ..., i-1, i+1, ..., n$. Each member then finds the Least Common Multiple (LCM) of the DH keys computed in the previous step. Let the LCM be lcm_i. U_i then randomly selects k_i, its share for the group key. It also selects two arbitrary numbers, D and D_p such that $D \neq k_i$ and $gcd(D_p, lcm_i) = 1$. Each member then solves the CRT

$$crt_i = k_i \bmod lcm_i$$

$$crt_i = D \bmod D_p$$

and broadcasts it to the group. Once U_i receives the CRT value from all the other members in the group, it can obtain their corresponding secret shares by computing $k_j = crt_j \bmod m_{ij}$, where $j \neq i$. It then computes the key as $GK = k_1 \oplus k_2 \oplus ... \oplus k_n$.

Explanations of the operations to be performed when a new member joins a group follow. Let us assume the member U_5 wishes to join an existing group of four members $\{U_1, U_2, U_3, U_4\}$.

- Step 1. All the current members (U_1, U_2, U_3, U_4) should compute the hash of the current key GK i.e. $h(GK)$. One of the existing (closest) members should transmit this hash value $h(GK)$ and all the DH public shares y_1, y_2, y_3, y_4 to the new member U_5. Note: h is a public cryptographic hash function.
- Step 2. U_5 will execute the steps given in the previous subsection and broadcast the CRT value crt_5 along with its public DH share y_5.
- Step 3. Existing members can compute the DH key they share with U_5 and thereby calculate the key share k_5 selected by U_5. The new

group key GK_{new} is computed by XORing the hash of the current key and the key share of the newly joining member U_5.

$$GK_{new} = h(GK) \oplus k_5$$

In case of multiple joins, all the joining members should execute the above steps to contribute their shares towards the group key. The existing members then XOR all key shares from the newly joining members to get the new group key. This makes multiple joins very efficient since existing members only perform XOR operations with all the contributed key shares. Also, the join operation (single/multiple) involves only two rounds of communication: one unicast message and one broadcast message.

The leave operation is similar to the join operation but consists of only one round. Let us assume U_2 is going to leave the group. Then the following operations need to be performed:

- Any one of the remaining members, say U_1, should redo the key agreement steps. Here, the LCM value is computed from the DH keys that a member shares with the other members in the group. For the leave operation, the DH key that U_1 shares with U_2 should be left out of this LCM computation. Then, U_1 selects a new key share k_1 and computes the CRT, which is broadcast to the group.
- The other members receive the crt_1 value from U_1 and calculate the new k_1 value. The new group key GK_{new} is computed as follows

$$GK_{new} = GK \oplus k_1$$

In case of multiple leaves, all the leaving members should be left out of the LCM computation as shown above. No extra computation is needed since the protocol need not be repeated for each leaving member. Thus, the CRTDH protocol efficiently supports leave operations and more importantly multiple leave operations in a single round of computation.

2.3.1.2 *Other Proposed Schemes*

Some of the schemes [Basagni *et al.* (2001); Asokan and Ginzboorg (2000); Pietro *et al.* (2002)] proposed for SGC over MANETs assume the existence of a pre-shared secret among the group members. Basagni et al. described the concept of secure pebblenets in [Basagni *et al.* (2001)]. Here, all the nodes in the network share a secret group identity key beforehand. Further, this key is stored in tamper-resistant devices that protect the key from attackers who may capture the mobile nodes. The paper also discussed various protocols for cluster formation. The proposed scheme is suitable in the case, where all the mobile nodes in the MANET are known beforehand. Furthermore, the overhead of such cluster formation protocols should be considered in highly dynamic MANETs.

A password-based multi-party key agreement scheme was proposed in [Asokan and Ginzboorg (2000)]. Here, all the participating members are assumed to share a weak password. The paper further discussed a scheme which derives a strong shared key starting from the already shared weak password. Pietro et al. in [Pietro *et al.* (2002)] discussed a group key management scheme based on the logical key hierarchy (LKH). This scheme also assumes the existence of a shared secret between each member and the GC.

Li et al. proposed a hybrid key agreement protocol in [Li *et al.* (2002)] which is based on GDH.2. The paper also discussed protocols for forming subgroups among ad hoc nodes using the dominating set concept. Though this scheme efficiently supports group formation and user join/leave, it suffers from the same drawbacks as GDH.2 such as the need for member serialization and a GC.

A tree based extension of the Diffie-Hellman scheme for key agreement over MANETs was proposed in [Hietalahti (2001)]. In this scheme a spanning tree is constructed among the participating nodes before the key agreement phase. The key agreement method described is similar to the Tree based Group Diffie Hellman (TGDH) scheme [Kim *et al.* (2000b)] (also see Section 2.2.3.1) though with some differences. Compared to the TGDH scheme, this approach is more centralized and the intermediate nodes are not virtual nodes but the members of the group. The study in [Hietalahti (2001)] does not discuss the aspects of node mobility or user join/leave and its effect on the key generation and tree formation. Its drawback, other than requiring member serialization, is that the root node (initiator of the group) of the tree also performs the role of a group controller in order to set up the group.

2.3.2   *Authenticated Key Exchange (AKE)*

Authenticated Key Exchange (AKE) refers to the protocols that allow a group of users within a larger insecure public network to establish a common group key in such a way that the authenticity of the users is guaranteed [Katz and Yung (2003)]. Authentication has been a crucial aspect for SGC. Substantial research has been carried out in this field and several provably authenticated protocols for group key exchange have been proposed. We discuss some AKE protocols in this section.

2.3.2.1 *AUTH-CRTDH*

We first describe AUTH-CRTDH, a key management scheme for mobile ad hoc networks with authentication capability. Auth-CRTDH is an improvement and extension to CRTDH discussed in Section 2.3.1.1. The users utilize the services of a central key generation center (KGC) for obtaining a secret corresponding to the ID. This central entity is different than a Group Controller (GC) (present in many schemes) as the services of the KGC are required only at system setup and it does not participate in the key agreement procedure. The operations performed at the KGC can be thought of as *offline* operations that need to be performed prior to the formation of any ad hoc environment. However, these operations ensure that each node in the ad hoc network can authenticate itself to any other node in the network. We also propose changes in the join and leave algorithms in CRTDH to make the scheme resistant to *Least Common Multiple* (LCM) attacks. The proposed scheme is described below. Before getting into AUTH-CRTDH, we describe the attacks on CRTDH including the LCM attacks as follows.

The CRTDH protocol, in its current form, lacks mutual authentication among members and hence is vulnerable to the Man-in-the-Middle attack. CRTDH also suffers from another kind of attack, which we call the LCM attack. The attack is possible due to the fact that the LCM for any given set of numbers is not unique to the given set. In other words, there could be many more numbers that could possibly be added to the set and still result in the same LCM value. This could cause problems in the member join and member leave operations.

- The LCM attack on member join. Assume that there exists a group of four members, $\{U_1, U_2, U_3, U_4\}$ who share the group key GK and a user U_5 wishes to join the group. The member join operation in CRTDH requires one of the members (closest to the newly added member) to provide the new member with the hash value of the current group key, along with the public DH shares of the current group members i.e. $h(GK)$ and y_1, y_2, y_3, y_4. User U_5 executes the steps in the key agreement procedure (as described previously) and broadcasts the CRT value crt_5 along with its DH public share y_5.

Existing members obtain the secret share selected by U_5 (k_5) after computing the DH key they share with it. The new group key is obtained by XORing the hash of the current group key and the key share of the newly joining member U_5.

The problem arises in the step where an existing user computes the DH key that it shares with the newly joined member. There could be a case where the addition of the shared DH key does not affect the LCM and hence the LCM value remains the same as before. This could lead to breaching of backward secrecy where the newly added member would be able to obtain the secret share of the existing member. To better explain the problem, assume that user U_4 computes the following after receiving the public share of U_5.

$\{U_4\} \rightarrow m_{41} = 6, m_{42} = 4, m_{43} = 8, m_{45} = 12$.

As can be observed, lcm_4 (=24) remains unchanged upon the addition of m_{45}. Hence, user U_5 could obtain the shared secret k_4, if it could capture previous messages sent by user U_4. Similarly, it is possible that the values for all other $lcms$ remain unchanged after U_5 joins, thus making it possible for U_5 to obtain all the previous key shares. This way U_5 can compute the previous group key.

- The LCM attack on member leave. In CRTDH, when an existing member of the group decides to leave, say U_i, the rekeying operation is performed in order to maintain forward secrecy. Any of the remaining members, say U_j, repeats the key agreement steps, wherein it selects a new k'_j and computes lcm_j again, but leaves the DH key it shares with U_i out of the LCM computation. It then solves the CRT and broadcasts it to the group. The idea here is that since the DH key shared between U_i and U_j i.e. m_{ij} is not included in the LCM and CRT computations, U_i would not be able to obtain the new key share k'_j.

  The problem arises once again due to the fact that there may be cases where the new LCM value for a user may still cover the DH key value that it shared with the departing member. In such a case, the departing member would still be able to decrypt new messages.

The AUTH-CRTDH scheme is able to solve the Man-in-the-Middle attack and the LCM attacks and is described below.

A. **Offline System Setup**

The users in the system are identified with a unique identity (ID). The scheme is analogous to RSA public key cryptosystem, with a value of $e=3$. The system setup procedure carried out at the KGC is described below.

- Step 1: Generate two large prime numbers p_1 and p_2, and let $n = p_1 \cdot p_2$.
- Step 2: Select the center's secret key d from the computation:

$$3 \times d \equiv 1 \bmod (p_1 - 1)(p_2 - 1).$$

- Step 3: Select an integer g that is a primitive element in Z_n^*.
- Step 4: Select a secure hash function h (i.e. one-way and collision-resistant) which is used to compute the extended identity (EID_i) of user U_i as:

$$EID_i = h(ID_i)$$

The hash function is made public.

- Step 5: Generate the user secret key S_i as

$$S_i = EID_i^d (\bmod n)$$

As a result of the above relations, the following equation holds.

$$EID_i = S_i^3 (\bmod n)$$

When a user U_i registers with the system, he sends his ID_i to the KGC, which performs the steps 4 and 5 mentioned above. The KGC sends (n, g, h, S_i) to U_i. U_i keeps S_i secret and stores the public information (n, g, h). In addition, the ID of each user is publicly known.

B. **Key Agreement**

In order to establish the group key for a group with m members, each member U_i should execute the following steps, where $i = 1, 2, ..., m$.

- Step 1: Select the Diffie-Hellman (DH) private share x_i, and compute the following values for the first broadcast.

$$A_i = S_i \cdot g^{2x_i} \ (\bmod n)$$
$$B_i = g^{3x_i} \ (\bmod n)$$

- Step 2: Broadcast A_i and B_i to all members of the group.
- Step 3: Receive the public shares A_j and B_j from other members in the group and authenticate the users. Each member U_i calculates $EID_j = h(ID_j)$ and checks the validity of the member's broadcast message through the following:

$$EID_j = A_j^3/B_j^2$$

If the equation holds true, then the user computes the DH shared secret with each of the members as follows:

$$m_{ij} = B_j^{x_i} \bmod n, \text{ where } j \neq i.$$

Otherwise, U_j's authentication fails and action would be initiated to remove user U_j from the group. Note: Step 6 and Step 7 conduct a second time verification on A_i.

- Step 4: Find the least common multiple (LCM) of all the DH keys calculated in Step 3 as lcm_i.
- Step 5: Select a random share for the group key k_i, such that $k_i < \min\{m_{ij}, \forall j \neq i\}$. Also select an arbitrary number D such that $D \neq k_i$ and another number D_p such that $gcd(D_p, lcm_i) = 1$ (similar to the original CRTDH scheme).
- Step 6: Solve the CRT: (as in the original CRTDH scheme)

$$crt_i \equiv k_i \bmod lcm_i$$
$$crt_i \equiv D \bmod D_p$$

For authentication purposes, the user also computes the following

$$
\begin{aligned}
X_i &= h(k_i) \cdot g^{2D} \cdot S_i \pmod n \\
Y_i &= g^{3D} \pmod n \\
Z_i &= \{A_i || X_i\}_{k_i}
\end{aligned}
$$

and broadcasts $\{X_i, Y_i, Z_i, crt_i\}$ to the group.

- Step 7: Receive the CRT values from all the other members in the group and calculate the following: (similar to the CRTDH scheme)

$$k_j = crt_j \bmod m_{ij}$$

for all $j \neq i$. To validate the authenticity of the key k_j, the user also computes EID_j and verifies the following equation

$$(h(k_j))^3 = X_j^3/(Y_j^2 \cdot EID_j)$$

In addition, $\{A_j || X_j\}_{k_j}$ will be computed and verified against Z_j. This aims at authenticating A_i (Step 1) and X_i.

After both of the above verifications succeed, the user then computes the group key (as in the CRTDH scheme)

$$GK = k_1 \oplus k_2 \oplus \ldots \oplus k_n$$

Thus the Chinese Remainder Theorem is used to send the secret key share of each user (disguised) to all the other members in the group. The mutual authentication is provided by using an ID based scheme.

2.3.2.2 *Other Proposed Schemes*

Katz and Yung [Katz and Yung (2003)] have proposed a scalable protocol for authenticated group key exchange among n parties. The work done by Katz and Yung has been motivated by the fact that the protocols that have been proposed in literature for SGC (like the GDH protocols, the CLIQUES protocol suite, the BD protocol etc.) have not been followed up with a rigorous proof of security. This fact has led to analysis of these protocols and certain flaws were found out in these protocols. The security analysis of CLIQUES was carried out early in 2001. The BD protocol was found out to be "heuristic" and had not been proven secure. The authors present a *constant round* and *scalable* protocol for group AKE and it is provably-secure in the standard model. The proposed protocol is indeed similar to the BD protocol and its security is provided via reduction to the Decisional Diffie-Hellman (DDH) assumption. The DDH assumption informally says that it is hard to distinguish between tuples of the form (g^x, g^y, g^{xy}) (called *Diffie Hellman tuples*) and $(g^x g^y g^z)$ (called *Random tuples*) where $z \neq x \cdot y$ is random. The authors also propose and analyze a scalable compiler that transforms any key-exchange protocol which is secure against a passive eavesdropper to one which is secure against a stronger and more realistic active adversary who controls all communication in the network. The complier adds only one round and $O(1)$ communication (per user) to the original scheme.

Bresson et al. in [Bresson *et al.* (2001)] study the provably authenticated group Diffie-Hellman key exchange for groups where the membership is dynamic, i.e. where members may join and leave the multicast group at any given time. The authors argue that a lot of schemes have been proposed for the problem of authenticated key exchange using group Diffie-Hellman protocol, but no formal treatment for this cryptographic problem has been suggested. The authors present a security model for this problem and use it to precisely define AKE. They further define the execution of an authenticated group Diffie-Hellman scheme and prove its security. The authors also discuss a generic transformation for turning an AKE protocol into a protocol that provides *mutual authentication*. The security of the transformation is also justified under certain assumptions. The model proposed by the authors assumes that the player of the protocol does not deviate from the protocol, the adversary is not a player and the adversary's capabilities are modeled by various queries.

Recently, in Asiacrypt 2004, Kim et al. proposed an efficient provably secure authenticated group key exchange (AGKE) scheme with constant round [Kim *et al.* (2004a)]. The paper discusses an authenticated group key exchange scheme for settings of ad-hoc networks where the group membership is highly dynamic and no central trusted party exists. According to the authors, most of the proposed schemes so far for AGKE have the number of rounds linear with respect to the number of members in the group. Hence, the schemes are neither scalable nor practical and are highly inefficient. The proposed scheme in the paper achieves AGKE in constant number of rounds (2 rounds for group operations like setup, join and leave) and is contributory and efficient. Each user executes at most three modular exponentiations and $O(n)$ XOR operations. For authentication, each group member generates 2 signatures and performs $2n$ signature verifications.

2.3.3   Self-Healing Key Distribution

The classical group key management schemes assume that the underlying networks are reliable and no member ever misses a key broadcast. But networks are not always reliable, especially in a dynamic wireless environment. In 2002, Staddon et al. [Staddon *et al.* (2002)] proposed a key distribution mechanism over unreliable networks that they called the self healing scheme. The basic idea behind self healing schemes is that if a user misses a session key broadcast, it should be able to recover that missed session key without interacting with the GC. The research community has been interested in such an idea and proposed several self healing schemes [Staddon *et al.* (2002); Blundo *et al.* (2004); Liu *et al.* (2003); More *et al.* (2003); Zhu *et al.* (2003)] since 2002.

2.3.3.1   *Self-Healing based on Polynomials and Secret Sharing*

We will discuss the pioneer scheme by Staddon et al. here. This scheme uses the Shamir's concept of secret sharing [Shamir (1979b)] to share current session key. Self healing is achieved by splitting any session key K into two polynomials $p(x) + q(x)$ and broadcasting the polynomials. The key polynomials are properly masked to ensure security.

- *Setup:* Let m be the number of sessions (this scheme achieves self healing over a cluster of m sessions), n the number of users (each one is assigned a unique index) and t the degree of polynomials. Let q be a large prime and N be an element of F_q that is not equal to any of user indices.

  The GC chooses m polynomials $p_1(x), \ldots, p_m(x)$ in $F_q[x]$, each of degree t, and m session keys, $K_1, \ldots, K_m \in F_q$ all at random and defines a polynomial in $F_q[x]$, $q_j(x) = K_j - p_j(x)$, for each session $j = 1, \cdots, m$. In addition, for each session j, the GC randomly chooses m polynomials in $F_q[x, y]$ $s_{i,j}(x, y)$ for $i \in \{1, \ldots, m\}$ as:

$$s_{i,j}(x, y) = a_{0,0}^{i,j} + a_{1,0}^{i,j}x + a_{0,1}^{i,j}y + \cdots + a_{t,t}^{i,j}x^t y^t$$

For each user U_i $(i = 1, \cdots, n)$, the GC computes and sends him/her the secret share securely:

$$S_i = \{N, i, s_{1,1}(i, i), \ldots, s_{m,1}(i, i), s_{1,2}(i, i), \ldots,$$

$$s_{m,2}(i, i), \ldots, s_{1,m}(i, i), \ldots, s_{m,m}(i, i)\}$$

- *Broadcast:* Let $A, R \subseteq \{U_1, \ldots, U_n\}, |R| \leq t$, denote the sets of active users and revoked users in session j respectively. The GC chooses $W = \{w_1, w_2, \ldots, w_t\} \subseteq F_q$ such that the indices of the users in R are contained in W and none of the indices of the users in A is contained in W and $N \notin W$. The broadcast in session $j \in \{1, \ldots, m\}$ is $B_j = B_j^1 \cup B_j^2$, where:

$$B_j^1 = \{p_{j'}(x) + s_{j',j}(N, x)\}_{j'=1,\ldots,j-1}$$

$$\cup$$

$$\{K_j + s_{j,j}(N, x)\}$$

$$\cup$$

$$\{q_{j'}(x) + s_{j',j}(N, x)\}_{j'=j+1,\ldots,m}$$

$$B_j^2 = \{w_\ell, \{s_{j',j}(w_\ell, x)\}_{j'=1,\ldots,m}\}_{\ell=1,\ldots,t}$$

- *Session key and shares recovery in session j:* For a user U_i belonging to A, U_i is able to recover the polynomial $s_{j,j}(x,i)$ as follows: 1) getting t points $\{(w_\ell, s_{j,j}(w_\ell, i))\}_{\ell=1,\dots,t}$ by setting $x = i$ respectively in polynomials $\{s_{j,j}(w_\ell, x)\}_{\ell=1,\dots,t}$, which are received from B_j^2; 2) along with $(i, s_{j,j}(i,i))$ in his/her secret share, the $t + 1$ points are interpolated to recover $s_{j,j}(x,i)$. Then U_i recovers K_j by evaluating $s_{j,j}(x,i)$ at $x = N$, and subtracting this value from $(K_j + s_{j,j}(N,x))|_{x=i}$. Similarly, U_i can interpolate to determine $\{s_{j',j}(x,i)\}_{j'=1,\dots,j-1,j+1,\dots,m}$ and therefore, recover the shares $\{p_{j'}(i)\}_{j'=1,\dots,j-1}$ and $\{q_{j'}(i)\}_{j'=j+1,\dots,m}$.

  The lost session key can be obtained as follows. Suppose U_i missed the broadcast for session j, but received the broadcast for session $j - r_1$ and the broadcast for session $j + r_2$. From broadcast $j - r_1$, U_i obtains the share $q_j(i)$ (one of the future key shares) and from broadcast $j + r_2$, U_i obtains the share $p_j(i)$ (one of the previous key shares). Then U_i can get $K_j = p_j(i) + q_j(i)$.

2.3.3.2   Other Proposed Schemes

In an effort to increase the efficiency of the Staddon's second Scheme [Staddon *et al.* (2002)], Liu et al. [Liu *et al.* (2003)] have proposed an efficient self-healing key distribution scheme which reduces the communication cost and storage overhead. An important requirement of Liu et al.'s scheme is that the set R_j of revoked group members must change monotonically. This means, $R_{j_1} \subseteq R_{j_2}$ for $1 \le j_1 \le j_2 \le m$. Otherwise, a group member who is revoked in session j, rejoins the group in a later session, can recover the session key for j. This means that the scheme is prone to a rejoin-collusion attack and does not allow temporary revocation.

Blundo et al. [Blundo *et al.* (2004)] have presented a study of self-healing key distribution schemes and proposed some new designs. It also pointed out that an attack is possible on Staddon's first scheme without using polynomial interpolation. It proposed a solution to the problem.

The scheme proposed by More et al. [More *et al.* (2003)] uses the same idea of splitting a session key into two polynomials as $K_j = p(x) + q(x)$. They introduced the concept of sliding window. A window in self-healing determines the range (the sessions) that the self-healing can apply to. Only the previous and subsequent sessions which are in the window can be used to recover the lost key of a session. In non-sliding window schemes, the windows are fixed, do not overlap, and are independent. The self-healing ability cannot pass across the boundary of windows, e.g. the end sessions in a window can not be used to recover the lost session key of the front sessions in the following window. In addition, at the beginning of each window, a system set up (which is complicated) needs to be done. In this sliding window scheme, any session has its own window and a session is the center of its window. Adjacent windows are heavily overlapped. The lost key of a session can be recovered from its previous and following sessions as long as these sessions are within the δ range. Also the expensive set up at the beginning of each window is eliminated. Finally, the scheme also improves Staddon's scheme [Staddon *et al.* (2002)] with reduction of the broadcast size and personal key sizes.

The scheme proposed in [Zhu *et al.* (2003)] uses the Subset Difference Rekeying method (SDR), is a separate class of self-healing key management schemes, and does not involve polynomials. SDR is based on the binary key tree key management scheme (i.e. LKH) (see Section 2.2.1.1) and its principle is as follows. The group manager maintains a binary key tree that contains all the users as leaves. Each group member receives from the group manager the subset cover keys of all possible subsets that the member might belong to. The binary tree is chosen large enough to accommodate the largest possible number of users. The group manager partitions the current group members into a minimum number of subsets during a rekeying operation. The group manager then encrypts the new group key with the common key of each subset separately. Therefore, the group member who belongs to one of these subsets and has the key of one of these subsets can decrypt the new group key. The self-healing capability is added to SDR as follows. Let $T(i)$ be the current rekeying time, and $K(i)$ is the new group key to be distributed. A simple method that enables a current member to recover the previous m group keys, i.e., $K(i-m), K(i-m+1), \ldots, K(i-2), K(i-1)$, is to encrypt these m keys with the current group key $K(i)$ individually and broadcast them to the group. Hence, when a user receives $K(i)$ reliably, it will be able to recover the previous m keys. Moreover, it is necessary to bind the time at which a user joined the group with its ability to recover a previous group key. This means, a user should only be allowed to recover the group keys that were used after he joined the group (but not the keys before he joined the group). To achieve this goal, the group manager encrypts each group key, $K(i-j)$, $1 \le j \le m$ with a key that is derived by XORing the current group key $K(i)$ with the group key $K(j-1)$ (i.e. the previous group key).

2.3.4 Block-free Group Key Management

A common problem with most group key management schemes (especially distributed ones) is that during the process of rekeying, all members stop data communication until the new group (root) key is distributed (formed) (this is called a *block*). We propose the concept of Block-free group key management for SGC which allows data communication to continue without interruption. The basic idea is as follows. (1) There are two kinds of keys: *front-end* key and *back-end* keys. The front-end key can be computed by all group members whereas for back-end keys, each member will have one key he/she cannot compute. (2) Whenever a member leaves[1], the remaining members *switch* to the *back-end* key the leaving member does not have *immediately*. And (3) Re-computation of all keys is performed in the *background*. There are two meanings of *background* here. One is that computation of keys is performed during the intervals between sending out packets and waiting to receive packets, thus utilizing idle computer time to compute new keys. The other meaning is that the rekeying materials are piggybacked on transmitted data packets and are only sent as independent packets unless there are no outgoing data packets, thus, saving network transmission bandwidth.

2.3.4.1 BF-TGDH

We discuss the following Block-Free TGDH mechanism (BF-TGDH) which is based on TGDH (See section 2.2.3.1): (1) the front-end key is the root key in TDGH and (2) the back-end keys are computed in an identical way to the root key as follows. Suppose the root key is denoted as $RK(a_1 \cdots a_i \cdots a_n)$ where $a_1, \cdots, a_i, \cdots, a_n$ (correspondingly $b_1 = g^{a_1}, \cdots, b_i = g^{a_i}, \cdots, b_n = g^{a_n}$) are private shares (correspondingly disguised public shares) of $U_1, \cdots, U_i, \cdots, U_n$ respectively. Imagine there are n *dummy members* $D_1, \cdots, D_i, \cdots, D_n$ and corresponding n *dummy private shares* $d_1, \cdots, d_i, \cdots, d_n$. The members can compute a back-end key, called *dummy root key* and denoted as $DRK_i(a_1 \cdots d_i \cdots a_n)$ $(i = 1, \cdots, n)$, in parallel with the computation of the root key $RK(a_1 \cdots a_i \cdots a_n)$. In DRK_i, the private share a_i is replaced by dummy private share d_i. Therefore, DRK_i can be computed by all members except U_i.

Suppose that every member U_i has a permanent Diffie-Hellman private share a_i and disguised public share b_i. Moreover suppose that there is an

---

[1] The join operation is generally much easier and more efficient to perform than the leave operation.

off-line Diffie-Hellman *shares generator*. The *shares generator* generates n (the maximum possible number of members in the group) Diffie-Hellman private shares $d_1, \cdots, d_n$ and their corresponding disguised public shares $e_1 = g^{d_1} \bmod p, \cdots, e_n = g^{d_n} \bmod p$. $e_1, \cdots, e_n$ are made public. These components are called dummy components. $d_1, \cdots, d_n$ are called *dummy private shares* and $e_1, \cdots, e_n$ are called *dummy disguised public shares*. We also imagine that there are n dummy members $D_1, \cdots, D_n$ who possess these dummy components $(d_1, e_1), \cdots, (d_n, e_n)$ respectively. Assume there is a public one-way function *POF*.

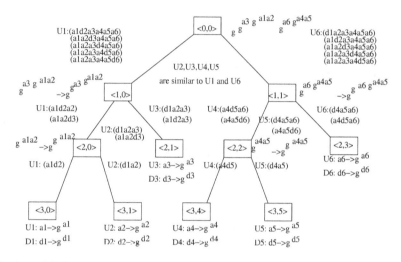

Fig. 2.10   Block-Free Tree-based Group Diffie-Hellman key agreement for seamless SGC.

Figure 2.10 shows an example of BF-TGDH. The notation $(a_1 \cdots d_i \cdots a_m)$ represents $k(a_1 \cdots d_i \cdots a_m) \rightarrow g^{k(a_1 \cdots d_i \cdots a_m)}$ where $k(a_1 \cdots d_i \cdots a_m)$ is a dummy secret key and $BK(a_1 \cdots d_i \cdots a_m) = g^{k(a_1 \cdots d_i \cdots a_m)}$ is a dummy blinded key. D_i's are dummy members and d_i's $(e_i = g^{d_i})$ are dummy private shares (dummy disguised public shares) which are generated by an off-line shares generator. For example, let us consider U_1. U_1 can compute $(a_1 d_2)$ (i.e., $g^{a_1 d_2} \rightarrow g^{g^{a_1 d_2}}$) and broadcast $BK(a_1 d_2) = g^{g^{a_1 d_2}}$. Then U_1 computes $(a_1 d_2 a_3)$ (i.e., $g^{g^{a_1 d_2 a_3}} \rightarrow g^{g^{g^{a_1 d_2 a_3}}}$ after receiving g^{a_3} from U_3) and $(a_1 a_2 d_3)$ from g^{d_3} which is generated by the off-line shares generator. Finally, U_1 computes $(a_1 d_2 a_3 a_4 a_5 a_6)$ (when receiving $g^{g^{a_4 g^{a_5 a_6}}}$), $(a_1 a_2 d_3 a_4 a_5 a_6)$ (when receiving $g^{g^{a_4 g^{a_5 a_6}}}$), $(a_1 a_2 a_3 d_4 a_5 a_6)$ (when receiving $g^{g^{d_4 g^{a_5 a_6}}}$), $(a_1 a_2 a_3 a_4 d_5 a_6)$ (when receiving $g^{g^{a_4 g^{d_5 a_6}}}$), and $(a_1 a_2 a_3 a_4 a_5 d_6)$ (when receiving $g^{g^{a_4 g^{a_5 d_6}}}$).

As in TGDH, each leaf node $< l, v >$ is associated with a member U_i. Moreover, $< l, v >$ is imagined to be associated with a dummy member D_i. As in TGDH, the group members compute the root key $RK(a_1 \cdots a_n)$, where $a_1, \cdots, a_n$ are permanent private shares of group members $U_1, \cdots, U_n$. Moreover, every member U_i can compute dummy root keys $DRK_j(a_1 \cdots d_j \cdots a_n)$, $j = 1, \cdots, i\text{-}1, i+1, \cdots, n$ in parallel with the computation of the root key RK with a little computation cost but no extra communication cost. For secure group communication, all group members pass the root key RK through the public one-way function POF to get the Data Encryption Key (DEK), i.e., $DEK = POF(RK(a_1 \cdots a_n))$ and then encrypt the message with DEK. Moreover, when a member broadcasts a message, it will sign the message using ElGamal signature protocol. All other members can authenticate the sender.

When a member joins the group, the member will broadcast a join request. After receiving the join request, every group member will pass the current DEK through the one-way function to get the new DEK $(=POF(DEK))$, and use the new DEK to encrypt and decrypt the messages without any interruption. The sponsor of the joining member is responsible for sending the new DEK to the joining member. Before sending the new DEK, the sponsor encrypts it with the Diffie-Hellman key between him/her and the joining member. As a result, the joining member can participate in the group communication immediately. During the data communication, the sponsor of the joining member will compute, *in the background*, the secret keys/dummy secret keys and blinded keys/dummy blinded keys on the path from his/her leaf node to the root node, and broadcast the blinded keys/dummy blinded keys to the group by appending the blinded keys/dummy blinded keys to out-going messages or a separate packet if there are no out-going messages. All the group members will compute the new root key and new dummy root keys after they receive the blinded keys/dummy blinded keys from the sponsor. The sponsor also sends blinded keys and dummy blinded keys, specifically, those keys corresponding to the nodes along the path from the joining member to the root, to the joining member so that the joining member can compute the new root key and new dummy root keys. Once a group member computes the new root key (and new dummy root keys), it computes the new $DEK = POF(RK(a_1 \cdots a_n))$ and uses the new DEK for communication (it is possible for him/her to use the old DEK to decrypt some messages encrypted with the old DEK for a while[2]).

When a member U_i leaves, after receiving the departure request, all remaining members will use the dummy root key DRK_i to get the new DEK (i.e., $DEK = POF(DRK_i)$) and use the new DEK to continue the communication without interruption. However, the leaving member U_i cannot decrypt these messages because its share is not in DRK_i. During the communication, the sponsor of the leaving member will recompute the secret keys/dummy secret keys and blinded keys/dummy blinded keys along the path from him/her to the root and broadcast all blinded keys/dummy blinded keys by appending them to out-going messages.

When multiple members join at the same time, all members will pass the current DEK through the one-way function to get the new DEK and use the new DEK to communicate. There will be multiple sponsors in general and a member may be the sponsor for several joining members. Each sponsor will encrypt the new DEK using the Diffie-Hellman key between him/herself and one of his/her joining members and send the DEK to the joining member. The joining members can participate in the communication immediately. During communication, the new root key and dummy root keys will be reestablished.

When multiple members (say, three) leave at the same time (suppose the members are U_1, U_4, U_6), all remaining members will get the new DEK as follows: multiply the three dummy root keys to get the product $PDRK = DRK_1 \times DRK_4 \times DRK_6$ and then pass the product $PDRK$ through the one-way function to get the new DEK. Since any leaving member will have one dummy root key missing, he/she cannot compute the new DEK. After the new DEK is computed, the group communication continues and the leaving members are excluded. During the process of communication, the sponsors will reestablish the new root key and dummy root keys. Note that if two leaving members collude, they have all dummy root keys for computing the new DEK, so BF-TGDH is not resistant to the collusion of leaving members who leave at the same time. However, this success due to collusion will persist just for a short time. Once the new root key and dummy root keys are reestablished, the leaving members are excluded completely.

When multiple members join and leave at the same time, the new DEK will be the one computed similar to the case of multiple leaves. This new

---

[2]The version number of the DEK used in the encryption may be included in the messages.

DEK will be sent to joining members immediately. Therefore, the group communication can continue without interruption.

2.3.5   Secure Dynamic Conferencing

Secure Dynamic conferencing refers to a scenario where given a group of members, any subset of members can form a privileged subgroup, and the members in a subgroup are able to communicate in such a way that any other individual not in the subgroup or any outsider is unable to read messages destined to the subgroup even when he/she can intercept the messages. The entire group is called the *universe* and each possible subgroup a *conference*. The first problem facing SDC is *conference key management* (CKM) since the members in a conference need to establish a conference key which is used to encrypt/decrypt the messages destined to the conference. The difficulty for this problem comes from the potential large (in fact, exponential) number of possible conferences, i.e., $2^n - n - 1$ for a group of size n, and dynamics that members can join or leave a conference, even the universe, dynamically.

It is worthy to mention that SDC is closely related to (SGC). SGC can be considered as a specific case of SDC where all group members form a single subgroup and communicate among all group members or to say, SDC is an extension to SGC. However, the CKM problem in SDC is much more difficult to deal with than the group key management (GKM) problem in SGC. As we know, GKM deals with only one SGC group but CKM deals with exponential number of possible SDC conferences.

There have been some CKM protocols for SDC proposed recently by researchers. We discuss some typical schemes in this section.

2.3.5.1   KTDCKM-SDC

We first present a scheme, called Key Tree based Distributed Conference Key Management for Secure Dynamic Conferencing (KTDCKM-SDC) [Adusumili and Zou (2005)]. The scheme is based on the principle of DGKD (See section 2.2.4). It manipulates the same binary key tree, maintains the same sponsor fields, and distributes conference keys in two multicast rounds. An initiator of a conference generates a random conference key and distributes the conference key to the co-distributors in the first round. Then the co-distributors distribute the conference key to corresponding conference members in a distributed/parallel manner in the second round.

In detail, KTDCKM-SGC performs the following steps to distribute the conference key (Suppose member U wants to initiate a conference of $\{U\} \cup \{U_{i_1}, \cdots, U_{i_l}\}$)

(1) U first determines the keys which cover exactly these members.
(2) If there is only one key determined (i.e. all the conference members are exactly covered under one subtree), the key will be used as the conference key. Otherwise, the following steps are performed.
(3) U selects a random conference key CK.
(4) For each of the above determined keys, U determines its co-distributor, which is the sponsor of the subtree rooted at the node corresponding to this key.
(5) U encrypts CK with the public keys of co-distributors respectively and multicasts the encrypted key.
(6) When a co-distributor receives the encrypted CK, it decrypts, reencrypts the CK with the key exactly covering the co-distributor and some other conference members, and broadcasts (all the co-distributors perform this step in a distributed/parallel way).
(7) The members covered by the key (thus, all the conference members covered by all the above keys) will get the conference key CK.

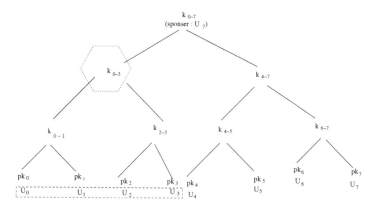

Fig. 2.11 U_0 initiates conference $\{U_0, U_1, U_2, U_3\}$ and k_{0-3} is used as the conference key CK.

Let us see two examples. In Figure 2.11, all the conference members $\{U_0, U_1, U_2, U_3\}$ are covered under key k_{0-3}. Thus, k_{0-3} is selected as the conference key for this conference. In Figure 2.12, $\{U_1, U_3, \cdots, U_7\}$ are covered by the keys pk_1, pk_3, and k_{4-7}. The sponsors corresponding to these key nodes are U_1, U_3, and U_7. U_1 is the initiator so U_3 and U_7 become the co-distributors of U_1. U_1 selects a random conference key CK, encrypts CK with the public keys of co-distributors, i.e., pk_3 and pk_7. Then the co-distributors, here only U_7, encrypts CK with k_{4-7} and distributes it. As a result, all the conference members will get CK.

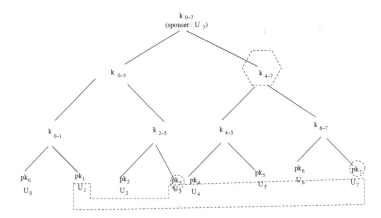

Fig. 2.12 U_1 initiates conference $\{U_1, U_3, \cdots, U_7\}$ and pk_3 and pk_7 are used to encrypt the conference key CK. Then U_7 encrypts CK with k_{4-7}.

KTDCKM-SDC is a distributed CKM scheme. There is a corresponding centralized CKM scheme, called Key Tree based Secure Dynamic Conferencing (KTSDC) scheme [Zou *et al.* (2004a,b)]. KTSDC is much like KTDCKM-SDC in the sense that (1) it contains two round transmission of keys and (2) the initiator of a conference computes the subtrees which together cover exactly the members of the conference. The differences here are also twofold: (1) a leaf key is the secret key shared between the leaf member and the GC and (2) the initiator sends the conference key (along with the subtrees indices) to the GC (by encrypting the conference key with the leaf key) in the first round and the GC distributes the conference key (which is encrypted by the keys of these subtrees) to conference members.

The following two examples illustrate the KTSDC principles. Let us first look at Figure 2.11 (note: the leaf (public) keys pk_i are substituted by (secret) keys k_i) and assume that U_0, U_1, U_2, U_3 want to form a conference. Since they are exactly covered under one subtree, key k_{0-3} will be the conference key. Then, let us look at Figure 2.12 and assume that U_1 initiates a conference including $U_1, U_3, \cdots, U_7$. Then U_1 selects a random conference key CK, encrypts CK with k_1, and send it (along with the indices $\{3, 4-7\}$

of $\{k_3, k_{4-7}\}$) to the GC. The GC decrypts CK and encrypts CK with k_3 and k_{4-7} and multicasts it. As a result, U_3 and U_4 to U_7 all get the conference key CK.

2.3.5.2 *Other Proposed Schemes*

Besides KTSDC and KTDCKM-SDC discussed above, there have been several proposed SDC CKM schemes in the literature. These schemes can be classified as naive solution [Desmedt and Viswanathan (1998)], public key based SDC (PKSDC) schemes including Chinese Remainder Theorem based SDC (secure lock) (SLSDC) scheme [Chiou and W.T.Chen (1989)], symmetric polynomial based schemes (SPSDC) [Blundo *et al.* (1998b, 1993); Zou *et al.* (2002a)], and interval based SDC scheme (ISDC) [Gouda *et al.* (2002a,b)]. Except for PKSDC and SLSDC, all others are centralized schemes. We briefly summarize them below.

The naive scheme proposed in [Desmedt and Viswanathan (1998)] assigns one (independent) key for each of $2^n - n - 1$ possible conferences, and gives each member $2^{n-1} - 1$ keys, one for each of the conferences the member can join. Whenever a member wants to communicate to the members in a conference, the member simply picks up the key corresponding to the conference and does it. The main problems with the naive solution are its exponential number of keys and no support for dynamics.

In PKSDC, whenever a member U_i wants to send a message M to a conference $C = \{U_{i_1}, \cdots, U_{i_\ell}\} \cup \{U_i\}$, U_i selects a random session key k, encrypts the message with k, and encrypts k with these members' public keys $P_{i_1}, \cdots, P_{i_\ell}$ respectively, and broadcasts $(\{E_{P_{i_1}}(k), \cdots, E_{P_{i_\ell}}(k)\}, \{M\}_k)$ to the group. An improved scheme, called secure lock based secure dynamic conferencing scheme (denoted as SLSDC), was proposed in [Chiou and W.T.Chen (1989)]. In SLSDC, the multiple encryptions of k, i.e., $\{E_{P_{i_1}}(k), \cdots, E_{P_{i_\ell}}(k)\}$ are combined into one value (called secure lock) using Chinese Remainder Theorem. The SLSDC scheme has two advantages over PKSDC: a receiver can compute the key directly and efficiently from the lock value and the conference members are hidden so that non conference members or outsiders can not know who are in the conference. The main problems with these kinds of schemes are the inefficiency of public key encryption and decryption and the requirement of PKI.

In a symmetric polynomial based secure dynamic conferencing scheme (denoted as SPSDC) [Zou *et al.* (2002a)], each member is initially given certain secret information (a share of a symmetric polynomial), from which (along with some public information) the member can compute any conference key the member can join later. The main problem with this scheme is the exponential size of secret information.

ISDC [Gouda *et al.* (2002a,b)] is similar to KTSDC in the sense that it is also based on the key tree scheme and also needs to determine the keys in the key tree which cover *exactly* the conference members. However, there are three main differences from KTSDC. One is that the GC in ISDC relays all the conference messages, i.e., decrypting the message, encrypting the messages (with (multiple) keys covering the conference members) and sending the messages. This will make the GC very busy and become a performance bottle-neck. The second difference is the way to determine the keys which *exactly* cover all conference members. ISDC finishes this by grouping the members into distinct intervals, then splitting each interval into basic intervals. This is inefficient compared to the KTSDC algorithm which computes the necessary keys directly without the concepts of intervals or basic intervals. The third difference is that the computation of intervals and basic intervals for every conference is performed by the GC, which increases GC's workload and worsens GC's performance.

It is worthy to discuss the power of SGC key management schemes. As mentioned previously, SDC and SGC have close relation: SGC is a specific case of SDC or SDC is an extension of SGC. By nature, a SDC scheme can be used directly for SGC. The only disadvantage of this utilization is the waste of capability of a SDC scheme or to say, the unnecessary high complexity. However, a SGC scheme is in general unable to be used for SDC. For most existing SGC schemes, it is required that each conference have a respective copy of the SGC key management scheme. Since there are potentially exponential number of conferences, there would be exponential number of copies of the SGC key management scheme. Thus, such kind of utilization is generally infeasible. The very power of DGKD is that this SGC scheme can be utilized for SDC in the identical and efficient way.

2.4   Conclusion

Secure group communication (SGC) is crucial to the success of collaborative applications of the future and is a critical component of the TCC framework. Encryption provides confidentiality of communication but requires keys to be distributed and managed efficiently in a dynamic environment. In this chapter, we have reviewed various classes of key management in quite detail. The key management schemes have greatly improved over time to become more efficient, scalable, practical and secure. SGC faces some practical challenges which need to be addressed, in order to realize the promise of taking collaborative computing applications to greater heights in the era of trusted collaborative computing.

Chapter 3

Cryptography based Access Control

As discussed in Introduction, trusted collaborative computing involves resource sharing and data exchange. However, sharing of resources and data among multiple participating entities must be in a finely-controlled manner to meet various and flexible access relations, in particular, many-to-many relation and hierarchical relation. In this chapter, we first overview general access control mechanisms and then focus our discussion on cryptography based access control schemes.

3.1 Overview of Access Control in Collaborative Computing

Access control is an intrinsic security problem in computing systems where users and resources are involved, such as file systems, operating systems, database systems, and networking systems. It means controlling users' access to certain resources by granting or preventing users' access to resources as required [Silberschatz *et al.* (2001)]. The resource being accessed is called an *object*[1] and the user or the program running on behalf of the user that accesses an object is called a *subject* [Sandhu and Samarati (1994)][2].

There are two access control models in TCC: differential access control (DIF-AC) and hierarchical access control (HAC). In DIF-AC, a user can (and only can) access certain resources and a resource can (and only can) be accessed by certain users (i.e, many-to-many relation). Typical DIF-AC schemes can be found in [Abdalla *et al.* (2000); Bar-Haim (2001); Huang *et al.* (2000); Kogan *et al.* (2003); Wool (2000)]. HAC occurs when resources (and users) have some hierarchical relation: resources are assigned

---

[1]We use the terms resources, data and objects interchangeably.

[2]We use the terms users, members and subjects interchangeably.

levels and a user who has the access right to a resource at one level is automatically granted access to the resources which are the resource's children or descendants at lower levels. A typical hierarchy has a partial order $\leq$, where $C_i \leq C_j$ means that a user at C_j can access resources at C_j as well as C_i. C_j is called an ancestor class of C_i whereas C_i is called a descendant class of C_j. A typical hierarchy is represented by a directed acyclic graph (DAG)[3] (see Figure 3.4).

Traditionally, access control has been implemented using noncryptographic techniques. These techniques are typically classified as the following categories [Sandhu and Samarati (1994); Tripunitara and Li (2004)]: Discretionary access control (DAC) [Harrison *et al.* (1976); Lampson (1974)], Mandatory access control (MAC) [Denning (1976)] and Role-based access control (RBAC) [Al-Kahtani and Sandhu (2004); Ferraiolo *et al.* (2001); Moyer and Ahamad (2001); Park and Hwang (2003); Sandhu *et al.* (1996)]. Some other (incremental or supplementary) access control models have been also proposed, such as Task-Based Access Control (TBAC), Team-Based Access Control (TBAC), Spatial Access Control (SAC) and Context-Aware Access Control (Context-AW) [Tolone *et al.* (2005)]. We briefly summarize them in the following.

(1) Discretionary Access Control (DAC). DAC [Harrison *et al.* (1976); Lampson (1974)] specifies which users can access which objects in which modes. A typical representation for DAC is Access Control Matrix (ACM) in which rows are subjects (i.e. users) and columns are objects (i.e. files) and row-column entries are access rights (e.g., read, write, and/or execute). Two concrete implementations of DAC are Access Control List (ACL) and Capability List (C-List). In ACL, for each object, a list of users, along with their respective access modes, are specified. This approach corresponds to storing the ACM by columns. In C-List, for each subject, a list of objects, along with their access modes, are specified. C-List corresponds to storing the ACM by rows. DAC is based on the notion that an individual user is owner of an object and therefore has complete discretion over who should be authorized to access the object and in which modes. DAC has an inherent weakness that information can be copied from one object to another, so access to a copy is possible even if the owner of the original does not provide access to the original [Sandhu and Samarati (1994)].

(2) Mandatory Access Control (MAC). MAC is an approach to controlling

---

[3]The nodes of a DAG represent classes in the hierarchy.

access to objects by subjects, contingent on a mandated formalized process, which is set by the system, but not by the owners of objects (like in DAC). The owner of an object must also abide by the system-specified access rules for the object. In this model, every user (and object) is assigned a security label. Access to an object by a subject is granted only if a certain relationship is satisfied between the security labels associated with the two [Sandhu and Samarati (1994)]. For example, suppose that λ signifies the security label of either a subject or an object, then the system may have the following mandatory rules [Sandhu (1993)]: (1) simple-security property (also called read-down): subject s can read object o only if $\lambda(s) \geq \lambda(o)$; (2) $\star$-property (also called write-up): subject s can write object o only if $\lambda(s) \leq \lambda(o)$. MAC is commonly represented by Lattice-based access control model [Denning (1976); Sandhu (1993)].

(3) Role-Based Access Control (RBAC). Different from DAC, which associates objects to subjects or even group of subjects directly, or MAC, which grants a subject's access to an object based on their security (confidential and clearance) labels, RBAC associates them indirectly via roles. A role is a semantic construct which forms the basis of access control policy [Sandhu *et al.* (1994)]. A role can represent specific task competency such as that of a doctor or can embody the authority and responsibility of, say, a project manager. Roles are created according to the job functions performed in a system or an organization. Then, access rights (permissions, or authorizations) are associated with roles and users are assigned roles on the basis of their specific job responsibilities and qualifications [Sandhu *et al.* (1994)].

(4) Task-Based Access Control (TBAC). TBAC considers that a task may consist of multiple steps. Each step is associated with a protection state containing a set of permissions based on the context the step is currently in. This model can be considered as an active model in which permissions dynamically change as a task progresses to completion. Unlike RBAC, TBAC supports type-based, instance, and usage-based access. In addition, authorizations have strict runtime usage, validity, and expiration features.

(5) Team-Based Access Control (TMAC). Different from RBAC, which defines a team as users who are associated with a same role, TMAC defines access rights directly for teams. Besides offering the advantages of RBAC, TMAC also provides fine-grained control on individual users in certain roles and on individual object instances. Moreover,

TMAC defines two important aspects of collaboration context: user context and object context. The former is used to identify specific users who play a role on a team at any time and the latter identifies specific objects needed for collaboration purposes. A further extension is Context-based TMAC (C-TMAC), which includes some other contextual information, such as time, place, etc.

(6) Spatial Access Control (SAC). In this model, the collaboration environments are taken into account and used to hide explicit security mechanisms from the end users. Two main components are contained in the model: a boundary and an access graph. The former is used to divide the collaboration environment into regions. It also accounts for both traversal and awareness within regions. The credentials are used to determine access rights within regions. The latter specifies the constraints on movement in the collaboration space and manage the access requirements in the environment.

(7) Context-Aware Access Control (Context-AW): This model emphasizes that access permissions should be based on the dynamic context that the subject and object under consideration are current in. This context can change along with pass of time, movement of location, and change of surroundings, and the access permissions also change accordingly. In particular, environment roles are introduced to capture environmental states. Similar to RBAC, these roles use role hierarchy, activation, separation, and so on to manage the policies and constraints that rely on the context of collaboration. Depending on environment conditions at the time of request, these roles are activated (or de-activated).

Collaborative computing environments pose some requirements on access control techniques. We identify some main requirements as follows.

- Distributed: the access control in collaborative computing should be applied and enforced in a distributed manner.
- Generic: the access control technique for CC should be generic to meet the needs of various collaborative tasks and enterprise models.
- Scalable: since CC environments can be varied in size, the access control technique for CC should be scalable and is able to accommodate large CC applications.
- Fine-grained and high-aggregated: the access control mechanism should be flexible enough to specify and enforce any detailed or any aggregated requirements of access rights on individual entities or group of entities.

- Transparent: transparent access to resources for authorized users in CC environments should be provided without users' worrying about where the resources are and how to access them. On the other hand, exclusion of unauthorized users should be strong, yet without constraining collaboration.

- Dynamic: one feature of CC environments is users can join, leave or move (resources can be added, removed, or moved) in the environments. The access rights of users to resources can change. Thus, the access control techniques in CC environments must be powerful enough to adapt the dynamic feature of CC environments.

- Efficient: due to the possible large scale and dynamics of CC environments, access control techniques must be efficient.

Cryptography based techniques are new mechanisms for enforcing (hierarchical) access control. The basic idea is to have a unique key for each resource class called *class key* or *node key*, such that all users belonging to a class are assigned the key of that class. When a user accesses a resource, the user provides the key. The provided key will be checked with the resource key. If (and only if) the key matches the resource key, the access to the resource is granted, otherwise, it is denied. In terms of hierarchical access control, all users belonging to the ancestor classes of a class can derive the key of that class, but the reverse is not permitted. As a result, the users in a parent class can access the resources of its child or descendant classes. Cryptography based techniques are applicable to a variety of domains including all the traditional domains. They have an advantage of data security offered by cryptography and well meet the above specified requirements. For example, cryptography based techniques do not require access matrix for storing accessibility information for each subject and object and hence are well suited for distributed environments where data / resources are dispersed and move across networks. Also the data security offered by cryptography makes it possible to have encrypted resources in public domains and still achieve access control.

In the following sections, we first present readers with a cryptography based Differential Access Control (DIF-AC) scheme. Then we examine and classify typical existing Cryptography based Hierarchical Access Control (CHAC) schemes. We also briefly present an efficient CHAC scheme recently proposed by Atallah [Atallah *et al.* (2005)]. The scheme elegantly utilizes a one-way hash function twice and achieves locality and efficiency for dynamic operations. Finally, we describe a uniform CHAC scheme based on access polynomial in detail.

3.2 An Efficient Differential Access Control (DIF-AC) Scheme

We assume here a random many-to-many relation between the users and resources. Suppose there are n users $U_1, U_2, \cdots, U_n$ and m resources $R_1, R_2, \cdots, R_m$. Each user can access multiple resources and each resource can be accessed by multiple users. As each resource is independent, it will be encrypted by a unique key. Thus, all the m resources must be encrypted by one unique key each, giving rise to m Resource Encryption Keys (REKs) $REK_1, REK_2, \cdots, REK_m$. We have one set of users associated with each resource, giving rise to m sets, which we term as m Resource Lists (RLs) $RL_1, RL_2, \cdots, RL_m$. The users in these RLs can overlap as different users subscribe to different combinations of resources. DIF-AC comes with the problem of distributing the different REKs to various subsets of users (RLs), because if a user subscribes to j resources, he/she is a member of j RLs and must get j REKs. Also, in a truly dynamic environment, users can add or drop subscriptions and the Group Controller can add or drop resources.

Based on the key tree group key management scheme (see chapter 2 section 2.2.1.1) and the KTSDC scheme (see chapter 2 section 2.3.5.1) , the following steps describe such an efficient DIF-FAC scheme.

3.2.1 *System Description and Initialization*

The GC will create and manage a Key Tree for these n users and efficient algorithms proposed in [Zou *et al.* (2002b)] will be implemented to allow bursty join and/or leaves. The nodes of the Key Tree will be numbered as follows: The root is numbered 0. For the rest of the nodes, node number of the left child of any node is obtained by left shifting the parent node number by 1-bit and adding one to it. Similarly node number of the right child is obtained by adding one to parent node number and then left shifting by one bit. For example if parent node number is 2, then its left child is $2 << 1 + 1$ i.e. 5 and right child is $(2+1) << 1$ i.e. 6 (See Figure 3.1). Due to this indexing scheme, indices of the left children nodes are odd and indices of the right children nodes are even. The GC will maintain the m resource lists (RLs) for m resources. Each RL will have a list of members who have subscribed for that resource. The RLs will be initialized to be empty at the start when the system is being set up. Every subscription request will be kept in an appropriate *RL*. Thus, *m RLs* will be created in a time interval and maintained by the GC. These *m RLs* correspond to *m* conferences.

At the end of time interval, the GC will run the algorithm to determine key indices of a conference (See Figure 3.2) for each *RL*. This algorithm starts by sorting the IDs of users in a conference (*RL*). In the first pass, pairs of users covered under the same node are identified and sorted in an array. In the next pass, the algorithm checks if two pairs are covered under one node. This continues until all the cover keys are identified.

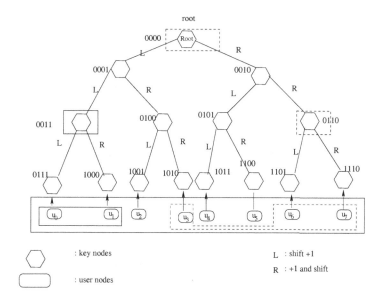

Fig. 3.1 Binary indexing of keys.

To identify if two users are covered under one node, the indexing scheme is helpful. If the first user's index is even, this means that the user will not share a key with any other user, since he/she is on a right branch. Thus, that user's index is put on the cover key list and the user's key is one of the cover keys. If the user's index is odd, the next user's index is checked to see if they share the key. After the first pass, the same operations are done but on pairs of users identified in the first pass. The next passes are similar and they either identify pairs that share node keys or are separate and, hence, cover keys. We can apply more optimization techniques here,

Algorithm 3.1.
/*RL: Resource List which stores members' IDs in an ascending
order */
    While (current member ID list is not empty) {
        if ($Current\_ID$ is even) {
            Store $Current\_ID$ (which is one key index needed)
            Remove $Current\_ID$ from current member ID list
            Move $Current\_ID$ to the next ID
        } **else** {
            if ($Next\_ID$ equals $Current\_ID$+1) {
                Find $Parent\_ID$ of $Current\_ID$
                Replace $Current\_ID$ by $Parent\_ID$
                Remove $Next\_ID$
                Move $Current\_ID$ to the next ID
            } **else** {
                Store $Current\_ID$ (which is one key index needed)
                Remove $Current\_ID$ from current member ID list
                Move $Current\_ID$ to the next ID
            }
        }
    }

Fig. 3.2   An efficient algorithm for determining the key indices for any RL.

such as if k RLs are identical, then the same REK can be used for all k
RLs.

For example, consider an e-newspaper offering 3 sections: sports, politics and stocks. Assume 8 members are registered with the GC and the GC
maintains a Key Tree as in Figure 3.1. If all the members subscribe to the
sports section (resource 1), then they are covered under the root key, hence
the REK for sports is the root key. If members m_0 and m_1 subscribe to
resource 2, i.e. politics, they will be put in RL_2. Now, members in RL_2 are
also covered by a single key k_3 which will be the REK for politics. Finally,
if members m_3, m_6, and m_7 subscribe to stocks (resource 3), the GC will
find the cover keys k_{10} and k_6. The GC will generate a REK for resource
3 and send it using the cover keys.

The basic idea behind our scheme is the fact that user subscriptions
to a resource can be viewed as a special case of SDC. Although SDC was
proposed for a different domain, it can be used efficiently for the domain

of Differential access control. The many-to-many relation between users and resources makes it extremely complex and discourages use of forced hierarchies. Allowing users to change subscriptions and the GC to change resources makes the Environment very dynamic. Once the central Key Tree and all the m Resource Lists (*RLs*) are set-up, the GC just has to maintain user joins and leaves and subscription changes. The next subsection describes the dynamic operation handling.

3.2.2 *System Dynamics and Maintenance*

We will assume that the GC will have a pre-defined time interval and all updates will be done only at the end of time interval. The time interval chosen should be large enough to avoid frequent updates and small enough to avoid loss of revenue. Choosing the time interval is application dependent. We will first deal with dynamics of subscription to resources. There are 3 possible cases:

(1) A member subscribes to one or more new resources to which he has not already subscribed.
(2) A member un-subscribes from one or more resources already subscribed.
(3) A member changes from subscribed resources.

To handle the subscription dynamics, the GC will have temporary *RLs* called as *TRLs* which will be initialized to be copies of corresponding *RLs* at the start of a time interval. These TRLs will be mapped to *RLs* at the end of time interval. To handle the first case, whenever the GC gets a *subscription* request from a registered member, the GC puts that member in the *TRLs* for the requested resources. Similarly for *un-subscription* requests, the GC just has to delete the member from the *TRLs* of the resources requested. To change subscription, the GC has to simply delete a member from the *TRLs* of the resources where he/she wants to unsubscribe and put him/her in the *TRLs* of the resources requested. For example, if a member sends a request to the GC for change of subscription from $\{r_i, r_j\}$ to $\{r_k, r_l\}$. The GC will delete that member from $\{TRL_i, TRL_j\}$ and add him/her to $\{TRL_k, TRL_l\}$.

At the end of time interval, the GC will run the efficient algorithm to find *REK* (See Figure 3.2) for each *TRL* where there was a change. One dirty bit per *RL* will help us detect the lists that were modified. All the changed *TRLs* will be mapped to corresponding *RLs*. The new cover keys will not differ from the original cover keys, as most of the users will be the same. This can be seen as a special case of some members leaving and joining from an ordinary Key Tree. In the maintenance operations described, it is assumed all the legal and technical formalities related to subscription, un-subscription and changes are taken care of.

Now let us describe resource dynamics. There are also only three possible cases:

(1) Adding one or more resources, like an e-newspaper, adding a soccer news section.
(2) Revoking a resource, like a broadcaster, revoking a 56Kbps quality broadcast.
(3) Changing a resource, like a broadcaster changing the 56Kbps quality broadcast to 128kbps.

The scheme makes it very simple to incorporate these resource dynamics. To add a resource, the GC just has to add a new Resource List RL corresponding to that resource to the existing RLs. To revoke a resource, the GC just deletes the corresponding RL. To change a resource, the GC does not have to do anything at all, as RLs are just like interfaces in the Object Oriented world and it is fine to change implementation as far as interface is same. Thus if a broadcaster wants to change a 28Kbps quality resource to 56Kbps resource, he/she is free to do so without affecting the subscribers and the system, or if an e-newspaper wants to replace a section like politics by world politics, only the resource changes and not any other part of the system.

In case a user wants to un-subscribe from all resources and leave the system all together, he/she can send a leave request to the GC. The GC will delete that leaving member from the RLs that he/she was part of and remove him/her from the central Key Tree updating all affected keys. This is like a normal leave from any Key Tree scheme with extra operation of deleting from RLs.

3.2.3 *Discussion*

We will discuss various performance and security issues of this DIF-AC scheme in this section. We will discuss the best, worst, and average case scenarios of finding the Resource Encryption Keys (REK) for each resource, followed by issues of scalability, number of keys and dynamics in terms of user join/leave and resource addition and revocation.

The *Best Case* of finding *REK*s is when all the users in a *RL* are covered under one key. Then that key from the efficient key tree for SGC becomes the *REK*. In the best case it is not required to construct a tree for distributing the *REK*. The *Worst Case* of finding *REK* is when we have $n = 2$ members in a *RL* in such a way that there is no shared key between any two members.

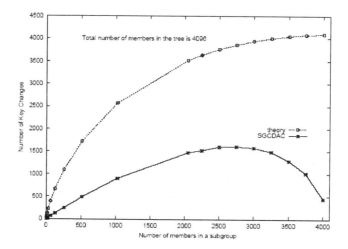

Fig. 3.3 Comparing number of shared keys with $Navg$.

In this case, the algorithm to find key cover returns $n = 2$ keys. In this case, it may be more efficient to construct a separate key tree with all the cover keys at leaf nodes and the *REK* at the root. In the average case, we will have more than one and less than $Navg = 2$ keys. Where, $Navg$ is the average number of keys to be changed in the batch rekeying scheme described in Chapter 3 of the book SGC over Data Networks [Zou *et al.* (2004b)].

$$N_{avg} = \sum_{l=0}^{h-1} 2^l \left(1 - \frac{\binom{\frac{n}{2l}}{m}}{\binom{n}{m}} \right).$$

where n is the total number of members in a key tree, h the height of the tree, and m the number of the changed members. Navg gives the total number of keys to be changed from the root to leaves of changed members. In our case, we just need to find the keys shared by members in a RL, hence the average number of keys is bound to be less than $Navg/2$. We are not concerned with all keys until the root.

We ran an experiment with the height h of a tree as 12 and the total number n of members as 4096. We changed the number (m) of members in subset from 8 to 4000. We calculated $Navg$ using the formula described above and the shared keys using the algorithm described in Figure 3.2. The results are plotted in Figure 3.3. As it can be seen from the figure, the average number of shared keys is far less than the expected value of $Navg/2$. Let us discuss the number of trees created. In the worst case, it will be $m + 1$, which is equal to the number of resources $+1$ for the central key Tree. In the average case, the number of trees will be less than $m + 1$, as some REKs will be either from a central key tree or without a need to create a tree. We can have a threshold value for the number of cover keys and we can construct a key tree for distributing REK if the number of cover keys exceeds the threshold.

In terms of the number of keys, all the members will have $log(n)$ keys for the central Key Tree. Besides that all members will have the REKs for the resources they subscribe. For example, if a member subscribes for i resources, he/she will have i REKs. In case some REKs are distributed by creating trees, all members subscribing to those resources will have keys from REK distribution trees. As we showed earlier, the worst case number of leaf nodes of a REK distribution tree is $n/2$. Hence, if a resource has a key tree associated with it, in the worst case a member must have $log(n/2)$ keys for that resource. Also it is possible to monitor the Resource Lists (RLs) and if some RLs have exactly the same members, we can have the same REK for all such resources.

Let us consider the number of rekeying messages in our scheme. As the central tree implements efficient algorithms for SDC, the number of rekeying messages are low. Moreover, we create a tree for distributing REKs when needed in order to minimize the number of messages. As a result, the number of messages flying across the system is minimal.

The scheme is certainly scalable, since the central key tree for SDC can be used for any number of users. Also, there can be any number of resources in the system, as the GC just maintains a list of users subscribing to each resource and then uses the efficient algorithm discussed in Figure 3.2.

In conclusion, this section presents a new, yet effective, scheme for key management for Differential Access Control in Dynamic Environments, based on principles of SGC Key Management and SDC. It also discussed the efficiency and scalability of the scheme in terms of number of trees, keys and rekeying messages. The scheme is compact, efficient, practical, and generic. The scheme scales better in a dynamic scenario when users change subscriptions or service providers add or revoke resources. The average number of shared keys found experimentally is far less than the one found theoretically. The scheme can be easily extended for resources with hierarchy.

3.3 Cryptographic Hierarchical Access Control (CHAC) Schemes

Besides the differential access (many-to-many) relation, collaborative computing systems involve intensively hierarchical access relation. In this section, we will discuss Cryptography based Hierarchical Access Control (CHAC). We begin with the general HAC model, proceed to summarize and classify typical CHAC schemes, and finally, discuss an efficient CHAC scheme due to its elegant locality feature associated with dynamic operations. In the next section, we will present an access polynomial based CHAC scheme which can deal with both dynamic hierarchy operations (node level) and user dynamically joining and leaving operations (user level) uniformly and efficiently.

3.3.1 *HAC Model*

A general HAC model is defined with a *directed acyclic graph* (DAG). A typical example of DAG can be shown in Figure 3.4. Each node represents a set of resources that can be accessed by users granted with certain rights. Here, we use words "nodes", "vertices", and "classes" interchangeably. Nodes are connected with links which represent a partial order set with relationship "$\leq$". For example, a relation $C_i \leq C_j$ implies that users with access right to resource C_j can also access resource C_i, but users with access right to resource C_i cannot access resource C_j. For simplicity, we just say "C_j can access C_i". We also use terminologies such as children, parents, descendants, ancestors, and siblings, which are commonly used in a DAG.

In this HAC model, we make the following assumptions, which are commonly used in other CHAC schemes,

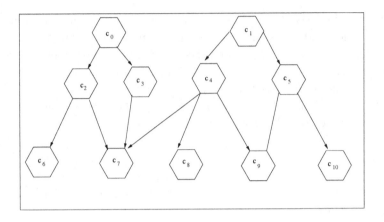

Fig. 3.4   A typical hierarchy represented as a DAG.

(1) There is one trusted *Central Authority* (CA) who is responsible for generating and distributing secret information for all nodes.
(2) There exists an underlying group key management mechanism which supports how keys/secret information are distributed to nodes and their users/resources in a secure manner (See Chapter 2).

The CHAC schemes can be typically classified as: unconditionally secure schemes and conditionally secure schemes [Zou *et al.* (2004b)] (also see Definition 1.3). In the first class of CHAC schemes, every vertex v_i in the hierarchy is assigned a unique key K_i. The keys among vertices are independent. Every resource associated with a node v_i is assigned a set of keys, denoted as R_i and $R_i \subseteq \{K_j : v_i \leq v_j\}$ and every user in a node v_i is assigned a set of keys, denoted as U_i and $U_i \subseteq \{K_j | v_j \leq v_i\}$. The assignment of keys to users and resources are performed in the following way: a user u_i can access a resource r_j if and only if $U_i \cap R_j \neq \emptyset$. How to assign the keys to users and resources are main concerns about this kind of CHAC schemes. Three generic schemes were proposed in [Zou *et al.* (2004b)]: user multiple key rekeying, resource multiple rekeying, and mixed rekeying. In particular, several concrete unconditionally secure schemes have been proposed [Karandikar *et al.* (2006); Sun and Liu (2004)]. The main advantages of this class scheme is its unconditional security and its independent selection of keys. However, since a resource or user is associated with multiple keys, the space requirement is higher and it is complicated to perform dynamic operations.

Thus, the research on CHAC schemes primarily focuses on the second class: i.e. conditionally secure schemes. These schemes are primarily based on one-way functions. There are two subclasses in this class: directly dependent key schemes and indirectly dependent key schemes. As for the first subclass, a node's key can be directly computed from the key of any of its parents using a one-way function. Thus, a node's key can be derived, directly or indirectly, from any of its ancestors' keys. However, due to the one-way feature of the function used, a descendent node cannot derive the keys of its ancestors. With regard to the second subclass, the keys of nodes are independently selected, but there are some parameters which are computed (by a central trusted authority) using a one-way function and reflect relationship between parent nodes and their child nodes. Thus, a node can compute the key of any of its descendants via the public parameters, but the reverse cannot be completed. The advantage of one-way function based schemes is that every resource or user is assigned just one key. A user, from its key, can derive all the keys of resources for which he is supposed to access (i.e. these resources belonging to the descendant nodes of the node the user belongs to). When a user wants to access a resource, the user computes the resource key from its own key and provides the key to the resource. The resource will check whether the provided key matches its own key. If matched, the access is granted, otherwise, denied.

3.3.2 *Directly Dependent Key Schemes*

The first CHAC scheme was proposed by Akl and Taylor in 1983 [Akl and Taylor (1983)]. Since then, many other CHAC schemes have been proposed [Atallah *et al.* (2005); Chien (2004); Chick and Tavares (1989); Mackinnon *et al.* (1985); Ray *et al.* (2002a); Sandhu (1988); Tzeng (2002); Zhong (2002); Zou *et al.* (2001, 2004b)] (Some schemes have been found insecure. For example, two schemes proposed in [Chien (2004); Tzeng (2002)] have the same collusion problem, as pointed out by Yi in papers [Yi (2005); Yi and Ye (2003)] respectively). Akl and Taylor's scheme belongs to directly dependent key class. We briefly introduce Akl and Taylor's scheme here. The central authority (also called as Group Controller GC) selects two large primes p and q and computes $M = pq$ which is made public. For every vertex v_i, the GC selects a distinct prime p_i and assigns p_i to v_i. Then for every vertex v_i, the GC computes $t_i = \prod_{v_j \npreceq v_i} p_j$ and makes all the t_i public. The root vertex v_0 is assigned $t_0 = 1$ (see Figure 3.5). Finally the GC randomly selects a large random integer k_0 as the key for the root vertex. The GC computes the key for each vertex v_i as $k_i = k_0^{t_i} \bmod M$. Each vertex v_i gets respective key k_i over a secure channel.

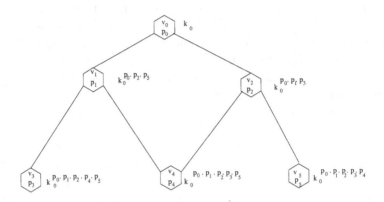

Fig. 3.5   Assignment of primes, t_is and keys k_is.

Due to the way t_i are computed the following condition is satisfied: $t_j | t_i$ (i.e. t_i is divisible by t_j) if and only if $v_i \leq v_j$. As a result, if $v_i \leq v_j$, then v_j can compute v_i's key k_i from k_j as follows: $k_j^{t_i/t_j} = (k_0^{t_j})^{t_i/t_j} = k_0^{t_i} = k_i$. However, v_i can not compute v_j's key k_j. Thus, hierarchical access control is enforced. It is worth mentioning that because of the modular operation, all k_i have the same magnitude whether they are computed from k_0 with larger exponent t_i or smaller t_i.

As for one-way functions used in CHAC schemes, some schemes (in particular, directly dependent key) are limited to specific one-way functions and some others (in particular, indirectly dependent key) can utilize any one-way functions. For example, Akl-Taylor's scheme [Akl and Taylor (1983)] binds and utilizes the RSA one-way trap door function in their scheme. Discrete Logarithm, cryptographic hash functions and pseudorandom functions are some popular one-way functions used, such as in [Lin (1997)] and [Atallah *et al.* (2005); Zhong (2002)]. Symmetric cryptosystems can be used as one-way functions such as in [Sandhu (1988); Chen and Chung (2002); Chen *et al.* (2004)], so do the Chinese Remainder Theorem [Chen and Chung (2002)] and quadratic residues [Chou *et al.* (2004)].

3.3.3   *Indirectly Dependent Key Schemes*

The scheme proposed by Lin [Lin (1997)] is one of the earliest indirectly dependent key schemes, following which are some extensions and improvements [Atallah *et al.* (2005); Zhong (2002)]. We briefly introduce Lin's scheme here.

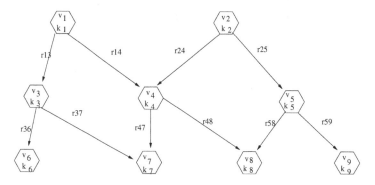

Fig. 3.6   Independent keys and the corresponding r_{ji}s.

Every vertex v_i selects its own independent key k_i which is sent to the GC securely. For all $v_i \leq v_j$, the GC computes an r_{ji} as follows: $r_{ji} = f(k_j, ID_i) \oplus k_i$ where f is a cryptographic hash function and ID_i is the identification of v_i. All r_{ji} are made public. Using r_{ji}, v_j can compute the key k_i of v_i as follows: $k_i = f(k_j, ID_i) \oplus r_{ji}$. However v_i cannot compute k_j efficiently because of the one-way property of f. Thus, hierarchical access control is enforced.

3.3.4   *Polynomial and Interpolation based Schemes*

Within the indirectly dependent key class, there is one specific category which utilizes polynomials and interpolation (and one-way function as well). The first such kind of a scheme was proposed in [Wu and Chang (2001)], immediately followed in [Shen and Chen (2002)]. Unfortunately, both schemes were found to have security holes [Hsu and Wu (2003)]. Hsu and Wu also provided an improvement. Furthermore, the authors in [Wang and Laih (2005)] found another kind of security hole existing in both schemes, even in the improved schemes. The paper [Das *et al.* (2005)] proposed a new scheme which is similar to the one in [Shen and Chen (2002)] but is more efficient and avoids security weakness.

Let us briefly introduce the scheme proposed in [Shen and Chen (2002)] here. The GC selects P as a large prime and g as a generator of Z_P^*. The GC also selects secret b_j and key k_j for every vertex v_j in the hierarchy. Now, the GC computes Newton's polynomial interpolation $I_j(x)$ for v_j by interpolating at points: $(ID_i \parallel (g^{k_j} \bmod P), b_i)$ for the relation $v_i \le v_j$. The GC publishes $I_j(x)$ and $Q_j = k_j^{1/b_j} \bmod P$ for every vertex v_j. Now a user at vertex v_j can derive the key of any descendant vertex v_i in two steps: (1) Get $b_i = I_j(ID_i \parallel (g^{k_j} \bmod P))$; (2) Get $k_i = Q_i^{b_i} \bmod P$.

The security flaw existed in the above scheme and pointed out in [Hsu and Wu (2003)] is as follows: if two classes have a same child class, one can access the data of the other's children who are not its children. For example, looking at Figure 3.4, C_2 and C_4 have a shared class C_7. So point $(ID_7 \parallel (g^{k_2} \bmod P), b_7)$ is contained in $I_2(x)$ and $(ID_7 \parallel (g^{k_4} \bmod P), b_7)$ is contained in $I_4(x)$. C_2 can compute b_7. Then by setting $I_4(x) = b_7$ and solving its roots, C_2 can obtain $ID_7 \parallel (g^{k_4} \bmod P)$. Thus, $(g^{k_4} \bmod P)$ can be found. As a result, C_2 can obtain the keys of C_4's other children such as C_8 as $b_8 = I_4(ID_8 \parallel (g^{k_4} \bmod P))$ and $k_8 = Q_8^{b_8}$. Similarly, C_4 will be able to access C_2's child C_6. The solution proposed in [Hsu and Wu (2003)] is simple: using a public cryptographic hash function f to change the first value of the points as $f(ID_i \parallel g^{k_j} \bmod P)$.

Moreover, there is another security flaw, found in [Wang and Laih (2005)] with the above schemes even including the improved scheme. For example, consider any class C_j, all its descendants' secrets are embedded in C_j's public polynomial $I_j(x)$, where these descendants' secrets are located at points only known to C_j. When some classes are added as or removed from C_j's descendant classes, $I_j(x)$ is updated to accommodate the change of embedded secrets. But, for those descendants, which remain as descendants of C_j, their secrets are still at the same points of the new updated $I_j(x)$. Consequently, if we generate a polynomial by taking the difference (or to say GCD) of the old and the new $I_j(x)$, we will obtain zeros at these points in this generated polynomial. In particular, if there is just one descendant which stays both before and after addition or deletion, its secret will be disclosed immediately without using any root finding algorithm. The solution to this problem is to integrate a random number z into the points as $(f(z \parallel ID_i \parallel (g^{k_j} \bmod P)), b_i)$. z is changed in every polynomial.

The authors in [Das et al. (2005)] modified the above scheme simply as follows: (1) instead publishing $I_j(x)$, make it only known to its class C_j; and (2) remove b_j and Q_j and change points to $(f(ID_i \parallel k_j), k_i)$.

Many other schemes for HAC have appeared in literature. Some schemes limit the HAC structure such as a tree [Atallah *et al.* (2005); Sandhu (1988)] or a DAG with one root [Akl and Taylor (1983)]. Some schemes can compute the keys of descendants in one step [Akl and Taylor (1983); Mackinnon *et al.* (1985); Harn and Lin (1990); Chick and Tavares (1989); Santis *et al.* (2004); Ray *et al.* (2002b); Santis *et al.* (2004); Hwang and Yang (2003); Hwang (1999); He *et al.* (2003); Chang and Buehrer (1993)] and others need to follow the path step by step from the node to its descendant [Atallah *et al.* (2005, 2006); Chang *et al.* (2004); Chien and Jan (2003); Lin (2001); Zhong (2002)].

3.3.5 *An Efficient CHAC Scheme with Locality*

The scheme proposed in [Atallah *et al.* (2005)] is an efficient CHAC scheme due to its locality in processing dynamics. This scheme is similar to Lin's scheme (see section 3.3.3) (thus, belonging to the indirectly dependent key CHAC class) with some elegant modifications: adding one more key to any node and using the public cryptographic hash function $f(x, y)$ one more time. The idea is as follows. Suppose every node v_i has one more key, i.e. a private key $\hat{k}_i$, which is distributed to the members of node v_i securely. Then the node key is defined as $k_i = f(\hat{k}_i, ID_i)$. Since the members in node v_i have the private key $\hat{k}_i$ and ID_i is public, every member can compute the node key k_i himself. As before, public edge values r_{ji} are defined on node keys as $r_{ji} = k_i - f(k_j, ID_i)$. A parent node can derive the node key k_i of its descendant v_i but not the private key $\hat{k}_i$. The change of ID_i can alter k_i easily. As a result, only when there are members who leave from v_i, $\hat{k}_i$ needs to be changed and distributed to the members in v_i (and k_i needs to be updated from new $\hat{k}_i$). All other changes to k_i can be easily done by just changing public ID_i. For example, when a member leaves v_j ($\hat{k}_j$ will be changed, so does k_j), k_i (not $\hat{k}_i$) of v_j's descendants v_i needs to be changed. But this change can be accomplished by just changing the public ID_i, which is very easy and efficient. In summary, the CHAC scheme in [Atallah *et al.* (2005)] is defined as follows:

- i) for every node v_i, it is assigned a private key $\hat{k}_i$, a public ID_i, and a node key k_i which is computed by itself as:

$$k_i = f(\hat{k}_i, ID_i), \tag{3.1}$$

- ii) for every edge from v_j to v_i, a public edge value r_{ji} is defined as:

$$r_{ji} = k_i - f(k_j, ID_i) \tag{3.2}$$

Fig. 3.7 illustrates an access hierarchy and the key and edge values. Each vertex represents a group of members formed from the first level.

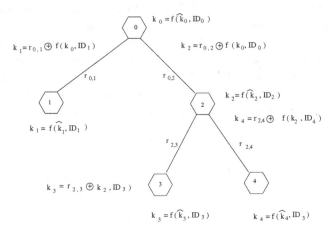

Fig. 3.7   An example of access hierarchy and their key and edge values.

Now, the access control and dynamic key update are ready. Let us show different operations.

- Key derivation: assume that vertex v_j is a parent node of vertex v_i, v_j can derive k_i by using its own node key and public information as:

$$k_i = r_{ji} + f(k_j, ID_i) \qquad (3.3)$$

  but vertex v_i cannot compute k_j because of the one-way feature of the cryptographic hash function.
- Similarly, if vertex v_j is an ancestor node of vertex v_i, following the path from v_j to v_i, v_j can derive v_i's key iteratively from its own key.
- When a vertex's key needs to be updated, the update does not affect the keys of other vertices but just the edge values of its adjacent vertices. Assume vertex v_j's key k_j needs to be changed, a new ID_j' is picked up and the new key k_j' is computed as $k_j' = f(\hat{k}_j, ID_j')$. Then, for v_j's parent vertex v_p (if any), $r_{pj} = k_j' - f(k_p, ID_j')$ is computed as public edge information. Similarly, the edge values to v_j's child node v_i (if any) are updated.
- Adding and removing a vertex can be processed in a similar way. If a new vertex v_j needs to be added, we just pick up a new private key $\hat{k}_j$ and a new ID_j and assign them to node v_j. Then, we compute

and publicize the edge values to its parent vertices and child vertices. Similarly, if an existing vertex v_j needs to be removed, we delete all edges adjacent to the vertex and then remove v_j.

- Adding/deleting an edge: adding an edge means computing and publicizing the edge value. As for deleting an edge, such as from v_j to v_i, if there exists another path from v_j to v_i, nothing needs to be done, since v_j still can compute v_i's key via other paths. But if this is the only path from v_j to v_i, v_j should not be able to compute v_i's key (and all v_i's descendants' keys) after deletion. This means that v_i's key and all v_i's descendants' keys need to be changed. This change can be done by changing their public IDs only without regenerating or resending the private keys.

The common feature of all existing schemes is that they proposed mechanisms about key update at the vertex level, but seldom provide the solution to the key distribution at the user level, i.e. once a node key is changed, how to distribute the changed node key to the users belonging to the node? In the following, we propose a dual level key management which is able to not only distribute the secret information to a group of users efficiently but also deal with the node level HAC effectively.

3.4 A Uniform CHAC Scheme Based on Access Polynomials

In this section, we will propose a novel concept/construction of an access polynomial (AP) and its utilization for a novel CHAC scheme. The scheme is applicable to a general hierarchy represented by a DAG (as in Figure 3.4). We do not pose any restrictions on structure of the hierarchy as some existing schemes do, making our scheme truly generic. Like other CHAC schemes, we assume the presence of a GC who generates polynomials and random keys, publicizes key materials, and maintains the system during dynamic operations. We also assume that each user in the system has a permanent personal secret ID (SID) and a corresponding secret value $H(SID)$, where $H(x)$ is a t degree polynomial in a finite field F_q (see the discussion below). The unique feature of the new scheme is that the access polynomial mechanism not only supports dynamic hierarchy operations, such as adding or deleting nodes in the hierarchy (called the node level dynamics), but also allows dynamic user operations, such as user joining or leaving (called the user level dynamics) to be finished in a uniform and efficient way.

3.4.1 *Principle*

The new scheme is based on polynomials over a finite field F_q [Lidl and Niederreiter (1986)], in particular, a novel concept/construction of an access polynomial (AP). Here q is a big prime as the system modulus and made public. All arithmetic operations will be performed with mod q, which is omitted for simplicity. The principle is as follows.

The GC selects a random t-degree polynomial $h(x)$, called masking polynomial, and keeps it secret ($t > 0$). Degree t determines the security of polynomials, hence the GC can select a large t to ensure security against collusion attacks. A large t will not significantly affect efficiency due to the linear complexity of our scheme in terms of t. For every vertex v_j in the hierarchy, the GC selects a unique (secret) identification $ID_j \in F_q$ and computes $h(ID_j)$ and gives $(ID_j, h(ID_j))$ to v_j securely (See Section 3.4.4 for the secure distribution using the same mechanism at the user level). The GC also selects a key k_j for every vertex v_j.

Now, for every vertex v_j, the GC constructs an access polynomial (AP) $A_j(x)$, using the ID of v_j and IDs of all v_j's ancestors v_i as follows:

$$A_j(x) = (x - ID_j) \times \prod_{v_j \leq v_i} (x - ID_i) + 1$$

This construction assures that $A_j(x = r) = 1$ for all $r \in \{ID_j$, IDs of v_j's ancestors$\}$ or a random value otherwise. The GC selects a random polynomial $S_j(x)$ of degree t and computes a polynomial $T_j(x) = k_j - S_j(x)$. Thus, $k_j = S_j(x) + T_j(x)$. This equation guarantees that when a user has a share of $S_j(x)$ and a share of $T_j(x)$ at the same value x, the key k_j will be recovered. Both $S_j(x)$ and $T_j(x)$ are kept secret. The GC then computes and publishes two polynomials as $P_j(x) = S_j(x) * A_j(x) + h(x)$ and $R_j(x) = T_j(x) + h(x)^4$. This construction makes sure that only v_j and its ancestors can derive key k_j (see the discussion below). We will discuss the security of our scheme in detail in section 3.4.5.

3.4.2 *Key Computation/Derivation*

A vertex v_j can compute its own key k_j by evaluating
  $S_j(ID_j) = P_j(ID_j) - h(ID_j)$

---

[4]The access polynomial $A_j(x)$ is just contained in $P_j(x)$ but not $R_j(x)$.

since
$$P_j(ID_j) = A_j(ID_j) * S_j(ID_j) + h(ID_j) = 1 * S_j(ID_j) + h(ID_j) = S_j(ID_j) + h(ID_j)$$
and $T_j(ID_j) = R_j(ID_j) - h(ID_j)$ first and setting $k_j = S_j(ID_j) + T_j(ID_j)$.

An ancestor v_i of v_j can derive v_j's key k_j by computing $S_j(ID_i) = P_j(ID_i) - h(ID_i)$ since
$$P_j(ID_i) = A_j(ID_i) * S_j(ID_i) + h(ID_i) = 1 * S_j(ID_i) + h(ID_i) = S_j(ID_i) + h(ID_i)$$
and $T_j(ID_i) = R_j(ID_i) - h(ID_i)$ first and setting $k_j = S_j(ID_i) + T_j(ID_i)$.

If a user with ID_r who is not in v_j or any of its ancestral nodes attempts to get key k_j, the user will end up with $S_j(ID_r) * A_j(ID_r) + T_j(ID_r)$, which is a random value and is useless. As a result, correct hierarchical access control is enforced. Next, we will discuss how the above AP scheme can support dynamic operations.

3.4.3   Node/Vertex Level Dynamics

There are two levels of dynamics: node level as well as user or resource level. Node level dynamics include adding, deleting, moving, merging, and splitting nodes and adding and deleting edges. User level dynamics include a user joining a node, leaving a node, and moving from one node to another. Correspondingly, the resource dynamics include adding a resource to a node, removing a resource from a node, and moving a resource from one node to another. The resource dynamics can be processed in the same way as the user dynamics, thus we ignore them for simplicity. Hence, we describe the node level dynamics in this subsection and then the user level dynamics in the next subsection.

- *Adding a node as a leaf*: The GC assigns the new leaf node a unique ID_{new}, $h(ID_{new})$ and key k_{new}. The GC constructs $A_{new}(x)$ including ID_{new} and ancestral IDs of the new node, computes $P_{new}(x)$ and $R_{new}(x)$, and makes them public. No other nodes are affected in any way.

- *Adding an intermediate node*: The only change from the above case is that all descendant nodes of the new node are affected. Each descendant v_j needs a new $A'_j(x)$ and hence new $P'_j(x)$ and $R'_j(x)$. Whether a new key k'_j is needed depends on application requirements. If the added node is allowed to access the previous key (thus the data) of its descendants, the old key k_j does not need to be changed. Otherwise, a new key k'_j is needed. Since $P'_j(x)$ and $R'_j(x)$ are public, changing and sending them to node v_j (or multicasting them to the users of v_j) is simple without any security complication.

- *Deleting a leaf node*: The GC can delete the node by simply discarding all its public and private parameters. (The discarded IDs and $h(ID)$s should be recorded somehow to prevent them from being re-used until the system polynomial is refreshed.)

- *Deleting an intermediate node*: The GC discards all its public and private parameters. No ancestor of the deleted node is affected in any way. For every descendant v_j of the deleted node, the GC changes key k_j and polynomials $A_j(x)$, $P_j(x)$, and $R_j(x)$. For the descendants of the deleted node, a policy is used to either place them as the descendants of the parent (if any) of the deleted node or as the descendants of some other nodes. We ignore the policy issue since it is irrelevant to our discussion here.

- *Adding an edge*: Suppose an edge from v_i to v_j is added, the GC recomputes $A'_j(x)$ with inclusion of IDs of v_i and v_i's ancestors who were not the ancestors of v_j, selects a new key k'_j, recomputes and publicizes $P'_j(x)$ and $R'_j(x)$. At the same time, the GC performs this for every descendant of v_j which was previously not a descendant of v_i.

- *Deleting an edge*: If an edge from v_i to v_j is deleted, the GC recomputes $A'_j(x)$ with exclusion of IDs of v_i and v_i's ancestors who will not be the ancestors of v_j, selects a new key k'_j (if needed), recomputes and publicizes $P'_j(x)$ and $R'_j(x)$. At the same time, the GC performs this for every descendant of v_j which will not be a descendant of v_i from now on.

- *Moving a node*: It is equivalent to a combination of deleting and adding a node.

- *Merging n nodes*: It is equivalent to deleting $n-1$ nodes and changing key materials of one node.

- *Splitting a node*: It is equivalent to adding a few new nodes and changing key materials of one node.

3.4.4   *User Level Dynamics*

The user level dynamics are important, as members can join/leave a vertex at any point in time. The join operation is generally easy and the GC simply gives the vertex ID and $h(ID)$ to the joining user. Then the user can compute its node key and derive its descendants' keys as well. However, when a user leaves from a vertex, all descendant node keys need to be changed. Otherwise, the leaving user may store those keys and continue to use them.

Let us consider a user's departure at a vertex v_i. The GC changes key k_i to k_i', ID_i to ID_i', and $h(ID_i)$ to $h(ID_i')$. The GC recomputes $P_i'(x)$ and $R_i'(x)$ according to the new k_i'. Thus the ancestors of v_i are not affected in any way. They can get v_i's key using (new) public polynomials $P_i'(x)$ and $R_i'(x)$ just as they did before. For every descendant v_j of v_i, key k_j needs to be changed to k_j'. The GC recomputes $A_j'(x)$ using the new ID_i' and computes and makes public the new $P_j'(x)$ and $R_j'(x)$.

It should be pointed out that once a node's ID is changed, the new ID (and its corresponding $h(ID)$) needs to be distributed to all its users securely. One elegant feature of our AP mechanism is that the scheme itself can be used to distribute ID and $h(ID)$ efficiently. As mentioned previously, every user in the system will be assigned a permanent personal secret identification SID and a corresponding $H(SID)$ (note: $H(x)$ is a masking polynomial at user level and multiple $H(x)$s can be selected/used, one for each node). Then the GC constructs an AP $A(x)$ which contains SIDs of all the users belonging to the node and computes and publicizes two pairs of polynomials
$\{P_1(x) = A(x) * S_1(x) + H(x), R_1(x) = T_1(x) + H(x)\}$ and
$\{P_2(x) = A(x) * S_2(x) + H(x), R_2(x) = T_2(x) + H(x)\}$
where $ID = S_1(x) + T_1(x)$ and $h(ID) = S_2(x) + T_2(x)$. Thus, the users of the node can obtain ID and $h(ID)$ securely.

3.4.5 *Security and Performance Analysis*

In this section, we will discuss the security and performance of our scheme. As we will see from the following discussion, because $S_j(x)$ is randomly selected and is changing every time, $T_j(x)$, $P_j(x)$, and $R_j(x)$ are constantly changing as well. Moreover, all public $P_j(x)$s are independent. Thus, an attacker or a malicious user cannot figure out secret information from public polynomials, regardless of the number of public polynomials the attacker collects. In addition, there is a strict value binding requirement among all these polynomials: $P_j(x)$, $S_j(x)$, $A_j(x)$, $h(x)$, $R_j(x)$, and $T_j(x)$. That is, only when each of them is evaluated at the same x value are their combinations meaningful. As a result, multiple malicious users cannot successfully collude since their known values are with different x and cannot be combined together. In summary, the security of the scheme is guaranteed. As for the complexity of the scheme, it mainly comes from computing polynomials $P_j(x)$ and $R_j(x)$. $P_j(x)$ has degree $m + t$ and $R_j(x)$ has degree t, so the complexity is in the order of $m + t$. This linear complexity makes the scheme efficient and allows a larger t to be used. We will discuss them in detail next.

3.4.5.1 *Security Analysis*

The attacks to the new scheme can come from either an individual or collusion of multiple users. Let us consider the single user attack first.

The key is split as $k_j = S_j(x) + T_j(x)$. To get the key k_j, any user needs a share of $S_j(x)$ and $T_j(x)$ at the same value of x say $x = ID_r$. The way that $S_j(x)$ and $T_j(x)$ are publicized via $P_j(x)$ containing $A_j(x)$ guarantees that only a valid user, i.e. the one belonging to vertex v_j or its ancestors, can get a share of them. Even if an invalid user succeeds in guessing a valid user's ID as say ID_{guess}, still the invalid user can not get the share of $S_j(x)$ (or $T_j(x)$) at $x = ID_{guess}$ since it is publicized via polynomial $P_j(x) = A_j(x) * S_j(x) + h(x)$ (or $R_j(x) = T_j(x) + h(x)$). The invalid user can only evaluate $P_j(x = ID_{guess}) = A_j(ID_{guess}) * S_j(ID_{guess}) + h(ID_{guess}) = S_j(ID_{guess}) + h(ID_{guess})$ (or $R_j(x = ID_{guess}) = T_j(ID_{guess}) + h(ID_{guess})$). Since the invalid user does not have $h(ID_{guess})$ and cannot compute $h(ID_{guess})$, the invalid user cannot get the share of $S_j(x)$ and $T_j(x)$ at the same value and hence key k_j. This security against guessing attacks is achieved by clever construction of the access polynomial and use of the masking polynomial.

Another single user attack can occur when an attacker or a malicious user tries to compute a vertex v_i's ID_i from multiple publicized polynomials in which ID_i is contained. There are three cases to consider. First, even though ID_i is contained in $A_i(x)$ and the format of $A_i(x)$ is known, $A_i(x)$ is totally hidden within $P_i(x)$ by two secret polynomials $S_i(x)$ and $h(x)$. Thus, any user other than the ones in v_i cannot figure out $A_i(x)$ from $P_i(x)$ and hence ID_i. Secondly, when k_i changes (to k_i'), $P_i(x)$ will be changed (to $P_i'(x)$). Even though $A_i(x)$ is contained in both $P_i(x)$ and $P_i'(x)$, they are independent due to the randomness of $S_i(x)$ and $S_i'(x)$ and independence between $S_i(x)$ and $S_i'(x)$. Therefore, any user other than the ones in v_i cannot figure out ID_i from multiple $P_i(x)$s. Finally, even though ID_i is contained at the same time in $P_i(x)$ and multiple $P_j(x)$s where v_j is a descendant of v_i, again, due to the independence among $P_i(x)$ and $P_j(x)$s, ID_i still cannot be figured out. In summary, due to the independence among the publicized polynomials, the attack of getting ID_i from them is void. Furthermore, even though ID_i were figured out, the attacker would still need to figure out $h(ID_i)$.

Let us consider collusion attacks now. The typical collusion is that two (or more) vertices try to attack their common ancestor. Assume two users a and b from two vertices with $(ID_a, h(ID_a))$ and $(ID_b, h(ID_b))$ collude to attack their common ancestor v_j for getting key k_j or ID_j. Since $P_j(x)$ contains neither ID_a nor ID_b, their collusion for getting k_j or ID_j from $P_j(x)$ is no stronger than any of them individually. Secondly, let us consider that they are trying to get ID_j from $P_a(x)$ and $P_b(x)$ in which ID_j is contained. The values both users know are ten elements: ID_a, ID_b, $P_a(ID_a)$, $P_b(ID_a)$, $P_a(ID_b)$, $P_b(ID_b)$, $S_a(ID_a)$, $S_b(ID_b)$, $h(ID_a)$, and $h(ID_b)$. Since $P_a(x) = S_a(x) * A_a(x) + h(x)$, which requires that x be substituted with the same value in all four polynomials $P_a(x), S_a(x), A_a(x)$, and $h(x)$, it is impossible for the two users to mix these ten known values to form informative equations. For example, the two users cannot form an equation $P_a(ID_b) = S_a(ID_a) * A_a(x) + h(ID_b)$ from $P_a(x)$. Thus, they cannot get information about $A_a(x)$ and hence ID_j. As a result, this security against collusion aiming at obtaining k_j or ID_j is achieved by binding the same x between $S_j(x)$ and $T_j(x)$ and among $P_j(x), S_j(x)$, $A_j(x)$ and $h(x)$.

The degree of a polynomial decides its collusion resistance. $h(x)$ is of degree t and so are $S_j(x)$ and $T_j(x)$. Thus, the proposed scheme can resist the collusion of up to t users. Since $S_j(x)$ and $T_j(x)$ are always changing, it is difficult and also useless for malicious users to collude to recover $S_j(x)$ or $T_j(x)$. Thus, the collusion attack will aim at $h(x)$. Since every user has an ID and $h(ID)$, more than t users can figure out the entire $h(x)$ using polynomial interpolation. In addition, it is possible for less than $t+1$ users, even one user, to figure out $h(x)$. As stated before, when a user departs from a vertex v_i, the vertex's ID_i and $h(ID_i)$ need to be changed. If there are more than $t-1$ times of user leaves from a vertex v_i, a user who stays always at vertex v_i will obtain at least t new pairs of $(ID_i, h(ID_i))$ and, plus its original $(ID_i, h(ID_i))$, is able to interpolate $h(x)$. To solve this problem, we can do as follows: (1) selecting larger t and (2) refreshing $h(x)$ once the number of ID changes reaches $t-1$. Thanks to the efficiency of our scheme, which allows a larger t to be selected, and thanks to the uniform feature of our scheme, which allows the refreshed ID and $h(ID)$ to be securely and efficiently distributed to users using the scheme itself, the problem can be solved without much difficulty. In addition, it is a good practice to refresh $h(x)$ periodically. How often to refresh $h(x)$ is an important issue which is related to security level, performance, and application domains. This is worthy of future study.

3.4.5.2   *Performance Analysis*

We will consider the efficiency of our scheme in terms of storage, computation, and communication complexities. Let us assume that there are n vertices in the hierarchy and the maximum number of ancestors any vertex can have is m.

A vertex v_j needs to store its secret parameters viz $\{ID_j, h(ID_j), k_j\}$. This means that the storage requirement for any vertex can be considered as $O(1)$, i.e., constant and independent from n (and m too) (in fact, $O(log\ q)$ since all these values are in F_q). Note, a vertex does not need to store information about the hierarchy of its descendants. In some other schemes, when a vertex derives its descendant's key, the derivation follows a chain from the vertex to its child, grandchild, $\cdots$, and finally, the descendant. So, a vertex in these schemes needs to remember/store exact information about its descendents and their hierarchical relation. However, in our scheme, the vertex only needs to substitute its ID in the polynomial directly and the descendant's key is revealed. It may be needed to store the indices of its descendants to indicate which vertices are its descendants but these indices are relatively small numbers. The GC needs to store the secret $t-$degree masking polynomial $h(x)$ (plus user level masking polynomial $H(x)$) and all n access polynomials $A_j(x)$, each of maximum degree m. To store the polynomials, it is only required to store the coefficients. Therefore, the storage requirement for the GC is $O(n*m+t)$. Considering the role of the GC, this is not a great amount of storage.

As far as computation complexity is concerned, one advantage of the proposed scheme is that both the node key computation and the descendant key derivation are directly evaluated in the same way. The evaluation for k_j consists of computing $P_j(ID)$ and $R_j(ID)$, two subtractions (subtracting $h(ID)$), and one addition $(S_j(ID) + T_j(ID))$. $P_j(x)$ has degree $t + m$ and $R_j(x)$ has degree t. So, the key computation/derivation complexity is $O(t+m)$, which is also independent from n. It is linear as well, which makes our scheme very efficient. In addition, the key computation/derivation is so efficient that we can have t be very large, which improves security of the new scheme. Thus, in our scheme, security and efficiency do not conflict with each other as they do in most existing schemes.

Regarding communication cost, whenever a vertex v_j's key k_j is up-

Table 3.1 Complexities of the newly proposed scheme.

Storage	Computation	Communication
$O(1)$ at users	$O(t+m)$ for key derivation	$O(t+m)$
$O(n*m+t)$ at GC	$O(t+m)$ for computing $P(x)$ and $R(x)$	

dated (due to the dynamics), $P_j(x)$ and $R_j(x)$ need to be publicized (or broadcast), which again is $O(t+m)$ and independent from n.

The complexities of the new scheme are summarized in Table 3.1. As a result, the complexities of our scheme is completely independent from n and thus, the new scheme is very efficient and scalable.

3.4.6 *An Illustrative Example and Experiment Results*

We implemented the above proposed scheme and give one example generated by the program in this section. We evaluated the running times and the results for different scenarios are also presented here.

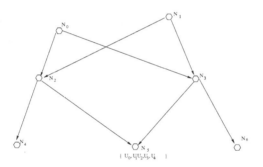

Fig. 3.8 An example

Suppose the access hierarchy is as Figure 3.8 and let $t = 10$ and $q = 251$. We will consider both node level operations and user level operations. Suppose the masking polynomial is:

$h(x) = 96x^{10} + 67x^9 + 191x^8 + 164x^7 + 41x^6 + 229x^5 + 234x^4 + 150x^3 + 205x^2 + 54x + 61$

and the secret node IDs and their corresponding $h(ID)$ for nodes $N_0, N_1, \cdots, N_6$ are:

$(ID_0 = 85, h(ID_0) = 136), (ID_1 = 119, h(ID_1) = 122), (ID_2 = 145, h(ID_2) = 177), (ID_3 = 30, h(ID_3) = 57), (ID_4 = 186, h(ID_4) = 3), (ID_5 = 160, h(ID_5) = 18), (ID_6 = 225, h(ID_6) = 88).$

Let us first consider node level key distribution and key derivation using node N_5 as an example. Supposing the GC randomly selects a node key for N_5 as $k_5 = 213$, it will distribute the key as follows:

- compute N_5's access polynomial as:
  $A_5(x) = (x - h(ID_0))(x - h(ID_1))(x - h(ID_2))(x - h(ID_3))(x - h(ID_5)) + 1 = x^5 + 214x^4 + 114x^3 + 141x^2 + 161x + 220.$
- select a random polynomial such as:
  $S_5(x) = 204x^{10} + 24x^9 + 167x^8 + 35x^7 + 110x^6 + 233x^5 + 131x^4 + 114x^3 + 38x^2 + 211x + 249$
  and compute:
  $T_5(x) = 47x^{10} + 227x^9 + 84x^8 + 216x^7 + 141x^6 + 18x^5 + 120x^4 + 137x^3 + 213x^2 + 40x + 215.$
- compute $P_5(x)$ and $R_5(x)$ respectively and publicize them:
  $P_5(x) = 204x^{15} + 6x^{14} + 196x^{13} + 5x^{12} + 116x^{11} + 1x^{10} + 55x^9 + 87x^8 + 156x^7 + 160x^6 + 88x^5 + 88x^4 + 129x^3 + 86x^2 + 219x + 123$ and
  $R_5(x) = 143x^{10} + 43x^9 + 24x^8 + 129x^7 + 182x^6 + 247x^5 + 103x^4 + 36x^3 + 167x^2 + 94x + 25.$

As a result, nodes N_0, N_1, N_2, N_3, N_5 can compute key k_5 from $P_5(x)$ and $R_5(x)$. For example, N_2 computes the key as:
$k_5 = (P_5(145) - h(145)) + (R_5(145) - h(145)) = (12 - 177) + (53 - 177) = -165 - 124 = -289 = 213\%251$
and N_5 also computes the key as:
$k_5 = (P_5(160) - h(160)) + (R_5(160) - h(160)) = (136 - 18) + (113 - 18) = 118 + 95 = 213 = 213\%251.$

However, other nodes which are not the ancestors of N_5 cannot compute the key. For example, N_4 obtains:
$(P_5(186) - h(186)) + (R_5(186) - h(186)) = (211 - 3) + (87 - 3) = 208 + 84 = 292 = 41\%251$ which is not the key.

Next, let us consider how the same access polynomial mechanism can be used to distribute the node ID and h(ID) to node users at the user level. Consider N_5 and assume that it involves 5 users U_0, U_1, U_2, U_3, U_4. Here assume that we have a different masking polynomial $H(x)$ for N_5 as:
$H(x) = 189x^{10} + 4x^9 + 244x^8 + 34x^7 + 163x^6 + 73x^5 + 83x^4 + 84x^3 + 125x^2 + 237x + 70.$

Moreover, assume that the users are assigned their $(SID, H(SID))$ as follows:
$(SID_0 = 5, H(SID_0) = 221), (SID_1 = 54, H(SID_1) = 23), (SID_2 = 189, H(SID_2) = 8), (SID_3 = 74, H(SID_3) = 199), (SID_4 = 140, H(SID_4) = 123).$

From these SIDs, the access polynomial at the user level can be formed as:

$$A(x) = \prod_{i \in \{0,4\}} (x - H(SID_i)) + 1 = x^5 + 40x^4 + 55x^3 + 23x^2 + 72x + 210.$$

In order to distribute $ID_5 = 160$ to these users securely, the GC constructs and publicizes polynomials $P(x)$ and $R(x)$ as:

$P(x) = 130x^{15} + 114x^{14} + 88x^{13} + 94x^{12} + 158x^{11} + 105x^{10} + 173x^9 + 140x^8 + 244x^7 + 58x^6 + 217x^5 + 87x^4 + 25x^3 + 140x^2 + 233x + 187$ and

$R(x) = 59x^{10} + 70x^9 + 148x^8 + 128x^7 + 80x^6 + 222x^5 + 202x^4 + 24x^3 + 165x^2 + 234x + 190$ where

$S(x) = 130x^{10} + 185x^9 + 96x^8 + 157x^7 + 83x^6 + 102x^5 + 132x^4 + 60x^3 + 211x^2 + 3x + 40$ and

$T(x) = 121x^{10} + 66x^9 + 155x^8 + 94x^7 + 168x^6 + 149x^5 + 119x^4 + 191x^3 + 40x^2 + 248x + 120$.

Thus, these users can obtain ID_5. For example, U_2 computes:

$ID_5 = (P_5(189) - H(189)) + (R_5(189) - H(189)) = (115 - 8) + (61 - 8) = 107 + 53 = 160 = 160\%251$.

Similarly, to distribute $h(ID_5) = 18$, the GC computes and publicizes polynomials $P(x)$ and $R(x)$ as:

$P(x) = 122x^{15} + 114x^{14} + 19x^{13} + 192x^{12} + 232x^{11} + 76x^{10} + 114x^9 + 41x^8 + 218x^7 + 174x^6 + 46x^5 + 55x^4 + 202x^3 + 196x^2 + 2x + 29$ and

$R(x) = 67x^{10} + 1x^9 + 27x^8 + 198x^7 + 103x^6 + 46x^5 + 18x^4 + 107x^3 + 205x^2 + 3x + 87$ where

$S(x) = 122x^{10} + 3x^9 + 217x^8 + 87x^7 + 60x^6 + 27x^5 + 65x^4 + 228x^3 + 171x^2 + 234x + 1$ and

$T(x) = 129x^{10} + 248x^9 + 34x^8 + 164x^7 + 191x^6 + 224x^5 + 186x^4 + 23x^3 + 80x^2 + 17x + 17$.

In the same way, these users can obtain $h(ID_5)$. For example, U_2 computes:

$h(ID_5) = (P_5(189) - H(189)) + (R_5(189) - H(189)) = (84 - 8) + (201 - 8) = 76 + 193 = 269 = 18\%251$.

If any other user wants to obtain ID_5 and $h(ID_5)$ using the same method, they will get useless values. It is worthy to mention that $q = 251$ and $t = 10$ were selected as such just for illustrative purposes. In real applications, they should be much larger. For example, in order to prevent a brute-force search attack on ID, $h(ID)$, q should be selected at least in the bit length of 128. Moreover, from Figures 3.9 and 3.11, t can be selected as 256 without affecting efficiency.

We implemented the proposed scheme in JAVA and did extensive experiments. P was selected to be 128 bits to guarantee enough security. The number of users and the degree of polynomial $h(x)$ are important factors affecting the performance of the scheme. Two main operations we considered are: (1) hiding the key via generating $P(x)$ and $R(x)$ (of course, which requires generating $S(x)$ and $T(x)$); (2) extracting the key. The program was run on a Dell Laptop computer with 1.8GHz CPU and 1.0G RAM. For obtaining stable running times, we ran each test case 100 times and averaged the running times. The results are shown in Figures 3.9 to 3.12.

From the figures, it can be seen that the running times for computing $P(x)$ and $R(x)$ to hide the secret key and for deriving the key from $P(x)$ and $R(x)$ are linear to both m and t. This validates the theoretical analysis in the previous section and proves that the scheme is computationally efficient. Large m indicates that the proposed scheme scales well to admit large group sizes or large number of ancestors and large t indicates that the scheme is able to defend collusion of large populations of malicious users.

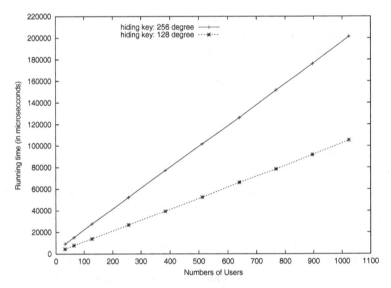

Fig. 3.9 Running times for hidding key: based on number of users.

3.4.7 *Discussion*

In this section, we will summarize the major properties of the proposed scheme.

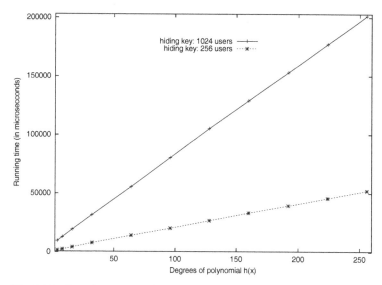

Fig. 3.10 Running times for hidding key: based on the polynomial degree.

- A good solution must be generic in the sense that it should have no restrictions on the hierarchy. The proposed scheme can be easily applied to any DAG, even those that have multiple roots.
- The best feature of the proposed scheme is the way in which it deals with user and node level dynamics in a uniform manner. All the cryptography based HAC schemes, including the newest one [Atallah *et al.* (2005)] so far, lack this capability.
- The Proposed scheme is scalable and does not limit the number of vertices or levels in the hierarchy. It can work well with a large number of vertices without loss of efficiency.
- Unlike many other schemes which derive keys via an iterative chain, the proposed scheme derives all keys directly.
- In most other HAC schemes including the most recent one [Atallah *et al.* (2005)], every vertex must know both its descendants and the exact hierarchical relation among these descendants, because these schemes derive their descendants' keys via an iterative derivation chain. However, the proposed scheme does not need to know the hierarchical relation of a node's descendants.
- The Proposed scheme is very efficient in terms of time and space com-

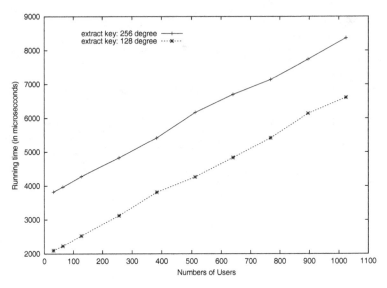

Fig. 3.11   Running times for extracting key: based on number of users.

plexity. Every node has just 3 secrets: its ID, $h(ID)$ and the key. All the other information is public. The computational and communication complexity is $O(t + m)$, which is far better than most of the existing schemes.

- The Proposed scheme does not have a problem from revoked members. Our scheme is truly dynamic and efficient.
- The Proposed scheme is very secure. Although most of the key derivation parameters are public, no one can derive keys unless they are allowed to. The degree of polynomials is assumed to be t which can be very large. Even with a large t, efficiency is better than any other t-secure scheme.

How large should t be? In general, t is applications dependent. In addition, collusion itself is not an easy task and the collusion of more than two users may be easily disclosed by the colluding users themselves. From the experiment, when t is 256, the times for hiding key and extracting key for a size of 1024 users are just 0.2 seconds and 0.008 seconds.

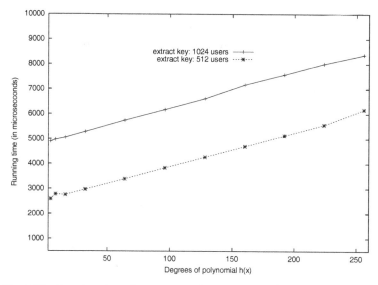

Fig. 3.12   Running times for extracting key: based on the polynomial degree.

3.4.7.1   *Enforcement of Other Access Models*

The hierarchical access model discussed so far is called "transfer up" [Atallah *et al.* (2005)], that is, the access permission of a vertex is transferred up to its ancestors. Some other models were proposed [Atallah *et al.* (2005); Bell and LaPadula (1973); Crampton (2003)], two of which are: 1) "transfer down", the access permission of a vertex is transferred down to its descendants and 2) "depth-limited transfer", the access permission of a vertex is transferred either up or down but only to a certain depth.

Both of the new models can be implemented as easily as the regular model is. For the "transfer down" model, the access polynomial $A(x)$ of a vertex is constructed to include the IDs of its descendants. For the "depth-limited transfer" model, the access polynomial $A(x)$ of a vertex is constructed to include the IDs of both its ancestors and descendants which are within the limited depth from the vertex.

In fact, it can be seen that the proposed scheme can be easily adapted to a "random" access model in the following sense: if a vertex v_i access permission is wanted to be transferred to a random other vertex v_j, regardless of the relation between the two vertices, simply include v_j's ID_j in the construction of $A_i(x)$.

In summary, the proposed scheme is highly secure, flexible, efficient, scalable, generic and practical. It conforms to the specifications of an ideal cryptography based scheme for hierarchical access control.

3.5   Conclusion

Enforcing correct and secure access to resources becomes more and more important and difficult in collaborative computing. The cryptography based access control technology is a good fit for the access control problem in such collaborative computing environments. Besides presenting an introduction to the cryptography based access control principles and summarizing typical existing hierarchical access control schemes, this chapter offered a Differential Access Control scheme (based on the key tree scheme and the secure dynamic conferencing principle) and a uniform hierarchical access control scheme (based on access polynomial). The security and performance analyses and experimental results were presented for both schemes.

Chapter 4

Intrusion Detection and Defense

4.1 Overview of Intrusion Detection and Defense

[1]Intruding attacks are serious problems associated with networked systems. Intruders attempt to break into a system to gain unauthorized access, misuse, and abuse the computer and networked system. The purpose of intrusion detection is to identify those intrusions of various kinds. After detecting the intrusions, the next step is to trace the location(s) of the intruders. Then, the follow-up warning and protection can be processed (such as blacklist, isolation, blocking etc.).

The intrusion detection problem is an inherent issue and becoming a more challenging task in CC environments, since CC environments are typically networked systems. Moreover, not only can there exist attacks from external attackers but malicious internal users in CC systems may also launch attacks. Thus, the book contributes this chapter for discussing intrusion detection and defense mechanisms.

Some main types of intrusions include Attempted break-ins, Masquerade attacks, Penetration of the security control system, Leakage, Denial of service, etc. [Denning (1987)]. The models to detect these intrusions can be classified as three categories [Bishop (2003)]: Misuse modeling, Anomaly modeling and Specification modeling. Many intrusion detection systems (IDS), including distributed intrusion detection systems (DIDS), have been proposed [Guangchun *et al.* (2003); Koutepas *et al.* (2004); Stillerman *et al.* (1999); Zhicai *et al.* (2004); Zhang *et al.* (2003)].

Among various intruding attacks, DoS (and Distributed DoS) attacks

---

[1]This chapter is mostly contributed by Scott Orr who is the Lead Network Engineer and Leah Cardaci who is a graduate student of Computer and Information Science Department at IUPUI.

are the most dangerous ones because such attacks are easy to launch by attackers but hard to defend from the server or victim. Some defending approaches include single-node defending methods [Bencsath and Vajda (2004); Jin *et al.* (2003b); Tanachaiwiwat and Hwang (2003)], multiple-node defending methods [Zhang and Dasgupta (2003)], and honeypot technology [Krawetz (2004); Spitzner (2003)].

In order to locate the intruders, two common traceback strategies have been proposed: the first type relies much on the routers in the network to send their identities to the destinations of certain packets, either encoding this information directly in rarely used bits of the IP header, or by generating a new packet to the same destination. The second type of solutions involves centralized management and logging of packet information on the network.

Intrusion detection and traceback systems themselves can be the (first) targets of attacks by intruders. Hence, they should be implemented to be secure and robust against attacks. Recently, a new powerful architecture for defending DoD/DDoS attacks, called Secure Overlay Service (SOS), was proposed [Keromytis *et al.* (2004)]. SOS hides the target server behind an overlay network and the client requests cannot go to the target server directly; instead, they must go to SOAPs (Secure Overlay Access Point) first, the edge of the overlay network, pass through several protecting/filtering layers, and finally arrive at the target server (if they pass all checks).

Thus, this chapter summarizes and classifies typical intruding attacks, typical intrusion detection modelings and traceback mechanisms. It further focuses on DoS (DDoS) attacks and their defending techniques. Finally, the chapter discusses some new DoS/DDoS resistant architectures, such as SOS.

4.2   Intruding Attacks

The intruding attacks can be typically classified as follows [Denning (1987)].

- Attempted break-in: an attacker attempts to break into a system by trying different passwords. This can be generally detected by abnormal behaviors, since the attempt may generate a high rate of password verification failures with respect to a single account or the system as a whole.
- Masquerading or successful break-in: an attacker breaks into a system

successfully via unauthorized account and password and masquerades as the legitimate user to do malicious things. This attack can be detected by abnormal profiles, strange behaviors, or violations of security constraints. The attacker may have a different login time, location, or connection type from that of the account's legitimate user. Moreover, the masquerader's actions may differ considerably from that of the legitimate user. For example, the legitimate user may spend most of his login time on editing or compiling and linking programs, whereas the masquerader may intensively browse directories and execute system status commands.

- Penetration by legitimate user: an authenticated user attempts to penetrate the security mechanisms in the system. This can be detected by monitoring for specific patterns of activity or violations of security constraints/system protections because such a malicious user may execute different programs or trigger more protection violations due to the attempts to access unauthorized files or programs. If his attempt is successful, he will have access to commands and files which are normally not permitted to him.

- Leakage by legitimate user: an authenticated user tries to leak sensitive information. This can be detected by abnormal use of system resources, because this kind of user may log into the system at unusual times or send data to a remote printer which is not normally used.

- Inference by legitimate user: an authenticated user attempts to obtain unauthorized data from a database through aggregation and inference. This can be detected by abnormal access behaviors, because this kind of user might retrieve more records than a usual amount.

- Trojan horse: a program that contains or installs a malicious program. Trojan horses may appear to be useful, interesting, or at the very least harmless programs to an unsuspecting user, but are actually harmful when executed. A Trojan horse planted in or substituted for a program may behave very differently from the legitimate program in terms of its CPU time or I/O activity and thus, can be detected by abnormal usage or activity patterns of system resources.

- Virus: a computer program written to alter the way a computer operates, without the permission or knowledge of the user, by hiding in other files containing executable codes. A true virus must have two features: replicate itself and execute itself. A virus planted in a system generally causes an increase of the frequency in terms of executable files rewritten, storage used by executable files, or a particular program being executed as the virus spreads. Some anti-virus software tries to detect and remove viruses. But new viruses continue to be created and spread.

- Denial of service (DoS): an intruder monopolizes a resource (e.g., network) so that the resource becomes unavailable to legitimate users. This kind of attack might have abnormally high activity with respect to the resource, whereas activity for all other users is abnormally low. DoS is one of the hardest intruding attacks. This chapter will mainly discuss it.

4.3   Intrusion Detection Models

In order to detect intrusions, an Intrusion Detection System (IDS) must have some model of known behavior, which can be compared to the events it is now analyzing. Then, based on the comparison, it can determine whether the activity is an attack and take appropriate actions. There are three types of modeling which current IDSs use to interpret activity [Bishop (2003)]: Anomaly Modeling, Misuse Modeling, and Specification Modeling [Sekar *et al.* (2002)]. Each model has its own advantages and drawbacks and many systems use a combination of models. The main advantage of anomaly modeling is its ability of detecting new attacks, while its drawback is the high rate of false positive alarms. This is mainly because previously unknown (yet legitimate) system behaviors are also identified as anomalies and hence flagged as potential intrusions. On the other hand, the main advantage of misuse modeling is that it can accurately detect known attacks, but it is unable to detect previously unknown attacks. Specification-based modeling combines the strengths of misuse and anomaly detection. This approach utilizes manually developed specifications to characterize legitimate program behaviors and to detect behavior deviations (from the specifications). Since it is based on legitimate behaviors, specification based modeling does not create false alarms when unusual (but legitimate) program behaviors are encountered. Moreover, it detects attacks as deviations from legitimate behaviors, so it has the potential to detect previously unknown attacks. The main disadvantage of specification modeling is that the process of developing specifications is manual, tedious and reliant on user-expertise. The following subsections discuss these three types of intrusion modeling in detail.

In general, there are two types of possible errors in an IDS's detection of attacks. A false positive occurs when the IDS identifies benign activity as an attack. A false negative occurs when the IDS fails to recognize an attack as objectionable activity. Each type of alarm errors has its own associated problems. The problem with the false negative is straightforward: an attack has gone through undetected, so the IDS has failed in its purpose. A false positive, while it does not involve a successful attack, also harms the operation of the system. It undermines the effectiveness of the IDS, as the impact of an alarm being generated is lessened as more false alarms are encountered. The different models used typically tend towards one type of error over the other, although, technically, each model could see either type of error.

From the architecture point view of IDS systems, two classes of modeling can be identified: Host based IDS (HIDS) and Network based IDS (NIDS). The original IDS models were host-based. That is, each IDS agent involved looked at the records generated by one or most hosts. Typical host-based records include system logs or application logs, and provide only a view of what is happening on one system. The IDS may look at a variety of activity such as system calls, file access, login information, and other host-based activity. In NIDS, the IDS agents look at all of the network traffic visible from their locations. Depending on the topology of the network, multiple agents may be needed to be able to see all of the traffic for the area which is supposed to be monitored. NIDS can gather information on the general nature of the traffic, or even examine the contents of the traffic. One future challenge for the latter approach may be the increase in encryption of network traffic, which will prevent the contents of packets from being readable. The first NIDS system was Network Security Monitor (NSM) [Heberlein *et al.* (1990)].

Of course, both types of IDSs have certain advantages and the ability to see certain types of attacks, which may be difficult or even impossible for the other to see. Clearly, it is easier for NIDS to see network based attacks, such as DoS/DDoS attacks and port scanning. In contrast, an HIDS is more likely to catch insider attacks, as such attacks may not generate any network traffic and therefore will not be visible to an NIDS. For this reason, some IDSs combine the two types to provide more thorough monitoring [Bishop (2003)].

The above models are, for the most part, centralized ones and have certain disadvantages. So, Distributed IDS (DIDS) models are proposed. In DIDS, monitoring of hosts, recording of audit data, and processing of data are performed in a distributed manner [Snapp *et al.* (1991)].

Some typical DIDS systems are Autonomous Agents For Intrusion Detection (AAFID) [Balasubramaniyan *et al.* (1998)] and its enhancement–Cooperative Itinerant Agent (CIA) [Pez *et al.* (2006)], a distributed intrusion detection system using mobile agents (DIDMA) [Kannadiga and Zulkernine (2005)], and Fault-tolerant Grid Intrusion Detection System (FGIDS) [Leu *et al.* (2006)].

Before going into detail, we introduce some related issues here.

4.3.1 *Anomaly Modeling*

Anomaly modeling uses the assumption that an attack will deviate in some way from the typical activity seen on the system. This model gathers information about the "normal" activity for the system or network and then compares the current activity it is examining to see if there is a deviation, or anomaly, from what is expected. Activity which, to a specified degree, does not match the model of normal activity is suspected as an attack. An advantage of anomaly detection is that it is able to detect new attacks. As it does not look for specific activity, just unusual activity, it is able to detect unseen anomalous behavior without being specifically trained to look for that activity. However, a disadvantage of this model is that it tends towards false positives. This is due to the fact that the system cannot tell the difference between benign behavior which is unusual and attacks which are unusual. For this reason, many anomaly IDS designs include measures to deal with false positives. Another problem is dealing with changes in normal behavior over time. If a static model is used, then the IDS will have an increased number of false positives. For this reason, some anomaly based models are designed to adjust their idea of normal behavior over time.

The above idea of finding attacks by looking for anomalies was introduced early on by Denning in the development of IDSs [Denning (1987)]. This anomaly model was designed to be a generic system, independent from the operating systems it was run on, the vulnerabilities it protected, or the types of attacks it detected. The system has six components: Subjects, Objects, Audit Records, Profiles, Anomaly Records, and Activity Rules. Audit Records were compared to Profiles. Overall, the anomaly model uses a statistical characterization and Profiles uses a variety of statistical metrics and models to define normal activities. The actions or states that are statistically unusual are classified as abnormal. Three basic model types proposed by Denning are threshold, statistical, and Markov models. In the threshold model [Denning (1987)], the simplest of the three approaches, the total of some metric over a given time period is applied to some fixed limit. If the current observations go over the fixed limit, the events are considered signs of an attack. One example of where a threshold model might be appropriate is in the number of times an attempted login fails. Depending on the environment, it may be appropriate to assume that more than x attempts to login are likely to indicate an attempt to break into an account [Bishop (2003)]. The second (i.e. statistical) model uses statistical moments, the first two of which are mean and standard deviation (and possibly higher moments for other measures of correlation). A behavior is classified as anomalous if the values representing the behavior fall outside the expected interval for a moment [Bishop (2003)]. Markov models assume that the system states or past history can (should) be used to detect anomalies and the statistical values are calculated based on not only the occurrence of individual events but also on sequences of events. In Markov models, a system is examined at a particular point in time. The events preceding that time have put the system in a particular state. The system transfers into a new state when the next event occurs. As a result, a state transition diagram (along with transition probabilities) can be developed. An event is deemed anomalous if the event will cause a transition that has a low probability [Bishop (2003)].

Some concrete IDS systems based on anomaly modeling include Haystack (a statistical model) [Bishop (2003)], Markov Chain Model [Ye (2000)], System Call Sequences based IDS [Forrest *et al.* (1996); Wagner and Soto (2002)], System Call Argument Based IDS [Mutz *et al.* (2006)], Immune Cell Detection Model [Hofmeyr and Forrest (1999)], Soft Computing Approaches (i.e. using artificial intelligence to allow the system to learn what is normal and decide if new activity falls outside those bounds) [Abraham and Jain (2004)], and POSEIDON [Bolzoni *et al.* (2006)].

4.3.2 *Misuse Modeling*

Misuse modeling is a complementary approach to anomaly detection. Rather than looking for events which go against the predefined normal patterns, it looks for activities which match a list of events which are against the local security policy. These events are considered 'misuse' of the system. Note: in some contexts, the term "misuse" refers to an attack by an internal or authenticated user. However, it means "rule-based detection" (or signature-based detection) here [Bishop (2003)]. Misuse modeling requires a knowledge of potential system vulnerabilities that attackers attempt to exploit. This knowledge is incorporated into the rule set of an IDS system. The IDS system applies the rule set to the monitored/collected data to determine if there is any match between a sequence of data and a rule. If so, a potential attack is reported [Bishop (2003)]. A disadvantage of this approach compared to anomaly detection is it cannot usually detect new attacks. As a new attack will not match any predefined violation of security policy, the system will not recognize it as unwanted activity. Another problem with misuse detection is that if an attacker knows the misuse signatures, it may be possible for the attacker to design attacks which can evade detection: the attack will be changed to perform equivalent steps but not match the signatures of attacks. The advantage of this approach is that it is less prone to false positives than anomaly detection. However, the misuse model must be carefully built to ensure that the rules/signatures properly define only policy violations and not some acceptable activity.

Some examples based on misuse modeling include Bro [Paxson (1999)] (note: Bro is also capable of anomaly detection), Colored Petri Nets [Kumar and Spafford (1994)], STAT (a State Transition Analysis Tool) and later implemented in USTAT and NetSTAT [Ilgun (1993)], and Genetic Algorithm Based Approach to Network Intrusion Detection [Gong *et al.* (2005)].

4.3.3 *Specification Modeling*

Specification modeling, initially proposed in [Ko *et al.* (1994)], takes a different approach to detecting intrusions. Instead of looking for general anomalies, or specific breaks in policy, it looks for actions which go against the specified appropriate behavior of a certain program or entity. Specification modeling implicitly assumes that if all programs in a site adhere to their own specifications, the site policy cannot be violated [Bishop (2003)]. In contrast, misuse modeling makes no such assumption and instead, focuses on overall site policy. In other words, specification modeling is a local form of misuse modeling [Bishop (2003)]. As a result, an attacker can design an attack in such a way that none of programs in the system violates its specification but the combined effect of execution of these programs violates the site policy. Such an attack would not be detected by specification modeling but might be detected by misuse modeling (and anomaly modeling).

How to develop specification of a program/system is a challenging task in specification modeling. In [Uppuluri and Sekar (2001)], specification development consists of the following steps:

(1) Developing generic specifications: Generic specification is a specification parameterized with respect to system calls and their arguments. Such specifications can be utilized to monitor almost any program if these parameters can be appropriately instantiated.
(2) Securing program groups: This step strengthens generic specifications by grouping programs that have similar security implications, such as setuid programs and daemons.
(3) Developing application-specific specifications: Some programs will more likely be attack targets than other programs. One example is servers that can be accessed from remote sites. For such applications, the effectiveness of IDS can be increased by developing more precise specifications.
(4) Customizing specifications for an operating system/site: Different operating systems and sites can have quite different characteristics and security policies. In order to enhance the detection accuracy and effectiveness of IDSs, specifications obtained from the previous steps are further customized to accommodate variations in operating systems and security policies specific to the site.
(5) Adding misuse specifications: It is likely that the detection of some attacks requires knowing attacker behavior. In such cases, specification modeling by itself may not be sufficient and thus, pure specifications can be augmented to contain misuse patterns to capture features of specific attacks and detect these specific attacks.

Some proposed techniques in this class include Specification Model Development Strategy [Uppuluri and Sekar (2001)], Specification Model for Network Attacks [Uppuluri and Sekar (2001)], Specification Model for AODV [Hassan *et al.* (2006)] and Specification-based anomaly detection [Sekar *et al.* (2002)] which combines specification-based and anomaly-based intrusion detection

The detection approaches (modelings) described above tend to be specific to one particular detection method which they were best suited for. However, some modeling approaches are general and can be used for more than one detection model, such as Data Mining Modeling [Lee *et al.* (1999)]. Data mining techniques could be a valuable tool for methodically building misuse and anomaly detection models without the typical need for enormous expert effort. In the case of anomaly detection, the techniques could be used to extract the pattern of normal behavior, while for misuse detection, they could extract the relevant information to see the signature of an attack.

4.4 Intrusion Response

Once an intrusion is detected, how can the intruded system be protected? How can the intrusion be stopped and the possible damage be minimized? The field of intrusion response deals with these challenges [Bishop (2003)].

Ideally, the detection of intrusions should be finished at the initial stage of the intrusion attempts and the action can be taken to stop the intrusions and prevent damage to the system (called intrusion prevention). This prevention requires closely monitoring the system and identifying the attack before it completes.

However, most intrusions would damage the system already when they are detected. The response is needed to repair damage, stop the intrusion, and recover the system. If possible, IDS systems can be augmented to thwart intrusions. Otherwise, the security officers/system administrators must respond to the attack and repair any damage.

In general, intrusion response consists of the following steps [Bishop (2003)]:

(1) Preparation. This is the first step and it plans and prepares for attacks. This step should occur even before any attacks are detected. It establishes rules, procedures and mechanisms for (detecting and) responding to attacks.
(2) Identification. This step tries to track and locate the attack source once an intrusion is detected. It will trigger the rest of steps. This may be one of the most challenging tasks in intrusion response. Section 4.7 will discuss traceback in detail.
(3) Containment. This step confines the attack by limiting the access of the attacker to the system and reducing the protection domain of the attacker as much as possible. To do so, the response engine must closely monitor the attack and constrain the attacker's actions. The former is passive and easy to do, but the latter is considerably more difficult. One typical technique is to use a honeypot [Spitzner (2003)]. When an IDS detects an attack, it takes actions to shift the attacker to a honeypot. The honeypot will isolate the attacker and the intruded system can recover and function normally.
(4) Eradication. Eradicating an attack means to stop the attack and block

further similar attacks. The usual mechanism is to either deny the access of the attacker to the system completely or kill the processes involved in the attack. In addition, it is important to ensure the attack does not immediately resume.

(5) Recovery. This step restores the system to its normal and secure state and brings the system back to normal operations.

(6) Follow-up. This last step involves taking actions external to the system against the attacker, identifying problems in the entire process of intrusion detection and response, and summarizing/recording learned lessons. It commonly involves legal actions, such as fining attackers, putting attackers into prison, or even execution, depending on the consequence of attacks.

4.5 DoS/DDoS Attacks

Among all intruding attacks, the Denial of Service (DoS) attack (along with its distributed form DDoS) is the most serious one, because such an attack is easy to launch but almost impossible to defend against. In fact, the victim may not initially realize that they are under attack and attribute access issues to network failures. In this subsection, we will discuss DoS/DDoS attacks in detail.

4.5.1 *Typical DoS Attacks*

DoS attacks have been around for some time. Typically launched from one host, if that host had more bandwidth than the target, the target was usually knocked offline. Occasionally the attacker used more than one host, but to do so, he needed to manually start the attack software on each system. Many DoS attacks in the wild take advantage of flooding, redirects, and service software bug [Costa-Requena (2001)].

4.5.1.1 *DoS Flooding Attacks*

TCP/IP Packet Flooding is the most common class of attacks. The goal is to overwhelm the target in such a way that all the available bandwidth, memory, processor time, or disk space is used when trying to fulfill attacker requests. What makes this type of attack so difficult to detect is that all the requests look legitimate.

(1) Mail Bombing. Mail bombing was one of the earliest forms of the attack against UNIX systems. All the attacker does is continually sending large emails to a system which supports SMTP connections. The same disk partition used to store incoming email messages was often the same one used by parts of the operating system to store temporary files. Should the partition fill up entirely, the system typically would crash. One advantage from the victim's point of view is that it is generally easy to determine where the attack originated. Even if the sender email address was forged, the message envelope contained the entire delivery history to include the attacker's IP address.

(2) Service Flooding. While the goal of mail bombing attacks is to deplete available disk space, other attacks focus on using all a computer's memory resources or to fully utilize the CPU so that no other programs can run. Most network daemons listen for incoming network service requests and each time one is received, the daemon forks a copy of itself to provide the desired information. Once that information has been transmitted, the forked copy terminates. The system has no way to determine whether the requests are legitimate; it simply answers each one. Knowing this, the attacker sends a continuous stream of requests to a particular service (e.g. HTTP). The victim cannot keep up with the flood of requests resulting in diminishing system performance and possibly application crashes.

This form of attack is not always intentional. Errors during the development of network client programs can have the same effect. One personal example occurred in the mid 1990s. A general purpose SunOS server running the finger daemon (an early user directory service) received a flood of requests from entry level Computer Science students learning how to fork processes. The assignment instructed them to use the finger client to connect to this system. In a matter of minutes, the server was unable to run any new programs.

(3) SYN Flooding. SYN floods are one of the most famous types of attacks and takes advantage of the basic design of TCP/IP communication. Each packet sent to a remote system includes a sequence number to uniquely identify itself. The sender then increments this number before sending the next packet. The recipient collects these packets and uses the sequence numbers to make sure the packets are processed in the proper order. Should one or more packets fail to be received within a preset time period or errors be found in the received packets, the recipient will request, by sequence number, that the sender retransmit

these packets. To make this model work, a client and server must first exchange initial sequence numbers. This is known as the SYN-Handshake. The client sends a SYN packet to the server requesting a new channel be created and includes an initial sequence number. The server acknowledges that it received the client's sequence number by sending a SYN-ACK packet and includes its own initial sequence number. Once the client acknowledges it received this information via an ACK packet, the actual service request can be sent.

In a SYN Flooding attack, the attacker sends a SYN packet to the target but never acknowledges the receipt of the target's SYN-ACK packets. The target must keep these "half-open" connections active for a set period before assuming a failure occurred and closing the port. Meanwhile, the attacker sends more SYN packets at a rate much faster than the failed connections are torn down. Eventually, the server can no longer receive any new communication requests from anyone. Of course, if the attacker uses his own IP address, the attack can be stopped fairly quickly by blocking that address at the server level, network border router, or firewall. To bypass this check, the attacker often randomly spoofs the sender address in the SYN packets. Doing so makes it impossible for the victim to determine which connection requests are legitimate and which are part of an attack [Costa-Requena (2001)].

(4) Land Attack. The Land attack is an interesting variation on SYN Floods. For SYN Floods to be effective, the attacker must continue to send SYN packets to the victim. Even with IP spoofing, the attacker's Internet Service Provider (ISP) may notice the increased volume of network traffic and block the attacker's connection. To reduce the number of packets the attacker must send, he spoofs the source IP address to match the destination of one of the victims. Now, the victim's system continually answered its own SYN packets until it eventually crashes. This vulnerability was first discovered in 1997 but recently the problem resurfaced in Microsoft Windows Server 2003 and XP SP2 [Kenney (1996)].

(5) Fraggle Attack. All the previous flood attacks have relied on TCP/IP packets which are connection oriented. In order for the attack to be launched, the victim's system must have some service listening on a particular port. UDP, on the other hand, is a connectionless protocol which does not require the session to be set up first, nor has the overhead required to make sure all packets are processed properly. When a

system receives a UDP packet, it checks to see what service or application is associated with the service port number and transfers the data to that daemon. If nothing is associated with that port, the system sends a "Destination-unreachable" ICMP packet to the sender. Recognizing this, the attacker will send a flood of UDP packets with spoofed IP source addresses to random ports in the victim. The victim will then eventually become overloaded and fail [Specht and Lee (2004)].

4.5.1.2 Redirection Attacks

Flooding attacks can be described as tier one attacks in that there is a direct connection between the attacker and the victim. This exposes the attacker to discovery, which he desperately would want to avoid. One way to minimize this problem is to add a layer between him and the victim. Taking advantage of TCP/IP design characteristics, the attacker can craft packets that can be used to turn intermediate systems into attack-launching platforms. This makes it difficult for the attacker himself to be traced [Specht and Lee (2004)].

(1) ICMP Redirects. Internet Control Message Protocol (ICMP) packets are used to provide diagnostic messages concerning packet delivery. The most common ones are echo request/reply messages which focus on the ability of one system to communicate with another. Another type is known as ICMP Redirects which, if accepted, modifies a system's routing table to send messages to a destination via a shorter route. The attack works by changing the route a victim host should use to reach its default gateway to an invalid path. The only systems that could then talk to the victim are those that are on the same local subnet [Specht and Lee (2004)].

(2) Smurf Attacks. Every TCP/IP subnet has a special address known as a broadcast address. Packets sent to this address are processed by every system on that subnet. One common use of it includes the address resolution protocol (ARP). This is used to map IP addresses to MAC ones within a subnet. To launch a Smurf Attack, the attacker will pick a random network and send an Echo-Request ICMP (ping) packet to that network's broadcast address. Normally each system on that network would send a response to the attacker but he also spoofs the source address to be that of the victim. By doing this, each system on the network instead sends its ICMP Echo-Reply packet to the victim.

The advantages of such an attack are two fold. Because the actual packets sent by the attacker are not received by the victim, it is more difficult to track the attack to its origin. The network also serves as an attack amplifier: one ICMP Echo Request may result in hundreds of reply packets directed at the victim [Patrikakis *et al.* (2004)].

(3) Chargen Attacks.   Chargen attacks [Specht and Lee (2004)] are a variation of the Fraggle one discussed in section 4.5.1.1. by taking advantage of the chargen service. Chargen is a special service bound to port 19 that was traditionally used to test network capacity. When a connection was made to this port, it would respond with a string of characters. While not used often anymore, many systems still include it as part of the operating system.

To launch this sort of attack, the attacker first searches for systems with the chargen service active. He then sends UDP Echo Request packets to port 19 after spoofing the source IP address as that of the victim. The intermediate host would respond with a character string to the Echo service port of the victim. As per the protocol, the victim would respond with that string. This sets up an endless loop until the victim system fails. Often one system is not enough to guarantee failure of the victim, so a number of intermediate systems may be used, just as with the Smurf Attack described previously [Costa-Requena (2001)].

4.5.1.3   *Service Exploits*

In both the previous attacks, the underlying technique used to disable the victim was to somehow overwhelm it with more network traffic than it can handle. Another way DoS attacks can be launched is through the careful crafting of packets that will exploit a flaw in the code that would process it. The advantage to this approach is that very few, perhaps even only one packet, is all that is required to be successful.

(1) WinNuke.   Microsoft systems use a set of proprietary protocols for name services and authentication information. On TCP/IP networks, these services were bound to ports 135-139. In early versions of the Windows operating systems, Microsoft failed to include error checking for data received on this port. Because of this, an attacker could send "out of band" traffic and cause the system to progressively get slower (Windows 95) or immediately reboot (NT). The code used to launch this attack was surprisingly small [Specht and Lee (2004)].

(2) Ping of Death. As mentioned previously, ICMP packets can be used to test network connectivity. Most commonly, the ping command would send Echo-Request packets and display the time it took to get an Echo-Reply response. The Echo-Request/Receive service was designed to allow packet sizes of up to 64KB for these tests. The problem came when an Echo Request packet exceeded the 64KB limit. Most systems didn't include code to address this problem, so the system would become unstable. Unlike other attacks, there was no need to develop exploit code to demonstrate this flaw. The ping command that came with early Microsoft Windows systems allowed for larger than 64KB size to be specified on the ping command line [Kenney (1996)].

(3) Teardrop Attack. This attack is associated with packet fragmentation. When a large TCP/IP packet needs to be transmitted across a subnet with less bandwidth, it can be broken down into smaller packets. When this happens, the TCP header includes offset information so that the larger packet can be reassembled later. It was assumed that the system that fragmented the packet did so correctly. The attack would take advantage of the fact that most systems didn't include error correction code to address situations when fragments overlapped. He would send two or more fragmented packets with the offsets modified to the victim. Usually this would be enough for the system to crash [Geng and Whinston (2000)].

4.5.2   *Distributed Denial of Service (DDoS) Attacks*

While DoS attacks were effective against small bandwidth targets like home computers, major company and ISP infrastructures would be largely unaffected. To successfully attack these sorts of sites would require the cooperation of many attackers using a multitude of systems. That was until the late 1990s. New tools were created that would allow one attacker to control numerous systems located across the Internet and simultaneously launch DoS attacks against a victim. To a degree, DDoS attacks are an extension of reflective DoS ones. There are unwitting systems used to launch the actual attack and it is more difficult to track the actual origin.

Over a period of time, the attacker breaks into systems all over the Internet. Once access has been gained, the attacker installs a DDoS client program that will be used later to launch the actual attack. There are two classes of client program, master stations and slaves (or zombies). The slaves are those systems which launch the actual attack. Systems selected to become slaves are usually those on networks with large amounts of band-width. The remaining ones run the master control program. The purpose of the master stations is to control the slaves. When slaves are created, they communicate with the master systems and receive commands (e.g. attack target or shutdown) from them. The attacker only communicates with the master stations. The whole system (sometimes referred to as a botnet) becomes a three tier structure providing the attacker added protection from discovery. A variation of this, known as a Distributed Reflective Denial of Service (DRDoS), describes situations when slaves send packets to networks vulnerable to launching Smurf or Chargen attacks. In these cases, there are four tiers between the attacker and the victim.

4.5.2.1 *DDoS Attack Steps*

In general, a DDoS attack takes three steps to conduct attacks [Mirkovic *et al.* (2004)]: Botnet Recruitment, Command and Control, and Attacks.

(1) Botnet Recruitment.   Unlike standard DoS attacks which can be launched at any time, DDoS attacks require time to set up. The attacker needs to find and compromise as many systems as possible in order to install DDoS client software. There are several ways to approach this: manual, semi-automated, and completely automated.
The first step in this process is to find potential candidates for the bot network. This is often done via some form of scanner. Early scanners did little more than probe the systems to determine which ports were open. In some cases, they may also identify which operating systems were being run (OS Fingerprinting). It was then up to the attacker to manually attempt to compromise each system using whatever tools he had on hand. Later versions of these scanners probed large networks automatically and included a number of vulnerability checks. The actual exploitation of vulnerabilities and installation of DDoS client programs were still left to the attacker, but the amount of time required lessened. Today many systems are compromised and added to existing botnets without any interaction with the attacker beyond the initial starting of the probe. This automated form of the attack is usually carried out by worms. Once the worm starts, it probes random networks for systems with specific vulnerabilities. Once a system is found to have the searched for weakness, it is automatically exploited and DDoS software installed. Sometimes this software is included with the worm itself,

others pull the source from a centralized server. After the software is installed, it makes contact with the master station and may even conduct probing operations on its own.

(2) Command and Control. With the DDoS software in place, the communication network needs to be established. Early versions of these tools would make use of the master stations to relay commands from the attacker to the slaves. The transmissions themselves were initially in plaintext, but later the tool authors added encryption. The reason for the added security features was this. When messages were passed in plaintext, it would be easy for anyone to intercept and third parties (including defenders) could forge their own commands to hijack or shut down entire botnets. In fact, this was a common occurrence when groups fought for control of various Internet Relay Chat (IRC) servers and social networks.

Encryption was not only used for communication but also to protect data stored on slave and master nodes. When a slave was activated, it needed to contact a master system to get further instructions, The only way early clients knew who to contact was via a file installed with the software that listed all the master station addresses. Of course, should that slave system be discovered, that file could then be used to identify other nodes that were part of the botnet. At that point, the attacker would lose control of everything he had built. By encrypting these files, the possibility of the entire botnet being compromised was lessened.

Even with encryption, botnets were susceptible to traffic analysis . Investigators could then use this information to find and shutdown masters and slave nodes. With a little luck, they might also be able to track down the attacker. So the attacker could avoid these problems, later DDoS tools started getting way from direct communication between masters and slaves and instead used IRC servers to exchange messages. IRC networks were an early real time chat network loosely modeled after Radio Frequency Citizens Band (CB) communication networks commonly used by the police and delivery truck drivers. In the case of IRC, a group of servers would form a virtual environment that might have hundreds or thousands of channels that users could join. Messages sent to these channels were viewable by everyone who had joined them, regardless of which server they initially connected to. Optionally, private messages could be sent between individual users.

DDoS botnets made use of this by creating their own channel on a IRC networks or created their own IRC server using a non-standard port on one node within the botnet. Masters and slaves would then join the IRC network and channel as specified in the DDoS software. Any message sent to the channel can be processed by any node. New masters could also be added to the botnet at any time. Should any node be discovered, forensic analysis or reverse engineering would not reveal the addresses of the master stations, only the channel being used and changing channels (or networks) would just be a matter of sending one command via the original channel.

(3) Attacks. For the most part, botnets remain dormant. As new nodes are added, they exchange information with master stations, but then they just wait until needed. The demands they place on the host systems is negligible, so end users are unaware that their system has been compromised. It isn't until the command comes that they begin to launch their attack.

Most DDoS slaves will utilize a number of the DoS flood and redirection attacks discussed in sections 4.5.1.1 and 4.5.1.2. The more they mix attack types, the harder it is for the victim to determine legitimate from attack traffic. Commands may also specify the duration of the attack. For example, it could say to use a smurf attack for 15 minutes then stop.

Not all attacks rely on communication channels to determine when to launch their attacks. Some DDoS worms will hard code attack target and time. Those, however, have a specific goal and afterward shutdown or await a tool upgrade via a new version of the worm.

4.5.2.2 *DDoS Tools*

There have been a number of DDoS tools in the wild since the late 1990s. In general, they all work in similar ways. The differences are in how they communicate and how they implement their attacks. What follows is a brief description of some of the more common ones found in the wild.

(1) Trinoo. This is one of the first tools to be discovered and created that later tools followed. Communication between attacker/masters and masters/slaves used dedicated ports and connections were password protected. Attacks consisted of UDP packets sent to random ports on the target for whatever duration the attacker chose [Dittrich (1999a)].

(2) Tribe Flood Network (TFN). The attacker connected directly to master stations via remote shells or telnet directly to the port used by the

master. Unlike Trinoo, no passwords were required. Commands were entered using a terminal style interface. These commands would then be sent to the slaves via encrypted messages embedded in ICMP Echo Reply packets. A variety of DoS attack methods could be directed against the target, including UDP Floods, SYN Floods, ICMP Echo (ping) Floods, and Smurf Attacks [Dittrich (1999c)].

(3) Tribe Flood Network 2000 (TFN2K). As the name suggests, this was an improved version of TFN. Some of the new features included a remote commands capability, IP source address spoofing (completely random address and random within a selected network), and the use of TCP, UDP, and ICMP packets to send commands. It would also send out decoy packets to make finding other master and slave nodes more difficult [Barlow and Thrower (2000)].

(4) Stracheldraht German for "barbed wire". This tool combined the features of Trinoo and TFN DDoS tools. One of the major modifications was that attackers communicated to the masters via an encrypted TCP channel. Masters and slaves used (unencrypted) TCP and ICMP packets to exchanges messages. The tool also included a mechanism for the slave code to be automatically updated [Dittrich (1999b)].

(5) Shaft. This one was another hybrid, combining the features of Trinoo, TFN, and Stacheldraht. However, it also added several new features of its own. The major one was the creation of a ticket system to help keep tracks of the slave stations. When the master station would send a command to a slave, it would include the slave's ticket as well as a weakly encrypted password. Before the slave would execute the command given it, the password and ticket must match those it stored internally. In addition, both master and slave nodes had the ability to change port numbers on command. The hope was this would make it more difficult for IDS to detect their presence. The attacks themselves would include any combination of UDP, SYN, and ICMP floods with spoofed IP source addresses in bursts of 100 packets per slave. An interesting extra component part of this system is that it also kept tracks of packet statistics [Dietrich *et al.* (2000)].

(6) Mstream. This tool worked like many of those previously discussed. Attackers contacted master stations via a password authenticated shell. The attack used TCP ACK packets with spoofed IP source addresses. When the victim received these packets, they immediately sent TCP RST packets back to the "source", using even more bandwidth [Dittrich *et al.* (2000); Korty (2000)].

(7) Trinity. This tool was the first to use IRC as the means of communication. When systems were compromised and the tool installed, they would connect to a public IRC server and await further commands. Attack payloads includes UDP, SYN, TCP ACK and RST floods as well as teardrop attacks [Alert (2000)].

(8) Phatbot. This is not a DDoS tool but major an entire arsenal of attack tools. Once a system is infected with this worm, it can be used as a vulnerability scanner and an email address harvester for spamming, (just to name a few) in addition to launching DDoS attacks. Attack payload includes SYN, UDP, and ICMP floods as well as a "targa" flood (a variation of the Teardrop attack), a "wonk" flood (sending a SYN packet followed by 1023 TCP ACK packets), and various HTTP "Get" floods (some with delay settings so to make these requests harder to differentiate from legitimate web page requests) [Group (2004)].

4.6 Typical DoS/DDoS Defense Mechanisms

Many methods have been suggested to defend against DoS/DDoS attacks. The defending methods can be implemented on a single node, such as the protected server, or on multiple collaborating nodes. In addition, a specific method, called a honeypot, has been developed to attract, analyze, and defend against DoS/DDoS attacks. We discuss these methods in this section.

4.6.1 *Single-node Defending Method*

The single-node defending methods [Wang *et al.* (2002); Jin *et al.* (2003a); Bencsath and Vajda (2004)] can observe attacking symptoms when the traffic to the victim accumulates to a warning level. They subsequently launch the traffic filtering to protect the victim. The hop-count filtering [Jin *et al.* (2003a)] is a solution relying on the fact that the number of hops between the attacking source and the victim is unchanged within a short period. The traffic level measurement [Bencsath and Vajda (2004)] protects a victim by dropping most incoming packets when total incoming traffic shoots to a high level. This measurement can identify attack sources by using statistical property of observed traffic flows. SYN flooding attacks can be observed at leaf routers that connect terminal hosts to the Internet [Wang *et al.* (2002)]. The attack detection is based on the fact that in normal network traffic, the SYN and FIN pair should appear symmetrically. To accumulate these pairs, they used a non-parameter CUSUM method that estimated the average duration time of TCP connections, which varied according to a network's status. These single-node defending methods, however, inevitably cause collateral damage on legitimate traffic destined for the victim that the system is trying to protect.

4.6.2 *Multiple-node Defending Methods*

The multiple-node defending methods require nodes (e.g., routers and servers) distributed in networks to cooperate in preventing DoS/DDoS attacks. Multiple routers can mark packets passing through them [Zhang and Dasgupta (2003); Yaar *et al.* (2006)]. As a result, the packets carry the path information, so it is feasible to detect packets with IP address spoofing and track back to real attacking source. Filtering schemes can be activated at the closest router to the attacking source to filter out illegitimate traffic and stop possible attacks. Intermediate routers can start to drop packets to a destination when the traffic reaches a certain threshold on a link relevant to the destination, as presented in [Ioannidis and Bellovin (2002)]. Mirkovic et al. [Mirkovic *et al.* (2003)] presented DefCOM (also see Section 4.8.4) that consisted of heterogeneous defensive nodes to detect and restrain attacking traffics. Three types of defensive nodes, alert generator nodes, core nodes and classifier nodes, are distributed in a peer-to-peer network and they must communicate frequently to achieve dynamic cooperative defense. Although these methods provide secure and efficient countermeasures to DDoS attacks, they require the modification and cooperation on routers and thus cause difficulties for deployment. Such intensive communications or expensive overhead are mainly consumed by the filtering functions in an intelligent manner to detect the DoS attacks and differentiate them from the legitimate traffics.

4.6.2.1 *Path Identification*

Here we describe one of the multiple-node defending methods: path identification proposed in [Yaar *et al.* (2003)]. In this method, multiple routers along the path from the source of a packet to the destination participate in the DDoS defense on a per packet basis. Each packet will have a path identifier (PI) which is a unique fingerprint for each path taken. In this case, all that needs to be done to mitigate the attack is to block all packets with PI's matching those coming from attack networks.

Like IP Packet Marking traceback 4.7.2, this system is one of traceback mechanisms and uses the ID Identification field of IP packet to store this path identifier. The PI itself is constructed as the packet passes through each router from source of the attack to the target. Every router will have its hash value of n bits ($n = 1$ or $n = 2$) which is the last n bits of an MD5 hash of the router's IP address. (Note for being more accurate, the n bit hash value of a router will be the last n bits of an MD5 hash of the router's IP address concatenated-is this a word? I'm not familiar with it and can't find it anywhere... with the last-hop router's IP address). When a packet comes to a router, the router will determine its n-bit portion in the ID Identification field according to the packet TTL (TTL%16 or TTL%8) and put its hash value there. Unless the source to target path is very long, the hash value for each router should be included in the ID field. Thus, all the packets arriving at the target along the same path will have the same PI.

There are a couple of problems with this approach. The first, as mentioned above, is that if the path is sufficiently long, hashed subsets representing the routers nearest the attacker could be overwritten by the those closest to the target. There are also compatibility issues using ID Identification field. If the packet needed to be fragmented, all router hash values would be lost. Finally, if any legitimate traffic also came from the attacker's network, those packets would also be dropped.

A recent revision of PI, StackPI [Yaar *et al.* (2006)], attempts to address the possibility of losing previous router data because they are overwritten by the closer routers. Instead of using the TTL to decide where router hash information should be placed within the ID field, that field is treated like a stack. Each new router pushes its data onto the stack until the packet reaches the border router of the destination or the stack fills. In this case, all the furthest most hop hash segments are preserved. This also helps address another problem with the original PI model. As long as all routers between the attack source and target supported PI markings, everything worked well. However, chances are that there would be at least a few routers that did not support this functionality. In the PI system, this would create holes within the hash data. StackPI doesn't suffer from this limitation. Only those routers supporting marking would push its data onto the ID field stack.

Even with this enhancement, you still do not have the data for those routers not supporting PI markings. To address that, StackPI also includes write-ahead functionality. Essentially a PI supporting router would not only push the hashed subset of its IP address onto the stack but since it knows what the next hop should be, it can also push that router's hash segment onto the stack as well. This solves the issue of having non-PI supporting routers in the path but for the neighboring routers supporting PI markings, you could have a lot of duplicate entries. To remedy this, before pushing any data onto the stack, it checks the hash value at the top of the stack, if that value matches the one it would push to identify itself, it skips that item and only pushes the hash data for the next router.

4.6.3 *Honeypot*

The honeypot technology proposed recently provides another perspective to detect and prevent the DoS/DDoS attacks in which a honeypot is a target to attract hackers to analyze ongoing attacking activities [Spitzner (2003)]. A honeypot can be defined as an information system resource whose value lies in unauthorized or illicit use of that resource [Spitzner (2003)]. Due to the nature of a honeypot, any traffic destined to it is most likely to be an attack and subsequent response schemes can be evoked to alarm it to the protected server and further reveal attacking origins. Usually, honeypots are fixed to locations and they are easily detected by sophisticated attackers [Krawetz (2004)]. If malicious attackers can detect honeypots, they can bypass detection and even can utilize them to attack other systems. A roaming honeypot technology, thus, can blur the detection and provide a more secure service, as proposed by Khattab et al. [Khattab et al. (2004)]. According to Khattab et al., honeypots are idle servers from a pool of servers and they keep changing to make the roaming honeypots unpredictable. This roaming scheme mitigates the service-level DoS attacks against back-ends (e.g., database servers) of private services. However, such scheme requests the servers in a sever pool to constantly change their roles, either as working servers or as honeypots, which could result in a high cost of maintaining data consistency among servers. Meanwhile, effective attackers can directly send traffic to back-end servers without passing through AG (access gateways) overlay networks to degrade the server's performance.

Honeypots take different forms to target different situations. According to the level of interaction an attacker is allowed to have with a honeypot, there are low-interaction and high-interaction honeypots, respectively. Low-interaction honeypots restrict the interaction between an attacker and the honeypot. This effectively limits the scope of the attacker's actions and minimizes the risk of compromise. On the other hand, high-interaction honeypots expose the whole system, including the operating system, to an attacker. On high interaction systems, attackers can gain full control of the system. Honeypots can also be categorized with respect to their implementations. A physical honeypot is a real machine with its own operating system and IP address, while a virtual honeypot is a machine which emulates system behavior and IP addresses. Virtual honeypots have a number of benefits: a single physical system can emulate more than one virtual honeypot; they can emulate more than one operating system; and they can emulate different IP addresses. Virtual honeypots require far less computational and network resources than physical honeypots, and they provide far greater flexibility in emulating various operating systems.

4.7 Defending against DoS/DDoS Attacks–Traceback

One important issue related to intrusion detection is the ability to track the source of the intrusion. This can result in the prosecution of the attacker or, at least, discovering other systems he or she has compromised and informing the appropriate parties. Also, it helps in mitigating DoS/DDoS attacks either by isolating the identified attack sources or by filtering attack packets far away from the victim as proposed in the IP traceback-based intelligent packet filtering technique [Sung and Xu (2003)]. There are many factors which help attackers to stay behind the scenes and hence complicate the process of traceback: the distributed anonymous nature of DDoS attacks, the stateless nature of the Internet, the destination oriented IP routing, and the fact of having millions of hosts connected to the Internet (implying huge search space) [Al-Duwairi and Govindarasu (2006)]. In particular, the most challenging factor in traceback is that attackers have developed many methods to hide the ultimate source of the attacks. Lee and Shields illustrated the different methods an attacker can use to hide the source of malicious traffic. First, if a connectionless attack, such as a flooding DoS attack, is involved, simple IP spoofing will work. If the attack requires two way communications, hiding the source becomes more difficult as there must be some way for the attacker to receive or properly respond to the target host's replies. Two simple methods are to guess that the proper replies were made and blindly follow the conversation with the host or to guess at the TCP sequence number and capture the packets assumed to be part of the communication (as many systems use a predictable series of 'random' sequence numbers, the latter is a plausible method). The attacker can also hijack an existing benign session and use this session to carry out the attack. Finally, the attacker can use an intermediate host which will alter the received packets in ways which can be simple or involved and then send the results to the target host [Lee and Shields (2001)]. They divided the problems of traceback into two fundamental challenges. The first is to discover the true upstream source of malicious packets. The second is, once a laundering host is found to be the source of an attack, to find the relationship between the traffic coming in and out of the host. This will mark the source of the commands which caused the laundering host to send the malicious traffic, and thus the next upstream step towards the ultimate source of the attack [Lee and Shields (2001)]. There are three important characteristics of the successful completion of tracing an attack. Precision relates to the degree to which the source of an attack can be traced, such as a user or just a host machine or even just a particular LAN. Accuracy measures how likely it is that the trace is correct. For example, there may be more than one possible source discovered in the course of the traceback. Timeliness relates to how soon the results of the traceback are available and complete [Lee and Shields (2001)].

Some intrusion detection systems are designed to track the source of the attacks themselves. When an intrusion is detected, they are able to take steps to track the path of the intrusion throughout the protected area. One such IDS system is an Intrusion Detection Agent system (IDA) [Asaka *et al.* (1999)]. However, this kind of approach will only work in the local area covered by the IDS architecture. On the other hand, another approach to traceback is to have a separate system to handle tracking the attack, typically involving modified routers. This approach can also be limited in scope as it will only be able to follow the path of the traffic through the modified routers. In this approach, once an IDS detects an attack, a request to track the traffic can be made. The traceback architecture will then attempt to track the attack. The actual data used for tracing may not be gathered until the request is made, or it may be gathered constantly. As many of these approaches focus on stopping denial of service attacks, their mechanisms often rely on a great deal of traffic to be able to construct a path. Such kind of traceback, when discussed in the domain of the Internet and TCP/IP architecture, is called IP traceback and requires modification of IP routers. IP traceback has three typical characteristics (or to say, challenges) [Savage *et al.* (2000)]: the modifications should not greatly increase the routers' overhead, the changes should be able to be implemented in stages, and the modified routers should still be able to work with unmodified parts of the network infrastructure.

Recently, a number of researchers have proposed various methods to track a packet back to the actual sender. In the following, we discuss some typical traceback techniques.

4.7.1   *ICMP Traceback*

An early proposal [Bellovin (2000)] to enable traceback was for routers to periodically select an incoming packet and generate a special ICMP packet with information about that packet, including the source address used, the network interface the packet arrived on, and some portion of the packet's contents. This packet would then be sent to the same destination as the packet it checked. So as not to put an undue load on the routers, the sampling size was chosen to be fairly small, e.g. 1/20,000. The idea was that because of the volume of traffic generated as part of a DoS/DDoS attack, chances were that some of the attack packets would be among those sampled. The site that was the target of the attack could then examine these packets to find the origins of the slave nodes and request they be blocked by the remote administrators.

One of the problems with this approach is that some sites block ICMP packets so this data would never be received. The addition of these packets, no matter how small the sample size is, could also contribute to the bandwidth issues faced by the target. While less likely, it is also possible for the ICMP packet to follow a different path than the original packet or be delayed because of ICMP bandwidth limiting mechanisms.

There was also a concern that the attacker could forge ICMP Traceback packets to create further confusion. To address this problem, true ICMP traceback messages could include some form of key to verify the packet's authenticity. In a revision of the original proposed method, HMAC hashing with a list of recently used keys was included in the ICMP packet.

Lee et al. [Lee *et al.* (2003)] suggested a modification to the above ICMP approach which was designed to make reconstructing the path of traffic easier. Instead of marking just one or two links in the path, the ICMP traceback message records the entire path taken by the message to the host. This is accomplished with a modified version of the ICMP traceback message, called the ICMP Traceback with Cumulative Path (ITrace-CP) [Lee *et al.* (2003)]. This message is sent to the next hop router rather than the destination address of the IP packet it traces. If the next hop router received both the traced message and the ITrace-CP message, it will modify the ITrace-CP message by adding its address to the massage and send it to the next hop router along the path followed by the IP packet being traced. If the router received the ITrace-CP message but not the traced packet, it will send an unaltered copy of the ITrace message to the destination address of the traced packet. This method allows for partial paths to reach the host and thus makes reconstructing the entire path of malicious traffic easier as less packets will be needed to perform the reconstruction [Lee *et al.* (2003)]. Another approach is to simply have each router store a log of each packet it has seen. However, given the large amount of packets in typical network traffic, storage space and the efficiency of checking for a packet becomes an issue.

4.7.2   *(Probabilistic) IP Packet Marking*

An alternative to sending special packets with trace information was simply to put tracing data into the selected packets themselves [Savage *et al.* (2000)]. The idea is as follows. When a packet arrives at a router, the router, with a probability p, selects the packet for marking, i.e. recording the router's IP address in the packet. Suppose the attack involves a great deal of traffic, such as flooding types of attacks. As long as a large amount of attacking packets are sent, there will be enough packets sampled and the victim will receive at least one sample for every router (in the path from the attacker to the victim). In addition, suppose the same sampling probability p is used in all routers, the probability that a packet is marked by a router and then left unchanged by all downstream routers is a strictly monotonic function of the distance to the victim (i.e. $p(1-p)^{d-1}$ where d is the distance from the router which samples the packet to the victim). As a result, the numbers of samples contributed by routers can be used to construct the actual path quite accurately.

The above marking method using router IP addresses is feasible but requires a large number of samples. In order to reduce the number of samples and identify attack origin quickly, the link information, i.e. from a router far away from the victim to another router closer to the victim, rather than router's IP addresses, can be used to mark a packet. Links not only provide information about routers on the path from the attacker to the victim but also relative locations between these routers. In addition, a distance of a router from the victim can be added in the marking information. When a router chooses to mark a packet, it sets the distance value to 0, and each router which does not choose to record a link in the packet will increment this value. When the packet arrives at the victim, the distance value indicates how many hops are in the path from the victim to that router. As a result, the path from the victim back to the attack origin can be more easily and quickly constructed. This method is called edge sampling [Savage *et al.* (2000)].

In order not to increase the packet length, the paper [Savage *et al.* (2000)] also suggests that the marking information be recorded in the ID Identification field in the IP header. Since the mark is part of the packet, it is unlikely that an attacker would attempt any forgeries.

The biggest problem with this approach would appear when the packet needed to be fragmented later in order to complete its journey. The marking system is incompatible with the fragmentation part of the protocol. Also, like ICMP Traceback, not every packet should be marked but only a small sample of them. The same sample rate was used as above.

4.7.3 *Hash Based Traceback*

Instead of selecting a small subset of packets to mark, this method proposes that each router should keep track of every packet it forwards, but only for a very short time. The method is called the "Source Path Isolation Engine" (SPIE) [Snoeren (2001)]. It would generate a 32 bit hash of the IP header with the exception of those fields that change during delivery (e.g. TTL and Checksum) and the first eight bytes of payload. As a result, all routers via which a packet travels will have identical hash for the packet. This identical hash can be used to traceback to the source of the packet.

In order to trace a malicious packet, a local IDS must first identify the packet as malicious. Then, it will submit a traceback request to the SPIE Traceback Manager (STM), which is responsible for the whole SPIE enabled area. The STM will then authenticate and verify the request, and then send out a request to all SPIE Collection and Reduction (SCAR) in its domain. Each SCAR, which is responsible for multiple SPIE enabled routers, will form a subgraph of the path of the packet, by querying all relevant routers in its part of the network. The SCARs will then send their subgraphs to the STM which will combine them to form a full graph of the path taken by the packet in the SPIE enabled network [Snoeren (2001)]. From this graph, the origin of malicious packets can be identified. Later work on SPIE looked at the changes needed to support SPIE for IPv6. In order to provide a sufficient amount of entropy, SPIE for IPv6 should include both the mutability of certain standard and extended IPv6 header fields and tunneling such as IPv6 over IPv4 and IPsec [Strayer *et al.* (2004)].

Since these hashes would only be available for a very short amount of time, the target of a DoS/DDoS attack would only have a brief period in which to trace the packets. Another concern about this approach is that routers already have a finite amount of memory and are busy forwarding packets. Calculating hashes, even weak ones, and storing them puts an additional burden on these devices. A revision proposed would be to have a port other than all the interfaces and add a separate device that would calculate and store the hashes. Those devices could also be on a different network to be queried and not interfere with the normal data flow to the target.

4.7.4   *Hybrid Approach*

The traceback techniques discussed above either record the route information in the packet itself, e.g. Probabilistic IP Packet Marking (PPM) (See section 4.7.2) and path identification (See section 4.6.2.1) or store the packet information in routers, e.g. Hash based traceback (See section 4.7.3). For PPM, the action of overwriting the information in the packet means that the information provided is most likely to be about the routers nearer the victim rather than the attacker. This is opposite of what is expected, which is to have more information about the routers closer to the attack source. Moreover, a considerable amount of packets must be collected at the victim before conducting the traceback process, which will also significantly increase the response time of countering an attack. For the method of storing the packet information in a router, storage and look-ups for the packet table are a problem. As a result, two hybrid schemes are proposed in [Al-Duwairi and Govindarasu (2006)]: Distributed Linked List Traceback (DLLT). and Probabilistic Pipelined Packet Marking (PPPM). We briefly discuss them below.

4.7.4.1   *Distributed Linked List Traceback (DLLT)*

In this scheme [Al-Duwairi and Govindarasu (2006)], a router probabilistically determines if it will mark a given packet. If it chooses to mark the packet, it will check to see if the packet has been marked by a previous router. If so, the router will store that information locally in its marking table and then insert its own mark into the packet. As a result, a link list is inherently built for a packet because the marking field in the packet serves as a pointer to the last router that did the marking for the packet and the marking table of that router contains a pointer (i.e., the IP address) to the previous marking router and so on. When a traceback request message is sent, it can be sent to the last router to mark the packet. This router can then confirm it forwarded the packet, add its information to the path list in the traceback request message, and then use its stored mark to look up the previous router marking the packet. In this manner the traceback request can follow the path of marking until a dead end is reached, at which point dead-end message will be sent back to the victim with the complete path up to the dead end.

4.7.4.2 *Probabilistic Pipelined Packet Marking (PPPM)*

Another hybrid approach to traceback with the same goal as DLLT is Probabilistic Pipelined Packet Marking (PPPM). The main idea for PPPM is to transfer the marking information for a certain packet by propagating the information from one marking router to another using subsequent packets traveling to the same destination [Al-Duwairi and Govindarasu (2006)]. Here the marking information contains not only the router's IP address, but also an ID for a packet and a $T\hat{T}L$ value. The ID of the packet is a randomly generated number by the first router which marks the packet and kept unchanged by all subsequent routers marking the same packet. Since one packet can bear just one mark, the marks by multiple routers (except the last making router) for the same packet will be carried to the destination by the subsequent packets. The unique packet ID in the marks of multiple packets will allow the destination to find the routers marking the packet. In addition, the $T\hat{T}L$ in the mark and original TTL in the IP header will allow the destination to determine its distance to the marking router. Thus, the order of routers can be discovered.

The marking process is as follows [Al-Duwairi and Govindarasu (2006)]. As in other approaches, a router R will probabilistically decide to mark a packet P. If there is no marking information which needs to be transferred to P's destination, then (1) if P is not already marked, then R writes into P its own mark (i.e. its own IP address, a randomly assigned ID, and a $T\hat{T}L$ value equal to that of P's current TTL); (2) otherwise (i.e. P is already marked), R buffers P's marking information in its destination-indexed table and then remarks it (note: the ID is kept intact). Otherwise (i.e. if there is marking information which needs to be transferred to P's destination), then

(1) if P is not already marked, R loads that information into P, (2) otherwise (i.e. P is already marked), R swaps the buffered mark information with P's current marking information. Note: R cannot perform its own marking on the packets for a destination when a buffered marking with the same destination exists. However, it is not a big problem, since we assume the attack involves a large number of packets and it is sufficient to obtain only one mark per router.

As can be observed, DLLT needs to keep the marking information in routers for a long time and the routers need to participate in the construction of packet path. In contrast, PPPM will clear the buffered marking information periodically or when it has been loaded. Furthermore, the destination itself can construct the packet path from the received packets.

4.7.5 *Intrusion Detection and Traceback in Wireless Networks*

The intrusion detection and traceback problem exists in wireless multi-hop networks, such as MANETs, wireless sensor networks, and wireless mesh networks, since these types of networks also face DoS/DDoS attacks. However, traditional methods do not work well in wireless networks due to the lack of stable infrastructure, the limited tolerance for additional storage and processing overhead, and the inability to trust nodes in such networks. Some intrusion detection and traceback approaches for wireless multihop networks have been proposed recently [Jin *et al.* (2006); Kim and Helmy (2006); Sun *et al.* (2003); Sy and Bao (2006)]. One example is Zone-based Intrusion Detection System for Mobile Ad hoc Networks (MANETs) (ZBIDS) [Sun *et al.* (2003)]. ZBIDS is a hierarchical IDS system. There are two levels in ZBIDS and the network in consideration is logically divided into non-overlapping zones. The high level is system level (i.e. interzone) and the low level is zone level (i.e. intrazone). The nodes which have physical connections to different zones are called gateway nodes (or interzone nodes). An IDS agent is attached to each node and each IDS agent performs the functionalities of low level ZBIDS. The agent of a node utilizes the local and trusted information and runs independently to monitor the node's local activities for abnormal behaviors and broadcasts the locally generated alerts inside the zone. In the high level, the gateway nodes of each zone aggregate and correlate the locally generated alerts inside the zone. A combining algorithm is introduced to aggregate the locally generated alerts based on their attribute similarities and thus, further improve the performance of ZBIDS. Source similarity plays an important role in aggregation and its probability distribution is utilized in making the final decisions to generate alarms. Once the aggregated alerts exceed certain thresholds, the gateway nodes will generate alarms.

Another example is CAPTRA, a CoordinAted Packet TRAceback mechanism [Sy and Bao (2006)]. Many other traceback techniques work better with a constant flow of traffic which is found in a persistent attack. However, Network-based attacks can also be sporadic. This kind of attack is sometimes easily detected but are hard to trace back. CAPTRA was designed to detect and traceback the origin of sporadic attacks [Sy and Bao (2006)]. It is suited for wireless sensor networks (WSNs) and takes advantage of the broadcasting nature of the packet transmissions in WSNs. CAPTRA remembers packets in multi-dimensional Bloom filters which are distributed in overhearing sensors. Later, it retrieves the information from Bloom filters and identifies the path of the packet transfers using a series of REQUEST-VERDICT-CONFESS message exchanges between the forwarding and overhearing nodes.

Intrusion detection and response for wireless multihop networks is a challenging area for future research and there will be plenty of new approaches proposed in the future.

4.7.6 *Pushback*

One of the problems with the traceback approaches is that while it may help identify the sources of a DoS/DDoS attack, it isn't able to do anything to stop them. Pushback [Mahajan *et al.* (2001)] is an attempt to address this. When a DoS/DDoS attack starts, the target's router looks at the volume of traffic coming from each upstream router and sends a message to those routers which seem to be sending an excessive amount of traffic. Each upstream router, in turn, does the same thing until the message received by the border routers for each of the networks involved in the attack. Those routers then block all systems responsible for attack traffic. The effect is essentially like pulling the plug on those offending networks. While waiting for the routers to stop the flow of traffic, the border router for the network being attacked will set up rules to put rate limits on those routers forwarding the attack packets.

Of course this system assumes that the network traffic is not equally distributed across all the interfaces. If it were, it would be much more difficult to discover the attack sources. Also, pushback only works if all routers support this feature. Otherwise the target network gets partial relief.

4.8 Exemplary DoS/DDoS Defense Research Projects and Systems

When looking at how to defend against DoS/DDoS attacks, two aspects should be addressed: prevention and reaction. This is a hard problem because of the very nature of the attack. How do you withstand the sheer number of attackers sending what on the surface seems like legitimate network traffic? In the movie Wargames, the NORAD computer, WOPR, came to the conclusion, after an exhaustive series of Nuclear War simulations, that the only way to win was not to play. This observation applies equally well to current Dos/DDoS defenses. In short, do not allow yourself to become an unwitting participant in the attack. Thus, this section will present best practice methods, and then illustrate exemplary DoS/DDoS defense research projects.

4.8.1 *Best Practice Methods*

(1) Secure Your Nodes. Recruitment is a key component in making any DDoS attack work. Without a large botnet army, no meaningful attack can take place. Remember that in all cases, systems must first be compromised before DDoS tools can be installed. The key first step then is to ensure that systems are patched on a regular basis. Attackers are typically not using zero-day exploits to compromise systems. Usually the vulnerabilities they exploit have have been around for weeks or months with patches having been published almost equally as long in most cases.

Once the systems have been patched, the next thing that needs to be done is to make sure virus scanners are installed and that their signature files are continually kept up to date. The advantage this provides is that, should malicious code find its way onto a system, these scanners can identify it immediately and either quarantine the tool or provide notification to the system user that the operating system may need to be reinstalled.

Additional integrity checkers like Tripwire can be installed to notify the user if any program, library, or configuration file had been modified.

The system works by taking the hash values of all key files when an operating system and key software packages are installed and storing these hashes in a database. These values are then periodically recalculated and compared to those in the database. If the values match, the files have not been modified. Otherwise, further investigation is warranted.

Finally, the system itself needs to be configured such that only those services which are needed are in place. In addition, operating system specific hardening measures should take place (e.g. SYN Cookies on Linux systems to prevent SYN Flood attacks). Tools like Microsoft's Baseline Security Analyzer and those freely available from the Center for Internet Security are particularly helpful to ensure operating systems and major network service daemons are properly configured and locked down.

(2) Egress/Ingress Filtering. Steps can also be taken at the network level to ensure systems within that network are not participating in an attack. Much can be done at the border routers. The first thing to do is to configure egress filter rules. Most people think of firewall and router packet filtering as focusing specifically on the traffic coming into a network. Egress filtering are those used to check packets leaving the local network. How this helps prevent a site from participating in a DDoS attack is that most of the DDoS attacks we've mentioned include IP source address spoofing. If the router sees a packet leaving the local network that has a source address that doesn't belong in the network's internal IP space, it should be discarded.

Likewise, Ingress filtering (filtering of incoming packets) can also minimize participation in DDoS attacks. DDoS attacks that use redirection techniques (e.q. Smurf Attacks) need to be able to send their packets to the broadcast address of intermediate networks. There is no reason such traffic should be allowed [Institute (2000)].

(3) Bogon Filtering. Ingress filtering can also help reduce the volume of traffic directed against your network. Again, since many source addresses are spoofed, chances are that many may be "bogons". Bogons are IP addresses that have not been assigned by the Internet Assigned Number Authority (IANA) or Regional Internet Registry (RIR). These include all address blocks that are available but have never been assigned to anyone as well as those defined by RFC 1918 and RFC 3330 for use in internal use only situations [WebSite (2006)].

While best practices could help significantly reduce the number and magnitude of DoS/DDoS attacks, it is unreasonable to assume all networks and computers would be configured properly. With DSL and Broadband cable becoming more popular to connect residential sites, the number of potential botnet members increases. That being the case, research into new techniques for Dos/DDoS defense and prevention are a must. Here is a brief summary of some of the stronger projects.

4.8.2 *D-Ward*

While in previous methods, the target network initiates action in response the attack, D-Ward [Mirkovic and Reiher (2005)] was designed for networks to act as the good neighbors. Basically, it works like an anomaly/misuse IDS looking at both incoming and outgoing traffic at the border router. Models are initially created based on normal application and protocol traffic levels and grouped into traffic patterns that are benign/legitimate, suspicious, or attack. The system then looks at network flows to remote sites as well as to individual nodes within the local network. If it sees anything that it deems as suspicious or as a potential attack based on the models, it imposes bandwidth rate limits (lesser ones for suspicious, stronger ones for potential attacks). Notice that the local systems are not blocked even if the traffic it is sending is suspected of being part of an attack. This is to minimize the effects of false positives.

4.8.3 *Netbouner*

This approach [Thomas *et al.* (2003)] is much like creating whitelists to allow access to local systems from others on the Internet. Before network traffic is allowed in from the outside, the sending node must first prove that it is an actual system. Many spoofed addresses don't correspond to systems that are active, so when Netbouncer sees a packet from a network not listed in its whitelist, it will send an ICMP packet to that node. If it gets a response, then Netbouncer knows that the remote node is a legitimate system and adds it to its whitelist. Further tests check to see if the network ports being used actually are appropriate for that protocol being received. If the remote system passes all these tests, then traffic is passed. This system is much like having to type in the distorted letters incorporated into an image as part of web form submissions.

The big problem with a system like this is an attack that spoofs an address of systems that were previously added to the whitelist. In those cases, the traffic would pass unhindered, especially if the attack itself was using a form of service flood.

4.8.4 *DefCom*

DefCom [Mirkovic *et al.* (2003)] uses a distributed model which incorporates defense mechanisms at both the victim and attack source networks as well as at core parts of the Internet backbone. When these components detect that an attack is underway, it counters by employing traffic rate limits on those packets found to be part of the attack.

There are three types of nodes used; alert generators to detect the occurrence of an attack, rate limiters which impose traffic limits on a traffic passing through it, and classifiers which try to identify and mark both attack and legitimate traffic. The alert generators and classifiers are positioned at the borders of local networks. Rate limiters are typically found as part of core routers. The alert generators (added to firewalls) detect the attack and through a backchannel, communicate with rate limiters and classifiers. The rate limiters near the victim network begin to limit the amount of traffic passed with additional rate limiters further upstream assisting later. All the filtering is based on the markings in the packets from the source networks. The classifiers, near the attack source networks, inject markings into each packet identifying it as either legitimate or suspicious. The rate limiters then give preferential treatment to those packets marked as legitimate followed by those labeled as suspicious. Any packets without any markings are limited the most.

4.8.5 *SIFF*

This approach [Yaar *et al.* (2004)] is similar to others in that it uses rate filtering based on the classification of the traffic being sent. What is different is that SIFF is not reactive but proactive. The basic idea is this: as part of the initial connection handshake, the two nodes would exchange capabilities. Packets between these nodes using these capabilities would then be viewed as privileged communication. Routers would monitor this and give less precedence to unprivileged packets. There would also be mechanisms in place to detect floods of "privileged" packets and if necessary, revoke the capabilities granted to the sending node. This helps to address situations when an attacker attempts to forge packets to make them seem to having been sent from a node part of an existing (privileged) session.

The only problem with this scheme is that it would require a fundamental change to the TCP/IP model in order to be effective. The authors suggest incorporating SIFF into IPv6 or creating modules that could be installed in IPv4 nodes and routers. To be effective, deployment would have to be widespread.

4.8.6 *Hop-Count Filtering*

The approach [Jin *et al.* (2003a)] also focuses on core TCP/IP usage, but unlike SIFF, does not require modifications to existing protocols. Every time a packet passes through a router, the Time to Live (TTL) value is decremented by 1. Should that value reach 0 before the packet reaches its destination, the packet is discarded. What this does is that on the recipient network, the TTLs of received packets are recorded and compared to a best guess as to what that value should be given the source address. If the difference between the two values is within a small threshold, it is assumed that the packet truly came from the node identified by the source address field of the packet. Otherwise, it is considered a forgery and discarded.

How the system makes its guess is to first see how many hops are between the source and destination networks. This value is then subtracted from a best guess as to what the initial TTL value was set to on the sending node. Each operating system has its own value that it uses on all outgoing packets so it should be quick to check the possibilities. On the other hand, it would be potentially difficult for an attacker to guess the right number of hops and include an appropriate value in any forged packets.

There is one significant flaw with this approach. It assumes that the source addresses used in an attack are forged. While that is often the case, it does not need to be. With botnets growing as quickly as they are, attacks can be launched using a subset in available systems and not spoofing any packets.

4.8.7 *PacketScore*

One of the problems with many of the research solutions thus far is that they are reactive. The victim determines that an attack is underway and attempts to block traffic using a series of router-based access control lists. To be effective though, network providers must all cooperate. Even models like SOS (see section 4.9) which selectively allow only legitimate traffic to reach core servers is only effective if the border routers are not completely overwhelmed.

PacketScore [Kim *et al.* (2004b)] is an attempt to use a model similar to that used to combat Spam. Each packet is scanned and a score computed. If that score exceeds a dynamic threshold, the packet is discarded. Packet information is collected by Detecting-Differentiating-Discarding routers (3D-R) found at the edge of all participating networks and thus forms a virtual security perimeter. When one router detects a potential attack, it communicates with a DDoS Control Server (DCS) and together compare the traffic to a normal traffic profile for that network. Statistical and "fine-grain" characteristics are examined for each packet and a score (CLP) is is generated via Bayesian analysis. That score is then compared to the threshold to determine whether the packet should be allowed into the target network. The threshold itself is dynamic and primarily based on target network's bandwidth capacity.

One of the problems with this approach is that as bandwidth has increased, it is becoming harder to score packets without introducing delays. A revision of PacketScore, called ALPI, attempts to address this. Instead of doing the Bayesian (CLP) checks, it observes current attributes and compares them to ones within the normal profile, the LB system (commonly used for traffic shaping) tracks the number of times attributes occur. If these values exceed what should be accepted, the packet is discarded.

An alternative included in ALPI [Ayres *et al.* (2006)], is the AV system, which attempts to look at variance in attributes from the norm. They modeled this approach after some of the current intrusion detection models were deployed. While more complex than LB, it was faster than CLP and in their experiments, proved to be more accurate in deciding which packets to drop.

4.8.8 *Speak-Up*

Speak Up [Walfish *et al.* (2006)] uses a unique approach that is counterintuitive. Many DDoS attacks are application centric. They flood the target with legitimate appearing service requests (e.g. HTTP GET) but never view the responses. The idea is that it is far more expensive for the server to fork copies of the daemon needed (and using up CPU and memory resources) than for an attacker to issue a simple request. Speak up deals with this by instead of trying to limit the flow of traffic from suspected attacks, encourages all clients to increase the amount of data being sent. Since the attackers will already be sending as much data as they could, only the legitimate clients would be able to increase their volume of traffic sent. How these clients do this is either by padding the requests or by sending lots of data via a separate payment channel. The net effect is that the good traffic will drown out the attack.

4.9   Secure Overlay Service (SOS)

As mentioned previously, new DoS/DDoS defense techniques need to be continuously investigated to defend existing attacks as well as newly appearing attacks. Secure Overlay Service (SOS) is one example of the new DoS/DDoS defense architectures, and we discuss it in this section.

SOS [Keromytis *et al.* (2004)] is a new and powerful architecture for mitigating DoS/DDoS attacks. SOS performs intensive filtering near the protected network edges, thus, pushing the attacking points far away from the protected server. In addition, SOS introduces randomness and anonymity into the forwarding architecture, thus, making it difficult for an attacker to target the nodes along the path to the protected server. The randomness also makes SOS robust in terms of node failure due to attacks or failures. In SOS, the server is protected by some firewall filters first and then overlay nodes in a network. The overlay nodes work together to forward legitimate packets to the protected server and block illegitimate packets. Besides forwarding capability, some nodes also play the roles as of the following three classes: secret servlets, beacons, and SOAP (Secure Overlay Access Point). The filters around the protected server just let the packets from the secret servlets get to the protected server but filter out all other packets. It is assumed that the secret servlets, selected by the protected server, are only made known to the beacon nodes, and thus the attackers cannot attack secret servlets nor send packets by spoofing as some secret servlet's IP address. The packets from legitimate users to the protected server are transmitted as follows. The legitimate users, assuming they know some SOAP nodes, send their packets to one of the SOAP nodes. The SOAP node performs verification, according to certain authentication protocols, to make sure the packets are coming from legitimate users. After verification is passed, the SOAP node routes the packets to one beacon node via overlay nodes by the way of "Chord". The beacon then forwards the packets to one of the secret servlets. Finally, the packets are sent by the secret servlet, filtered by some firewalls, and arrive at the protected server.

In summary, this approach has the same goal as Netbouncer in that only traffic found to be from a legitimate client should be allowed to pass. The way SOS handles this is to first set up a virtual network within the real one. Since the target of most DDoS attacks are servers (e.g. web servers), these are what are protected. When a client makes a request for a service, its packets get to some SOAP point first, pass through beacons and servlets, and finally arrive at the server. The SOS system includes redundancy features such that if any node in the system were to fail, another can take its place [Keromytis *et al.* (2004)].

This model has since been extended to allow for authenticated access to resources. Specifically, WebSOS [Stayrou *et al.* (2005)] enables clients to gain access through the overlay network after first authenticating to the network. This authentication takes the form of a Graphical Turing Test (GTT). The model used is called CAPTCHA (Completely Automated Public Turing test to Tell Computers and Humans Apart) which displays a morphed image of letters and requires the client type them in. After successfully authenticating, these clients receive a signed applet which connects them to the beacon network via a SSL encrypted channel.

A more general model of WebSOS can be used by ISPs to protect entire networks from DDoS attacks. In many situations, if an ISP detects an attack on one of its clients, it can simply direct its routers to drop all packets destined for that network. This is often called blackholing. While this does not help the client who is being attacked, it does protect other clients of the ISP from experiencing performance problems. The SOS architecture Gore [Chou *et al.* (2005)] adds proxies and a gore center to the ISP infrastructure to help attacked clients remain accessible. When the ISP detects an attack, the gore routers reroute all traffic for the target network to the gore center. The center then attempts to determine which are legitimate and which should be discarded. Proxies can be used in the same manner as WebSOS. Clients can authenticate either by a GTT or centralized authentication server (e.g. RADIUS Server) to get priority access. All allowed traffic then passes to internal servers much like the original SOS model.

An interesting extra feature for ISPs is that the proxy capability of WebSOS and Gore can be offered to clients as a paid for added feature.

4.10   Conclusion

Intruding attacks have been and will continue to be a serious problem in the security field, in particular, collaborative computing environments. As a result, intrusion detection and defense have been and will continue to be an important research area for security, in particular, trusted collaborative computing. This chapter discussed typical intruding attacks, detection models, response mechanisms, and defense architectures. In particular, the chapter discussed DoS/DDoS attacks and typical DoS/DDoS defending mechanisms.

New and collaborative intrusion detection and defense technologies need to be investigated for existing intruding attacks and for the new attacks as well. Detection and defense mechanisms should be designed to defend themselves from attacking. The cryptographic mechanisms and trusted collaborative computing techniques should be combined into collaborative defense schemes to enhance their defending capability.

Chapter 5

Reliability in Grid Computing

As a representative of collaborative computing, grid computing is a newly developed technology for complex systems with large-scale resource sharing, wide-area communication, and multi-institutional collaboration. Although the developmental tools and infrastructures for the grid have been widely studied, grid reliability analysis and modeling are not easy because of its largeness, complexity and stiffness. This chapter introduces the Grid computing technology, analyzes different types of failures in a grid system and their influence on its reliability and performance. The chapter then presents models for a star-topology grid, considering data dependence, and a tree-structure grid, considering failure correlation. Evaluation tools and algorithms are developed, based on Universal Generating function, Graph theory, and Bayesian approach. Illustrative numerical examples are presented to show the grid modeling and reliability/performance evaluation.

5.1 Overview of Reliability in Grid Computing

Grid computing [Foster and Kesselman (2003)] is a newly developed technology for complex systems with large-scale resource sharing, wide-area communication, and multi-institutional collaboration [Kumar (2000); Das et al. (2001); Foster et al. (2001, 2002); Berman et al. (2003)]. Many experts believe that the grid technologies will offer a second chance to fulfill the promises of the Internet.

The real and specific problem that underlies the Grid concept is coordinated resource sharing and problem solving in dynamic, multi-institutional virtual organizations [Foster et al. (2001)]. The sharing that we are concerned with is not primarily file exchange, but rather direct access to computers, software, data, and other resources. This is required by a range of collaborative problem-solving and resource-brokering strategies emerging in industry, science, and engineering. This sharing is highly controlled by the resource management system [Livny and Raman (1998)], with resource providers and consumers defining what is shared, who is allowed to share, and the conditions under which the sharing occurs.

Recently, the Open Grid Service Architecture [Foster *et al.* (2002)] enables the integration of services and resources across distributed, heterogeneous, dynamic, virtual organizations. A grid service is desired to complete a set of programs under the circumstances of grid computing. The programs may require using remote resources that are distributed. However, the programs initially do not know the site information of those remote resources in such a large-scale computing environment, so the resource management system (the brain of the grid) plays an important role in managing the pool of shared resources, in matching the programs to their requested resources, and in controlling them to reach and use the resources through wide-area network.

The structure and functions of the resource management system (RMS) in the grid have been introduced in details by [Livny and Raman (1998); Cao *et al.* (2002); Krauter *et al.* (2002); Nabrzyski *et al.* (2003)]. Briefly stated, the programs in a grid service send their requests for resources to the RMS. The RMS adds these requests into the request queue [Livny and Raman (1998)]. Then, the requests are waiting in the queue for the matching service of the RMS for a period of time (called waiting time) [Abramson *et al.* (2002)]. In the matching service, the RMS matches the requests to the shared resources in the grid [Ding *et al.* (2002)] and then builds the connection between the programs and their required resources. Thereafter, the programs can obtain access to the remote resources and exchange information with them through the channels. The grid security mechanism then operates to control the resource access through the Certification, Authorization and Authentication, which constitute various logical connections that causes dynamicity in the network topology.

Although the developmental tools and infrastructures for the grid have been widely studied [Foster and Kesselman (2003)], grid reliability analysis and evaluation are not easy because of its complexity, largeness and stiffness. The gird computing contains different types of failures that can make a service unreliable, such as blocking failures, time-out failures, matching failures, network failures, program failures and resource failures. This chapter thoroughly analyzes these failures.

Usually the grid performance measure is defined as the task execution time (service time). This index can be significantly improved by using the RMS that divides a task into a set of subtasks which can be executed in parallel by multiple online resources. Many complicated and time-consuming tasks that could not be implemented before are working well under the grid environment now.

It is observed in many grid projects that the service time experienced by the users is a random variable. Finding the distribution of this variable is important for evaluating the grid performance and improving the RMS functioning. The service time is affected by many factors. First, various available resources usually have different task processing speeds online. Thus, the task execution time can vary depending on which resource is assigned to execute the task/subtasks. Second, some resources can fail when running the subtasks, so the execution time is also affected by the resource reliability. Similarly, the communication links in grid service can be disconnected during the data transmission. Thus, the communication reliability influences the service time as well as data transmission speed through the communication channels. Moreover, the service requested by a user may be delayed due to the queue of earlier requests submitted from others. Finally, the data dependence imposes constraints on the sequence of the subtasks' execution, which has significant influence on the service time.

This chapter first introduces the grid computing system and service, and analyzes various failures in grid system. Both reliability and performance are analyzed in accordance with the performability concept. Then, the chapter presents models for star- and tree-topology grids, respectively. The reliability and performance evaluation tools and algorithms are developed based on the universal generating function, graph theory, and Bayesian approach. Both failure correlation and data dependence are considered in the models.

5.2 Grid Service Reliability and Performance

5.2.1 *Description of the Grid Computing*

Today, the Grid computing systems are large and complex, such as the IP-Grid (Indiana-Purdue Grid) that is a statewide grid (http://www.ip-grid.org/). IP-Grid is also a part of the TeraGrid that is a nationwide grid in the USA (http://www.teragrid.org/). The largeness and complexity of the grid challenge the existing models and tools to analyze, evaluate, predict and optimize the reliability and performance of grid systems. The global grid system is generally depicted by the Figure 5.1. Various organizations [Foster *et al.* (2001)], integrate/share their resources on the global grid. Any program running on the grid can use those resources if it can be successfully connected to them and is authorized to access them. The sites that contain the resources or run the programs are linked by the global network as shown in the left part of Figure 5.1.

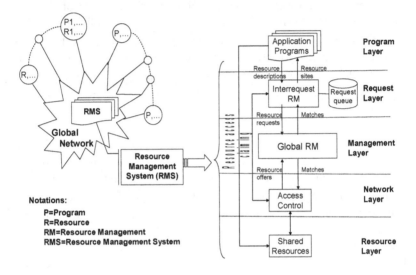

Fig. 5.1   Grid computing system.

The distribution of the service tasks/subtasks among the remote resources are controlled by the Resource Management System (RMS) that is the "brain" of the grid computing [Livny and Raman (1998)]. The RMS has five layers in general, as shown in Figure 5.1: program layer, request layer, management layer, network layer and resource layer.

(1) *Program layer*: The program layer represents the programs of the customer's applications. The programs describe their required resources and constraint requirements (such as deadline, budget, function etc). These resource descriptions are translated to the resource requests and sent to the next request layer.
(2) *Request layer*: The request layer provides the abstraction of "program requirements" as a queue of resource requests. The primary goals of this layer are to maintain this queue in a persistent and fault-tolerant

manner and to interact with the next management layer by injecting resource requests for matching, claiming matched resources of the requests.

(3) *Management layer*: The management layer may be thought of as the global resource allocation layer. It has the function of automatically detecting new resources, monitoring the resource pool, removing failed/unavailable resources, and most importantly matching the resource requests of a service to the registered/detected resources. If resource requests are matched with the registered resources in the grid, this layer sends the matched tags to the next network layer.

(4) *Network layer*: The network layer dynamically builds connection between the programs and resources when receiving the matched tags and controls them to exchange information through communication channels in a secure way.

(5) *Resource layer*: The resource layer represents the shared resources from different resource providers including the usage policies (such as service charge, reliability, serving time etc.)

5.2.2 *Failure Analysis of Grid Service*

Even though all online nodes or resources are linked through the Internet with one another, not all resources or communication channels are actually used for a specific service. Therefore, according to this observation, we can make tractable models and analyses of grid computing via a virtual structure for a certain service. The grid service is defined as follows:

Grid service is a service offered under the grid computing environment, which can be requested by different users through the RMS, which includes a set of subtasks that are allocated to specific resources via the RMS for execution, and which returns the result to the user after the RMS integrates the outputs from different subtasks.

The above five layers coordinate together to achieve a grid service. At the "Program layer", the subtasks (programs) composing the entire grid service task initially send their requests for remote resources to the RMS. The "Request layer" adds these requests in the request queue. Then, the "Management layer" tries to find the sites of the resources that match the requests. After all the requests of those programs in the grid service are matched, the "Network layer" builds the connections among those programs and the matched resources.

It is possible to identify various types of failures on respective layers:

(1) *Program layer*: Software failures can occur during the subtask (program) execution; see e.g. [Xie (1991); Pham (2000)].
(2) *Request layer*: When the programs' requests reach the request layer, two types of failures may occur: "blocking failure" and "time-out failure". Usually, the request queue has a limitation on the maximum number of waiting requests [Livny and Raman (1998)]. If the queue is full when a new request arrives, the request blocking failure occurs. The grid service usually has its due time set by customers or service monitors. If the waiting time for the requests in the queue exceeds the due time, the time-out failure occurs [Abramson *et al.* (2002)].
(3) *Management layer*: At this layer, "matching failure" may occur if the requests fail to match with the correct resources, [Xie *et al.* (2004)] (pp. 185-186). Errors, such as incorrectly translating the requests, registering a wrong resource, ignoring resource disconnection, misunderstanding the users' requirements, can cause these matching failures.
(4) *Network layer*: When the subtasks (programs) are executed on remote resources, the communication channels may be disconnected either physically or logically, which causes the "network failure", especially for those long time transmissions of large dataset [Dai *et al.* (2002)].
(5) *Resource layer*: The resources shared on the grid can be of software, hardware or firmware type. The corresponding software, hardware or combined faults can cause resource unavailability.

5.2.3 *Grid Service Reliability and Performance*

Most previous research on distributed computing studied performance and reliability separately. However, performance and reliability are closely related and affect each other, in particular under the grid computing environment. For example, while a task is fully parallelized into m subtasks executed by m resources, the performance is high but the reliability might be low because the failure of any resource prevents the entire task from completion. This causes the RMS to restart the task, which reversely increases its execution time (i.e. reduces performance). Therefore, it is worthwhile to assign some subtasks to several resources to provide execution redundancy. However, excessive redundancy, even though improving the reliability, can decrease the performance by not fully parallelizing the task. Thus, the performance and reliability affect each other and should be considered together in the grid service modeling and analysis.

In order to study performance and reliability interactions, one also has to take into account the effect of service performance (execution time) upon the reliability of the grid elements. The conventional models [Kumar *et al.* (1986); Chen and Huang (1992); Chen *et al.* (1997); Lin *et al.* (1997)] are based on the assumption that the operational probabilities of nodes or links are constant, which ignores the links' bandwidth, communication time and resource processing time. Such models are not suitable for precisely modeling the grid service performance and reliability.

Another important issue that has much influence on performance and reliability is data dependence that exists when some subtasks use the results from some other subtasks. The service performance and reliability is affected by data dependence because the subtasks cannot be executed totally in parallel. For instance, the resources that are idle in waiting for the input to run the assigned subtasks are usually hot-standby because cold-start is time consuming. As a result, these resources can fail in waiting mode.

The considerations presented above lead the following assumptions that lay in the base of grid service reliability and performance model.

Assumptions:

(1) The service request reaches the RMS and is being served immediately. The RMS divides the entire service task into a set of subtasks. The data dependence may exist among the subtasks. The order is determined by precedence constraints and is controlled by the RMS.

(2) Different grid resources are registered or automatically detected by the RMS. In a grid service, the structure of virtual network (consisting of the RMS and resources involved in performing the service) can form star topology with the RMS in the center or, tree topology with the RMS in the root node.

(3) The resources are specialized. Each resource can process one or multiple subtask(s) when it is available.

(4) Each resource has a given constant processing speed when it is available and has a given constant failure rate. Each communication channel has constant failure rate and a constant bandwidth (data transmission speed).

(5) The failure rates of the communication channels or resources are the same when they are idle or loaded (hot standby model). The failures of different resources and communication links are independent.

(6) If the failure of a resource or a communication channel occurs before the end of output data transmission from the resource to the RMS, the subtask fails.

(7) Different resources start performing their tasks immediately after they get the input data from the RMS through communication channels. If same subtask is processed by several resources (providing execution redundancy), it is completed when the first result is returned to the RMS. The entire task is completed when all of the subtasks are completed and their results are returned to the RMS from the resources.

(8) The data transmission speed in any multi-channel link does not depend on the number of different packages (corresponding to different subtasks) sent in parallel. The data transmission time of each package depends on the amount of data in the package. If the data package is transmitted through several communication links, the link with the lowest bandwidth limits the data transmission speed.

(9) The RMS is fully reliable, which can be justified to consider a relatively short interval of running a specific service. The imperfect RMS can also be easily included as a module connected in series to the whole grid service system.

5.2.4 *Grid Service Time Distribution and Indices*

The data dependence on task execution can be represented by $m \times m$ matrix H such that $h_{ki} = 1$ if subtask i needs for its execution output data from subtask k and $h_{ki} = 0$ otherwise (the subtasks can always be numbered such that $k < i$ for any $h_{ki} = 1$). Therefore, if $h_{ki} = 1$ execution of subtask i cannot begin before completion of subtask k. For any subtask i one can define a set ϕi of its immediate predecessors: $k \in \phi_i$ if $h_{ki} = 1$.

The data dependence can always be presented in such a manner that the last subtask m corresponds to the final task processed by the RMS when it receives output data of all the subtasks completed by the grid resources.

The task execution time is defined as time from the beginning of input data transmission from the RMS to a resource to the end of output data transmission from the resource to the RMS.

The amount of data that should be transmitted between the RMS and resource j that executes subtask i is denoted by ai. If data transmission between the RMS and the resource j is accomplished through links belonging to a set γ_j, the data transmission speed is

$$s_j = \min_{L_x \in \gamma_j} (b_x) \qquad (5.1)$$

where b_x is the bandwidth of the link Lx. Therefore, the random time tij of subtask i execution by resource j can take two possible values

$$t_{ij} = \hat{t}_{ij} = \tau_j + \frac{a_i}{s_j} \qquad (5.2)$$

if the resource j and the communication path γ_j do not fail until the subtask completion and $t_{ij} = \infty$ otherwise. Here, τ_j is the processing time of the j-th resource.

Subtask i can be successfully completed by resource j if this resource and communication path γ_j do not fail before the end of subtask execution. Given constant failure rates of resource j and links, one can obtain the conditional probability of subtask success as

$$p_j(\hat{t}_{ij}) = e^{-(\lambda_j + \pi_j)\hat{t}_{ij}} \qquad (5.3)$$

where π_j is the failure rate of the communication path between the RMS and the resource j , which can be calculated as $\pi_j = \sum_{x \in \gamma_j} \lambda_x$, λ_x is the failure rate of the link L_x . The exponential distribution is common in software or hardware components' reliability that had been justified in both theory and practice [Xie *et al.* (2004)].

These give the conditional distribution of the random subtask execution time t_{ij} : $\Pr(\ t_{ij} = \hat{t}_{ij}) = p_j(t_{ij})$ and $\Pr(\ t_{ij} = \infty) = 1 - p_j(t_{ij})$.

Assume that each subtask i is assigned by the RMS to resources composing set ω_i. The RMS can initiate execution of any subtask j (send the data to all the resources from ω_i) only after the completion of every subtask $k \in \phi_i$. Therefore the random time of the start of subtask i execution T_i can be determined as

$$T_i = \max_{k \in \phi_i}(\tilde{T}_k) \qquad (5.4)$$

where $\tilde{T}_k$ is random completion time for subtask k. If $\phi_i = \emptyset$, i.e. subtask i does not need data produced by any other subtask, the subtask execution starts without delay: $Ti = 0$. If $\phi_i \neq \emptyset$, T_i can have different realizations $\hat{T}_{il}$ $(1 \leq l \leq Ni)$.

Having the time T_i when the execution of subtask i starts and the time t_{ij} of subtask i executed by resource j, one obtains the completion time for subtask i on resource j as

$$\tilde{t}_{ij} = T_i + t_{ij} \qquad (5.5)$$

In order to obtain the distribution of random time $\tilde{t}_{ij}$ one has to take into account that probability of any realization of $\tilde{t}_{ij} = \hat{T}_{il} + \hat{t}_{ij}$ is equal to the product of probabilities of three events:

(1) execution of subtask i starts at time $\hat{T}_{il}$: qil=Pr($T_i = \hat{T}_{il}$);
(2) resource j does not fail before start of execution of subtask i: $pj(\hat{T}_{il})$;
(3) resource j does not fail during the execution of subtask i: $pj(\hat{t}_{ij})$.

Therefore, the conditional distribution of the random time $\tilde{t}_{ij}$ given execution of subtask i starts at time $\hat{T}_{il}$ ($T_i = \hat{T}_{il}$) takes the form
$$\Pr(\tilde{t}_{ij} = \hat{T}_{il} + \hat{t}_{ij}) = pj(\hat{T}_{il})pj(\hat{t}_{ij}) = pj(\hat{T}_{il} + \hat{t}_{ij}) = e^{-(\lambda_j + \pi_j)(\hat{T}_{il} + \hat{t}_{ij})}$$
$$\Pr(\tilde{t}_{ij} = \infty) = 1 - pj(\hat{T}_{il} + \hat{t}_{ij})$$

$$= 1 - e^{-(\lambda_j + \pi_j)(\hat{T}_{il} + \hat{t}_{ij})} \tag{5.6}$$

The random time of subtask i completion $\tilde{T}_i$ is equal to the shortest time when one of the resources from ω_i completes the subtask execution:

$$\tilde{T}_i = \min_{j \in \omega_i}(\tilde{t}_{ij}) \tag{5.7}$$

According to the definition of the last subtask m, the time of its beginning corresponds to the service completion time, because the time of the task proceeds with RMS is neglected. Thus, the random service time Θ is equal to T_m. Having the distribution (pmf) of the random value $\Theta \equiv T_m$ in the form $q_{ml} = \Pr(T_m = \hat{T}_{ml})$ for $1 \le l \le N_m$, one can evaluate the reliability and performance indices of the grid service.

In order to estimate both the service reliability and its performance, different measures can be used depending on the application. In applications where the execution time of each task (service time) is of critical importance, the system reliability $R(\Theta*)$ is defined (according to performability concept in [Meyer (1997); Grassi *et al.* (1980); Tai *et al.* (1980)] as a probability that the correct output is produced in time less than $\Theta*$. This index can be obtained as

$$R(\Theta*) = \sum_{l=1}^{N_m} q_{ml} \cdot 1(\hat{T}_{ml} < \Theta*) \tag{5.8}$$

When no limitations are imposed on the service time, the service reliability is defined as the probability that it produces correct outputs without respect to the service time, which can be referred to as $R(\infty)$. The conditional expected service time W is considered to be a measure of its performance, which determines the expected service time given that the service does not fail, i.e.

$$W = \sum_{l=1}^{N_m} \hat{T}_{ml} q_{ml} / R(\infty) \tag{5.9}$$

5.3 Star Topology Grid Architecture

A grid service is desired to execute a certain task under the control of the RMS. When the RMS receives a service request from a user, the task can be divided into a set of subtasks that are executed in parallel. The RMS assigns those subtasks to available resources for execution. After the resources complete the assigned subtasks, they return the results back to the RMS and then the RMS integrates the received results into the entire task output which is requested by the user.

The above grid service process can be approximated by a structure with star topology, as depicted by Figure 5.2, where the RMS is directly connected with any resource through respective communication channels. The star topology is feasible when the resources are totally separated so that their communication channels are independent. Under this assumption, the grid service reliability and performance can be derived by using the universal generating function technique.

5.3.1 *Universal Generating Function*

The universal generating function (u-function) technique was introduced and proved to be very effective for the reliability evaluation of different types of multi-state systems [Levitin (2003)].

The u-function representing the pmf of a discrete random variable Y is defined as a polynomial

$$u(z) = \sum_{k=1}^{K} \alpha_k z^{y_k} \tag{5.10}$$

where the variable Y has K possible values and α k is the probability that Y is equal to yk.

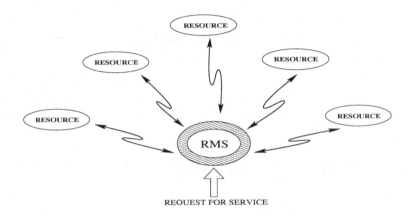

Fig. 5.2   Grid system with star architecture.

To obtain the u-function representing the pmf of a function of two independent random variables $\varphi\,(Yi,\ Yj)$, composition operators are introduced. These operators determine the u-function for $\varphi\,(Yi,\ Yj)$ using simple algebraic operations on the individual u-functions of the variables. All of the composition operators take the form

$$
\begin{aligned}
U(z) &= u_i(z) \underset{\varphi}{\otimes} u_j(z) = \sum_{k=1}^{K_i} \alpha_{ik} z^{y_{ik}} \\
&\underset{\varphi}{\otimes} \sum_{h=1}^{K_j} \alpha_{jh} z^{y_{jh}} = \sum_{k=1}^{K_i} \sum_{h=1}^{K_j} \alpha_{ik}\alpha_{jh} z^{\varphi(y_{ik},y_{jh})}
\end{aligned}
\tag{5.11}
$$

The u-function $U(z)$ represents all of the possible mutually exclusive combinations of realizations of the variables by relating the probabilities of each combination to the value of function $\varphi\,(Yi,\ Yj)$ for this combination.

In the case of grid system, the u-function $u_{ij}(z)$ can define pmf of execution time for subtask i assigned to resource j. This u-function takes the form

$$
u_{ij}(z) = p_j(\hat{t}_{ij})z^{\hat{t}_{ij}} + (1 - p_j(\hat{t}_{ij}))z^{\infty}
\tag{5.12}
$$

where $\hat{t}_{ij}$ and $p_j(\hat{t}_{ij})$ are determined according to Eqs. (5.2) and (5.3) respectively.

The pmf of the random start time T_i for subtask i can be represented by u-function $U_i(z)$ taking the form

$$
U_i(z) = \sum_{l=1}^{L_i} q_{il} z^{\hat{T}_{il}}
\tag{5.13}
$$

where

$$q_{il} = \Pr(T_i = \hat{T}_{il}) \tag{5.14}$$

For any realization $\hat{T}_{il}$ of T_i the conditional distribution of completion time $\hat{t}_{ij}$ for subtask i executed by resource j given $T_i = \hat{T}_{il}$ according to (5.6) can be represented by the u-function

$$\tilde{u}_{ij}(z, \hat{T}_{il}) = p_j(\hat{T}_{il} + \hat{t}_{ij})z^{\hat{T}_{il}+\hat{t}_{ij}} + (1 - p_j(\hat{T}_{il} + \hat{t}_{ij}))z^{\infty}.$$

The total completion time of subtask i assigned to a pair of resources j and d is equal to the minimum of completion times for these resources according to Eq. (5.7). To obtain the u-function representing the pmf of this time, given $T_i = \hat{T}_{il}$, composition operator with $\varphi(Yj, Yd) = \min(Yj, Yd)$ should be used:

$$\begin{aligned}
\tilde{u}_i(z, \hat{T}_{il}) &= \tilde{u}_{ij}(z, \hat{T}_{il}) \underset{\min}{\otimes} \tilde{u}_{id}(z, \hat{T}_{il}) \\
&= [p_j(\hat{T}_{il} + \hat{t}_{ij})z^{\hat{T}_{il}+\hat{t}_{ij}} + (1 - p_j(\hat{T}_{il} + \hat{t}_{ij}))z^{\infty}] \\
&\quad \underset{\min}{\otimes} [p_d(\hat{T}_{il} + \hat{t}_{id})z^{\hat{T}_{il}+\hat{t}_{id}} + (1 - p_d(\hat{T}_{il} + \hat{t}_{id}))z^{\infty}] \\
&= p_j(\hat{T}_{il} + \hat{t}_{ij})p_d(\hat{T}_{il} + \hat{t}_{id})z^{\hat{T}_{il}+\min(\hat{t}_{ij}, \hat{t}_{id})} \\
&\quad + p_d(\hat{T}_{il} + \hat{t}_{id})(1 - p_j(\hat{T}_{il} + \hat{t}_{ij}))z^{\hat{T}_{il}+\hat{t}_{id}} \\
&\quad + p_j(\hat{T}_{il} + \hat{t}_{ij})(1 - p_d(\hat{T}_{il} + \hat{t}_{id}))z^{\hat{T}_{il}+\hat{t}_{ij}} \\
&\quad + (1 - p_j(\hat{T}_{il} + \hat{t}_{ij}))(1 - p_d(\hat{T}_{il} + \hat{t}_{id}))z^{\infty}.
\end{aligned} \tag{5.15}$$

The u-function $\tilde{u}_i(z, \hat{T}_{il})$ representing the conditional pmf of completion time $\hat{T}_i$ for subtask i assigned to all of the resources from set $\omega_i = \{ j_1, \ldots, j_i \}$ can be obtained as

$$\tilde{u}_i(z, \hat{T}_{il}) = \tilde{u}_{ij_1}(z, \hat{T}_{il}) \underset{\min}{\otimes} \ldots \underset{\min}{\otimes} \tilde{u}_{ij_i}(z, \hat{T}_{il}) \tag{5.16}$$

$\tilde{u}_i(z, \hat{T}_{il})$ can be obtained recursively:

$$\tilde{u}_i(z, \hat{T}_{il}) = \tilde{u}_{ij_1}(z, \hat{T}_{il}),$$

$$\tilde{u}_i(z, \hat{T}_{il}) = \tilde{u}_i(z, \hat{T}_{il}) \underset{\min}{\otimes} \tilde{u}_{ie}(z, \hat{T}_{il})$$

for $e = j_2, \ldots, j_i$.

Having the probabilities of the mutually exclusive realizations of start time T_i, $q_{il} = \Pr(T_i = \hat{T}_{il})$ and u-functions $\tilde{u}_i(z, \hat{T}_{il})$ representing corresponding conditional distributions of task i completion time, we can now obtain the u-function representing the unconditional pmf of completion time $\tilde{T}_i$ as

$$\tilde{U}_i(z) = \sum_{l=1}^{N_i} q_{il} \tilde{u}_i(z, \hat{T}_{il}) \tag{5.17}$$

Having u-functions $\tilde{U}_k(z)$ representing pmf of the completion time $\tilde{T}_k$ for any subtask $k \in \phi_i = \{k_1, ..., k_i\}$, one can obtain the u-functions $U_i(z)$ representing pmf of subtask i start time T_i according to (5.4) as

$$U_i(z) = \tilde{U}_{k_1}(z) \underset{\max}{\otimes} \tilde{U}_{k_2}(z)... \underset{\max}{\otimes} \tilde{U}_{k_i}(z) = \sum_{l=1}^{N_i} q_{il} z^{\hat{T}_{il}} \tag{5.18}$$

$U_i(z)$ can be obtained recursively:

$$U_i(z) = z^0,$$

$$U_i(z) = U_i(z) \underset{\max}{\otimes} \tilde{U}_e(z)$$

for $e = k1, \ldots, ki$.

It can be seen that if $\phi_i = \emptyset$ then $U_i(z) = z^0$.

The final u-function $Um(z)$ represents the pmf of random task completion time T_m in the form

$$U_m(z) = \sum_{l=1}^{N_m} q_{ml} z^{\hat{T}_{ml}} \tag{5.19}$$

Using the operators defined above one can obtain the service reliability and performance indices by implementing the following algorithm:

(1) Determine $\hat{t}_{ij}$ for each subtask i and resource $j \in \omega_i$ using Eq. (5.2);

Define for each subtask i $(1 \le i \le m)$ $\tilde{U}_i(z) = U_i(z) = z^0$.

(1) For all i:

If $\phi_i = 0$ or if for any $k \in \phi_i$ $\tilde{U}_k(z) \ne z^0$ (u-functions representing the completion times of all of the predecessors of subtask i are obtained)

2.1. Obtain $U_i(z) = \sum_{l=1}^{N_i} q_{il} z^{\hat{T}_{il}}$ using the above recursive procedure;

2.2. For $l = 1, \ldots, Ni$:

2.2.1. For each $j \in \omega_i$ obtain $\tilde{u}_{ij}(z, \hat{T}_{il})$ using Eq. (5.14);

2.2.2. Obtain $\tilde{u}_i(z)$ using recursive procedure;

2.3. Obtain $\hat{U}_i(z)$ using Eq. (5.17).

3. If $U_m(z) = z^0$ return to step 2.

4. Obtain reliability and performance indices $R(\Theta\,^*)$ and W using equations (5.8) and (5.9).

5.3.2 *Illustrative Example*

This example presents analytical derivation of the indices $R(\Theta\,^*)$ and W for simple grid service that uses six resources. Assume that the RMS divides the service task into three subtasks. The first subtask is assigned to resources 1 and 2, the second subtask is assigned to resources 3 and 4, the third subtask is assigned to resources 5 and 6:

$\omega_1 = \{\,1,2\,\}$, $\omega_2 = \{\,3,4\,\}$, $\omega_3 = \{\,5,6\,\}$.

The failure rates of the resources and communication channels and subtask execution times are presented in Table 5.1.

Table 5.1 Parameters of grid system for analytical example.

No of sub i	No of res j	$\lambda\,j + \pi\,j$ (sec-1)	$\hat{t}_{ij}$ (sec)	$p_j(\hat{t}_{ij})$
1	1	0.0025	100	0.779
	2	0.00018	180	0.968
2	3	0.0003	250	-
	4	0.0008	300	-
3	5	0.0005	300	0.861
	6	0.0002	430	0.918

Subtasks 1 and 3 get the input data directly from the RMS, subtask 2 needs the output of subtask 1, the service task is completed when the RMS gets the outputs of both subtasks 2 and 3: $\phi_1 = \phi_3 = \emptyset$, $\phi_2 = \{1\}$, $\phi_4 = \{2,3\}$. These subtask precedence constraints can be represented by the directed graph in Figure 5.3.

Since $\phi_1 = \phi_3 = \emptyset$, the only realization of start times $T1$ and $T3$ is 0 and therefore, $U1(z) = U2(z) = z0$. According to step 2 of the algorithm we

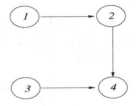

Fig. 5.3 Subtask execution precedence constraints for analytical example.

can obtain the u-functions representing pmf of completion times $\tilde{t}_{11}$, $\tilde{t}_{12}$, $\tilde{t}_{35}$ and $\tilde{t}_{36}$. In order to determine the subtask execution time distributions for the individual resources, define the u-functions $u_{ij}(z)$ according to Table 5.1 and Eq. (5.9):

$$\tilde{u}_{11}(z,0) = \exp(-0.0025 \times 100)z^{100}$$
$$+ [1 - \exp(-0.0025 \times 100)]z^{\infty}$$
$$= 0.779z^{100} + 0.221z^{\infty}.$$

In the similar way we obtain
$\tilde{u}_{12}(z,0) = 0.968z^{180} + 0.032z^{\infty}$;
$\tilde{u}_{35}(z,0) = 0.861z^{300} + 0.139z^{\infty}$;
$\tilde{u}_{36}(z,0) = 0.918z^{430} + 0.082z^{\infty}$.

The u-function representing the pmf of the completion time for subtask 1 executed by both resources 1 and 2 is
$\tilde{U}_1(z) = \tilde{u}_1(z,0) = \tilde{u}_{11}(z,0) \underset{\min}{\otimes} \tilde{u}_{12}(z,0) = (0.779z^{100} + 0.221z^{\infty}) \underset{\min}{\otimes}$
$(0.968z^{180} + 0.032z^{\infty})$
$=0.779z^{100} + 0.214z^{180} + 0.007z^{\infty}$.

The u-function representing the pmf of the completion time for subtask 3 executed by both resources 5 and 6 is
$\tilde{U}_3(z) = \tilde{u}_3(z,0) = \tilde{u}_{35}(z) \underset{\min}{\otimes} \tilde{u}_{36}(z) = (0.861z^{300} + 0.139z^{\infty}) \underset{\min}{\otimes}$
$(0.918z^{430} + 0.082z^{\infty})$
$=0.861z^{300} + 0.128z^{430} + 0.011z^{\infty}$.

Execution of subtask 2 begins immediately after completion of subtask 1. Therefore,

$U2(z) = \tilde{U}_1(z) = 0.779z^{100} + 0.214z^{180} + 0.007z^{\infty}$

(*T*2 has three realizations 100, 180 and ∞).

The u-functions representing the conditional pmf of the completion times for the subtask 2 executed by individual resources are obtained as follows.

$$\tilde{u}_{23}(z, 100) = e^{-0.0003 \times (100+250)} z^{100+250}$$

$$+ [1 - e^{-0.0003 \times (100+250)}] z^{\infty}$$

$$= 0.9z^{350} + 0.1z^{\infty};$$

$$\tilde{u}_{23}(z, 180) = e^{-0.0003 \times (180+250)} z^{180+250}$$

$$+ [1 - e^{-0.0003 \times (180+250)}] z^{\infty}$$

$$= 0.879z^{430} + 0.121z^{\infty};$$

$$\tilde{u}_{23}(z, \infty) = z^{\infty};$$

$$\tilde{u}_{24}(z, 100) = e^{-0.0008 \times (100+300)} z^{100+300}$$

$$+ [1 - e^{-0.0008 \times (100+300)}] z^{\infty}$$

$$= 0.726z^{400} + 0.274z^{\infty};$$

$$\tilde{u}_{24}(z, 180) = e^{-0.0008 \times (180+300)} z^{180+300}$$

$$+ [1 - e^{-0.0008 \times (180+300)}] z^{\infty}$$

$$= 0.681z^{480} + 0.319z^{\infty};$$

$$\tilde{u}_{24}(z, \infty) = z^{\infty}.$$

The u-functions representing the conditional pmf of subtask 2 completion time are:

$$\tilde{u}_2(z, 100) = \tilde{u}_{23}(z, 100) \underset{min}{\otimes} \tilde{u}_{24}(z, 100)$$

$$= (0.9z^{350} + 0.1z^{\infty}) \underset{min}{\otimes} (0.726z^{400} + 0.274z^{\infty})$$

$$= 0.9z^{350} + 0.073z^{400} + 0.027z^{\infty};$$

$$\tilde{u}_2(z, 180) = \tilde{u}_{23}(z, 180) \underset{\min}{\otimes} \tilde{u}_{24}(z, 180)$$

$$= 0.879z^{430} + 0.121z^{\infty}) \underset{\min}{\otimes} (0.681z^{480} + 0.319z^{\infty})$$

$$= 0.879z^{430} + 0.082z^{480} + 0.039z^{\infty};$$

$$\tilde{u}_2(z, \infty) = \tilde{u}_{23}(z, \infty) \underset{\min}{\otimes} \tilde{u}_{24}(z, \infty) = z^{\infty}.$$

According to Eq. (18) the unconditional pmf of subtask 2 completion time is represented by the following u-function

$$\tilde{U}_2(z) = 0.779\tilde{u}_2(z, 100) + 0.214\tilde{u}_2(z, 180) + 0.007z^{\infty}$$

$$= 0.779(0.9z^{350} + 0.073z^{400} + 0.027z^{\infty}) + 0.214(0.879z^{430} + 0.082z^{480}$$

$$+ 0.039z^{\infty}) + 0.007z^{\infty}$$

$$= 0.701z^{350} + 0.056z^{400} + 0.188z^{430} + 0.018z^{480} + 0.037z^{\infty}$$

The service task is completed when subtasks 2 and 3 return their outputs to the RMS (which corresponds to the beginning of subtask 4). Therefore, the u-function representing the pmf of the entire service time is obtained as

$$U_4(z) = \tilde{U}_2(z) \underset{\max}{\otimes} \tilde{U}_3(z)$$

$$= (0.701z^{350} + 0.056z^{400} + 0.188z^{430} + 0.018z^{480} + 0.037z^{\infty}) \underset{\max}{\otimes}$$

$(0.861z^{300} + 0.128z^{430} + 0.011z^{\infty}) = 0.603z^{350} + 0.049z^{400} + 0.283z^{430} + 0.017z^{480} + 0.048z^{\infty}$.

The pmf of the service time is:

$\Pr(T4 = 350) = 0.603; \Pr(T4 = 400) = 0.049;$
$\Pr(T4 = 430) = 0.283; \Pr(T4 = 480) = 0.017;$
$\Pr(T4 = \infty) = 0.048.$

From the obtained pmf we can calculate the service reliability using Eq. (5.8):

$R(\Theta*) = 0.603$ for $350 < \Theta* \le 400$;
$R(\Theta*) = 0.652$ for $400 < \Theta* \le 430$;
$R(\Theta*) = 0.935$ for $430 < \Theta* \le 480$;
$R(\infty) = 0.952$

and the conditional expected service time according to Eq. (5.9):

$$W = (0.603 \times 350 + 0.049 \times 400 + 0.283 \times 430 + 0.017 \times 480)/0.952$$

$$= 378.69 \text{ sec.}$$

5.4   Tree Topology Grid Architecture

In the star grid, the RMS is connected with each resource by one direct communication channel (link). However, such approximation is not accurate enough even though it simplifies the analysis and computation. For example, several resources located in a same local area network (LAN) can use the same gateway to communicate outside the network. Therefore, all these resources are not connected with the RMS through independent links. The resources are connected to the gateway, which communicates with the RMS through one common communication channel. Another example is a server that contains several resources (has several processors that can run different applications simultaneously, or contains different databases). Such a server communicates with the RMS through the same links. These situations cannot be modeled using only the star topology grid architecture.

In this section, we present a more reasonable virtual structure which has a tree topology. The root of the tree virtual structure is the RMS, and the leaves are resources, while the branches of the tree represent the communication channels linking the leaves and the root. Some channels are commonly used by multiple resources. An example of the tree topology is given in Figure 5.3 in which four resources (R1, R2, R3, R4) are available for a service.

The tree structure models the common cause failures in shared communication channels. For example, in Figure 5.4, the failure in channel L6 makes resources R1, R2, and R3 unavailable. This type of common cause failure was ignored by the conventional parallel computing models, and the above star-topology models. For small-area communication, such as a LAN or a cluster, such assumption that ignores the common cause failures on communications is acceptable because the communication time is negligible compared to the processing time. However, for wide-area communication, such as the grid system, it is more likely to have failure on communication channels. Therefore, the communication time cannot be neglected. In many cases, the communication time may dominate the processing time due to the large amount of data transmitted. Therefore, the virtual tree structure is an adequate model representing the functioning of grid services.

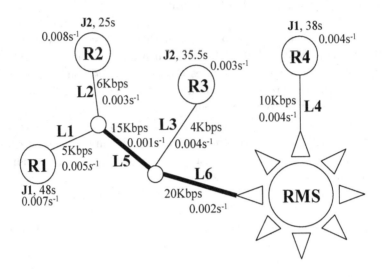

Fig. 5.4   A virtual tree structure of a grid service.

5.4.1   *Algorithms for Determining the pmf of the Task Execution Time*

With the tree-structure, the simple u-function technique is not applicable because it does not consider the failure correlations. Thus, new algorithms are required. This section presents a novel algorithm to evaluate the performance and reliability for the tree-structured grid service based on the graph theory and the Bayesian approach.

5.4.1.1   *Minimal Task Spanning Tree (MTST)*

The set of all nodes and links involved in performing a given task form a task spanning tree. This task spanning tree can be considered to be a combination of minimal task spanning trees (MTST), where each MTST represents a minimal possible combination of available elements (resources and links) that guarantees the successful completion of the entire task. The failure of any element in a MTST leads to the entire task failure.

For solving the graph traversal problem, several classical algorithms have been suggested, such as Depth-First search, Breadth-First search, etc. These algorithms can find all MTST in an arbitrary graph [Dai *et al.* (2002)]. However, MTST in graphs with a tree topology can be found in a much simpler way because each resource has a single path to the RMS, and the tree structure is acyclic.

After the subtasks have been assigned to corresponding resources, it is easy to find all combinations of resources such that each combination contains exactly m resources executing m different subtasks that compose the entire task. Each combination determines exactly one MTST consisting of links that belong to paths from the m resources to the RMS. The total number of MTST is equal to the total number of such combinations N, where

$$N = \prod_{j=1}^{m} |\omega_j| \qquad (5.20)$$

(see Example 5.4.2.1).

Along with the procedures of searching all the MTST, one has to determine the corresponding running time and communication time for all the resources and links.

For any subtask j, and any resource k assigned to execute this subtask, one has the amount of input and output data, the bandwidths of links, belonging to the corresponding paths γ_k, and the resource processing time. With these data, one can obtain the time of subtask completion (see Example 5.4.2.2).

Some elements of the same MTST can belong to several paths if they are involved in data transmission to several resources. To track the element involvement in performing different subtasks and to record the corresponding times in which the element failure causes the failure of a subtask, we create the lists of two-field records for each subtask in each MTST. For any MTST Si $(1 \leq i \leq N)$, and any subtask j $(1 \leq j \leq m)$, this list contains the names of the elements involved in performing the subtask j, and the corresponding time of subtask completion y_{ij} (see Example 4.2.3). Note that y_{ij} is the conditional time of subtask j completion given only MTST i is available.

Note that a MTST completes the entire task if all of its elements do not fail by the maximum time needed to complete subtasks in performing which they are involved. Therefore, when calculating the element reliability in a given MTST, one has to use the corresponding record with maximal time.

5.4.1.2 *pmf of the Task Execution Time*

Having the MTST, and the times of their elements involvement in performing different subtasks, one can determine the pmf of the entire service time.

First, we can obtain the conditional time of the entire task completion given only MTST Si is available as

$$Y_{\{i\}} = \max_{1 \le j \le m} (y_{ij}) \text{ for any } 1 \le i \le N : (23)$$

For a set ψ of available MTST, the task completion time is equal to the minimal task completion times among the MTST.

$$Y_\psi = \min_{i \in \psi}(Y_{\{i\}}) = \min_{i \in \psi}\left[\max_{1 \le j \le m}(y_{ij})\right] \qquad (5.21)$$

Now, we can sort the MTST in an increasing order of their conditional task completion times $Y_{\{i\}}$, and divide them into different groups containing MTST with identical conditional completion time. Suppose there are K such groups denoted by $G_1, G_2, ..., G_K$ where $1 \le K \le N$, and any group G_i contains MTST with identical conditional task completion times Θ_i ($0 \le \Theta_1 < \Theta_2 < ... < \Theta_K$). Then, it can be seen that the probability $Q_i = \Pr(\Theta = \Theta_i)$ can be obtained as

$$Q_i = \Pr(E_i, \bar{E}_{i-1}, \bar{E}_{i-2}, ..., \bar{E}_1) \qquad (5.22)$$

where E_i is the event when at least one of MTST from the group G_i is available, and $\bar{E}_i$ is the event when none of MTST from the group G_i is available.

Suppose the MTST in a group G_i are arbitrarily ordered, and F_{ij} ($j=1,2,...,N_i$) represents an event when the j-th MTST in the group is available. Then, the event E_i can be expressed by

$$E_i = \bigcup_{j=1}^{N_i} F_{ij} \qquad (5.23)$$

and Eq. (5.22) takes the form

$$\Pr(E_i, \bar{E}_{i-1}, \bar{E}_{i-2}, ..., \bar{E}_1) = \Pr(\bigcup_{j=1}^{N_i} F_{ij}, \bar{E}_{i-1}, \bar{E}_{i-2}, ..., \bar{E}_1) \qquad (5.24)$$

Using the Bayesian theorem on conditional probability, we obtain from Eq. (5.24) that

$$Q_i = \sum_{j=1}^{N_i} \Pr(F_{ij}) \cdot \Pr\left(\bar{F}_{i(j-1)}, \bar{F}_{i(j-2)}, ..., \bar{F}_{i1}, \bar{E}_1, \bar{E}_2, \cdots, \bar{E}_{i-1} \mid F_{ij}\right)$$

$$(5.25)$$

The probability $\Pr(F_{ij})$ can be calculated as a product of the reliabilities of all the elements belonging to the j-th MTST from group Gi.

The probability $\Pr\left(\bar{F}_{i(j-1)}, \bar{F}_{i(j-2)}, ..., \bar{F}_{i1}, \bar{E}_1, \bar{E}_2, \cdots, \bar{E}_{i-1} \mid F_{ij}\right)$ can be computed by the following two-step algorithm (see Example 5.4.2.4).

Step 1: Identify failures of all the critical elements' in a period of time (defined by the start and end time), during which they lead to the failures of any MTST from groups Gm for $m=1,2,...i\text{-}1$ (events $\bar{E}_m$), and any MTST Sk from group Gi for $k=1,2,...,j-1$ (events $\bar{F}_{ik}$), but do not affect the MTST Sj from group Gi.

Step 2: Generate all the possible combinations of the identified critical elements that lead to the event $\bar{F}_{i(j-1)}, \bar{F}_{i(j-2)}, ..., \bar{F}_{i1}, \bar{E}_1, \bar{E}_2, \cdots, \bar{E}_{i-1} \mid F_{ij}$ using a binary search, and compute the probabilities of those combinations. The sum of the probabilities obtained is equal to $\Pr\left(\bar{F}_{i(j-1)}, \bar{F}_{i(j-2)}, ..., \bar{F}_{i1}, \bar{E}_1, \bar{E}_2, \cdots, \bar{E}_{i-1} \mid F_{ij}\right)$. When calculating the failure probabilities of MTSTs' elements, the maximal time from the corresponding records in a list for the given MTST should be used. The algorithm for obtaining the probabilities $\Pr\{\bar{E}_1, \bar{E}_2, \cdots \bar{E}_{i-1} \mid E_i\}$ can be found in Dai *et al.* [Dai *et al.* (2002)].

Having the conditional task completion times $Y_{\{i\}}$ for different MTST, and the corresponding probabilities Q_i, one obtains the task completion time distribution (Θ_i, Q_i), $1 \leq i \leq K$, and can easily calculate the indices (5.8) & (5.9) (see Example 5.4.2.5).

5.4.2 *Illustrative Example*

Consider the virtual grid presented in Figure 5.4, and assume that the service task is divided into two subtasks J1 assigned to resources R1 & R4, and J2 assigned to resources R2 & R3. J1, and J2 require 50Kbits, and 30Kbits of input data, respectively, to be sent from the RMS to the corresponding resource; and 100Kbits, and 60Kbits of output data respectively to be sent from the resource back to the RMS.

The subtask processing times for resources, bandwidth of links, and failure rates are presented in Figure 5.4 next to the corresponding elements.

5.4.2.1 *The Service MTST*

The entire graph constitutes the task spanning tree. There exist four possible combinations of two resources executing both subtasks: { R1, R2 } , { R1, R3 } , { R4, R2 } , { R4, R3 } . The four MTST corresponding to these combinations are: $S1$: { R1, R2, L1, L2, L5, L6 } ; $S2$: { R1, R3, L1, L3, L5, L6 } ; $S3$: { R2, R4, L2, L5, L4, L6 } ; $S4$: { R3, R4, L3, L4, L6 } .

5.4.2.2 *Parameters of MTSTs' Paths*

Having the MTST, one can obtain the data transmission speed for each path between the resource, and the RMS (as minimal bandwidth of links belonging to the path); and calculate the data transmission times, and the times of subtasks' completion. These parameters are presented in Table 5.2. For example, resource R1 (belonging to two MTST $S1$ & $S2$) processes subtask J1 in 48 seconds. To complete the subtask, it should receive 50Kbits, and return to the RMS 100Kbits of data. The speed of data transmission between the RMS and R1 is limited by the bandwidth of link L1, and is equal to 5 Kbps. Therefore, the data transmission time is 150/5=30 seconds, and the total time of task completion by R1 is 30+48=78 seconds.

Table 5.2 Parameters of the MTSTs' paths.

Elements	R1	R2	R3	R4
Subtasks	J1	J2	J2	J1
transmission speed (Kbps)	5	6	4	10
Data transmission time (s)	30	15	22.5	15
Processing time (s)	48	25	35.5	38
Subtask complete time (s)	78	40	58	53

5.4.2.3 *List of MTST Elements*

Now one can obtain the lists of two-field records for components of the MTST.

$S1$: path for J1:(R1,78); (L1,78); (L5,78); (L6,78); path for J2: (R2,40); (L2,40); (L5,40); (L6,40).

$S2$: path for J1: (R1,78), (L1,78), (L5,78), (L6,78); path for J2: (R3,58), (L3,58), (L6,58).

$S3$: path for J1: (R4,53), (L4,53); path for J2: (R2,40), (L2,40), (L5,40), (L6,40).

$S4$: path for J1: (R4,53), (L4,53); path for J2: (R3,58), (L3,58), (L6,58).

5.4.2.4 *pmf of Task Completion Time*

The conditional times of the entire task completion by different MTST are $Y1=78$; $Y2=78$; $Y3=53$; $Y4=58$.

Therefore, the MTST compose three groups:

$G1 = \{ S3 \}$ with $\Theta 1 = 53$; $G2 = \{ S4 \}$ with $\Theta 2 = 58$; and $G3 = \{ S1, S2 \}$ with $\Theta 3 = 78$.

According to Eq. (5.22), we have for group $G1$: $Q1=\Pr(E1)=\Pr(S3)$. The probability that the MTST $S3$ completes the entire task is equal to the product of the probabilities that R4, and L4 do not fail by 53 seconds; and R2, L2, L5, and L6 do not fail by 40 seconds.

$\Pr(\Theta =53)=Q1=\exp(- 0.004 \times 53)\exp(- 0.004 \times 53)\exp(- 0.008 \times 40)$
$\times \exp(- 0.003 \times 40)\exp(- 0.001 \times 40)\exp(- 0.002 \times 40) = 0.3738$.

Now we can calculate $Q2$ as

$Q2= \Pr(E_2, \bar{E}_1) = \Pr(F_{21}) \Pr(\bar{E}_1 | F_{21}) = \Pr(F_{21}) \Pr(\bar{F}_{11} | F_{21}) = \Pr(S_4) \Pr(\bar{S}_3 | S_4)$

because $G2$, and $G1$ have only one MTST each. The probability that the MTST $S4$ completes the entire task $\Pr(S_4)$ is equal to the product of probabilities that R3, L3, and L6 do not fail by 58 seconds; and R4, and L4 do not fail by 53 seconds.

$$\Pr(S_4) = \frac{\exp(-0.004 \times 53) \exp(-0.003 \times 58) \exp(-0.004 \times 53)}{\exp(-0.004 \times 58) \exp(-0.002 \times 58)}$$
$$= 0.3883$$

To obtain $\Pr(\bar{S}_3 | S_4)$, one first should identify the critical elements according to the algorithm presented in the Dai *et al.* [Dai *et al.* (2002)]. These elements are R2, L2, and L5. Any failure occurring in one of these elements by 40 seconds causes failure of $S3$, but does not affect $S4$. The probability that at least one failure occurs in the set of critical elements is

$\Pr(\bar{S}_3 | S_4) = 1 - \exp(-0.08 \times 4) \exp(-0.03 \times 4) \exp(-0.01 \times 4) = 0.3812$.

Then,

$\Pr(\Theta = 58)= \Pr(E_2, \bar{E}_1) = \Pr(S_4) \Pr(\bar{S}_3 | S_4)$
$= 0.3883 \times 0.3812 = 0.1480$.

Now one can calculate $Q3$ for the last group $G3 = \{\ S1,\ S2\ \}$ corresponding to $\Theta 3 = 78$ as

$$Q3 - \Pr(E_3, \bar{E}_2, \bar{F}_1) = \Pr(F_{31})\Pr\left(\bar{E}_1, \bar{E}_2 | F_{31}\right)$$
$$+ \Pr(F_{32})\Pr\left(\bar{F}_{31}, \bar{E}_1, \bar{E}_2 | F_{32}\right)$$
$$= \Pr(S_1)\Pr\left(\bar{S}_3, \bar{S}_4 | S_1\right) + \Pr(S_2)\Pr\left(\bar{S}_1, \bar{S}_3, \bar{S}_4 | S_2\right)$$

The probability that the MTST $S1$ completes the entire task is equal to the product of the probabilities that R1, L1, L5, and L6 do not fail by 78 seconds; and R2, and L2 do not fail by 40 seconds.

$$\Pr(S_1) = \exp(-0.007 \times 78)\exp(-0.008 \times 40)$$
$$\times \exp(-0.005 \times 78)\exp(-0.003 \times 40)$$
$$\times \exp(-0.001 \times 78)\exp(-0.002 \times 78) = 0.1999.$$

The probability that the MTST $S2$ completes the entire task is equal to the product of the probabilities that R1, L1, L5, and L6 do not fail by 78 seconds; and R3, and L3 do not fail by 58 seconds.

$$\Pr(S_2) = \exp(-0.007 \times 78)\exp(-0.003 \times 58)$$
$$\times \exp(-0.005 \times 78)\exp(-0.004 \times 58)$$
$$\times \exp(-0.001 \times 78)\exp(-0.002 \times 78) = 0.2068.$$

To obtain $\Pr\left(\bar{S}_3, \bar{S}_4 | S_1\right)$, one first should identify the critical elements. Any failure of either R4 or L4 in the time interval from 0 to 53 seconds causes failures of both $S3$, and $S4$; but does not affect $S1$. Therefore,
$$\Pr\left(\bar{S}_3, \bar{S}_4 | S_1\right) = 1 - \exp(-0.004 \times 53)\exp(-0.004 \times 53) = 0.3456.$$

The critical elements for calculating $\Pr\left(\bar{S}_1, \bar{S}_3, \bar{S}_4 | S_2\right)$ are R2, and L2 in the interval from 0 to 40 seconds; and R4, and L4 in the interval from 0 to 53 seconds. The failure of both elements in any one of the following four combinations causes failures of $S3$, $S4$, and $S1$, but does not affect $S2$:

(1) R2 during the first 40 seconds, and R4 during the first 53 seconds;
(2) R2 during the first 40 seconds, and L4 during the first 53 seconds;
(3) L2 during the first 40 seconds, and R4 during the first 53 seconds; and
(4) L2 during the first 40 seconds, and L4 during the first 53 seconds.

Therefore,
$$\Pr\left(\bar{S}_1, \bar{S}_3, \bar{S}_4 | S_2\right) = 1 - \prod_{i=1}^{4}\left[1 - \prod_{j=1}^{2}[1 - \exp(\lambda_{ij} \cdot t_{ij})]\right] = 0.1230,$$
where λ_{ij} is the failure rate of the j-th critical element in the i-th combination $(j{=}1,2)$, $(i{=}1,2,3,4)$; and t_{ij} is the duration of the time interval for the corresponding critical element.

Having the values of $\Pr(S_1)$, $\Pr(S_2)$, $\Pr\left(\bar{S}_3, \bar{S}_4 | S_1\right)$, and $\Pr\left(\bar{S}_1, \bar{S}_3, \bar{S}_4 | S_2\right)$, one can calculate

$\Pr(\Theta = 78) = Q3 = 0.1999 \times 0.3456 + 0.2068 \times 0.1230 = 0.0945$.

After obtaining $Q1$, $Q2$, and $Q3$, one can evaluate the total task failure probability as

$\Pr(\Theta = \infty) = 1 - Q1 - Q2 - Q3 = 1 - 0.3738 - 0.1480 - 0.0945 = 0.3837$,

and obtain the pmf of service time presented in Table 5.3.

Table 5.3 pmf of service time.

Θ_i	Q_i	$\Theta i Q_i$
53	0.3738	19.8114
58	0.1480	8.584
78	0.0945	7.371
∞	0.3837	∞

5.4.2.5 *Calculating the Reliability Indices.*

From Table 5.3, one obtains the probability that the service does not fail as

$$R(\infty) = Q_1 + Q_2 + Q_3 = 0.6164,$$

the probability that the service time is not greater than a pre-specified value of $\theta* = 60$ seconds as

$$R(\theta*) = \sum_{i=1}^{3} Q_i \cdot 1(\Theta_i < \theta*) = 0.3738 + 0.1480 = 0.5218,$$

and the expected service execution time given that the system does not fail as

$$W = \sum_{i=1}^{3} \Theta_i Q_i / R(\infty) = 35.7664/0.6164 = 58.025 \text{ seconds}.$$

5.4.3 *Parameterization and Monitoring*

In order to obtain the reliability and performance indices of the grid service, one has to know such model parameters as the failure rates of the virtual links and the virtual nodes, and bandwidth of the links. It is easy to estimate those parameters by implementing the monitoring technology.

A monitoring system (called *Alertmon Network Monitor*, http://www.abilene.iu.edu/noc.html) is being applied in the IP-grid (Indiana Purdue Grid) project (www.ip-grid.org), to detect the component failures, record service behavior, monitor the network traffics and control the system configurations.

With this monitoring system, one can easily obtain the parameters required by the grid service reliability model by adding the following functions in the monitoring system:

(1) Monitoring the failures of the components (virtual links and nodes) in the grid service, and recording the total execution time of those components. The failure rates of the components can be simply estimated by the number of failures over the total execution time.

(2) Monitoring the real time network traffic of the involved channels (virtual links) in order to obtain the bandwidth of the links.

To realize the above monitoring functions, network sensors are required. We presented a type of sensors attaching to the components, acting as neurons attaching to the skins. It means the components themselves or adjacent components play the roles of sensors at the same time when they are working. Only a little computational resource in the components is used for accumulating failures/time and for dividing operations, and only a little memory is required for saving the data (accumulated number of failures, accumulated time and current bandwidth). The virtual nodes that have memory and computational function can play the sensing role themselves; if some links have no CPU or memory then the adjacent processors or routers can perform this data collecting operations. Using such self-sensing technique avoids overloading of the monitoring center even in the grid system containing numerous components. Again, it does not affect the service performance considerably, since only a small part of computation and storage resources is used for the monitoring. In addition, such self-sensing technique can also be applied in monitoring other measures.

When evaluating the grid service reliability, the RMS automatically loads the required parameters from corresponding sensors and calculates the service reliability and performance according to the approaches presented in the previous sections. This strategy can also be used for implementing the Autonomic Computing concept.

5.5 Conclusion

Grid computing is a newly developed technology for complex systems with large-scale resource sharing, wide-area communication, and multi-institutional collaboration. Although the developmental tools and techniques for the grid have been widely studied, grid reliability analysis and modeling are not easy because of their complexity of combining various failures.

This chapter introduced the grid computing technology and analyzed the grid service reliability and performance under the context of performability. The chapter then presented models for a star-topology grid with data dependence and a tree-structure grid with failure correlation. Evaluation tools and algorithms were presented based on the universal generating function, graph theory, and Bayesian approach. Numerical examples are presented to illustrate the grid modeling and reliability/performance evaluation procedures and approaches.

Future research can extend the models for grid computing to other large-scale distributed computing systems. After analyzing the details and specificity of corresponding systems (e.g. NASA ANTS missions), the approaches and models can be adapted to real conditions. The models are also applicable to a wireless network that is more failure prone.

Hierarchical models can also be analyzed in which output of lower level models can be considered as the input of the higher level models. Each level can make use of the proposed models and evaluation tools.

Chapter 6

Security in Grid Computing

Grid computing environments are typical CC paradigms that users offer and share their resources. In this omnipresent environment, security becomes a critical factor to its success. This chapter introduces the Grid Security problem, its challenges and requirements. Moreover, we present a dual level key management scheme which can offer secure grid communication and fine-grained access control to shared grid resources. How grid services are supported by this scheme is also presented by some examples of typical grid services.

6.1 Overview of Security in Grid Computing

As mentioned in the previous chapter 5, Grid computing [Foster and Kesselman (2003)] is a newly developed technology for complex systems with large-scale resource sharing and multi-institutional collaboration, see e.g. [Kumar (2000); Das et al. (2001); Foster et al. (2001, 2002); Berman et al. (2003)]. It harnesses existing isolated systems from local personal computers to super computers to let end users share the resources and data across geographical and organizational boundaries [Ramakrishnan (2004); Foster et al. (2005)]. The emerging technology/methodology could transform heterogeneous platforms into omnipresent and all pervasive computing environments for commercial organizations. For organizations, grid computing might have economic or profit reasons for them to share resources, but they would be unlikely to use it until they can rely on the confidentiality of communication, security and integrity of their data and, privacy of their sensitive information. In other words, security in Grid computing is an essential element for its acceptance at a large-scale commercial level [Li and Cordes (2005); Power et al. (2006)].

The Internet and networks are not security-oriented by design. Numerous hackers constantly explore security holes existing in hardware, software, processes, or systems to launch various attacks. There are two types of attacks: passive and active [Bishop (2003); Kaufman *et al.* (2002)]. Passive attackers steal useful information by eavesdropping and/or performing traffic analysis. Active attacks interfere with legal communication and are typically in the forms of masquerading, replaying, modification, and denial of services (DOS). The countermeasures against attacks utilize encryption/decryption for confidentiality, message authentication code for integrity, digital signature for authentication, undeniable digital signature for non-repudiation, access control for authorization, and intrusion detection/defense for availability/DOS [Pfleeger and Pfleeger (2003)]. The Internet-based grid computing encounters the same attacks and involves all the security requirements discussed above. Furthermore, grid computing systems are group-oriented, including a large number of users and shared resources. They are also complex, dynamic, distributed, and heterogeneous. As a result, the attacks to grid systems may become more serious and to defend them becomes more difficult. As examples, (1) Firewalls have been used by many organizations to protect their networks and local resources from external threats, but a seminal concept of grid computing sharing resources across organizational boundaries makes firewalls and similar techniques contradictory; (2) In a grid environment, trust relations are agreed upon at the organizational level instead of user level. Therefore, designing security at a user level many times proves to be difficult; (3) The grid nodes are dynamic and unpredictable in nature, imposing restrictive policies would make the grid architecture rigid and therefore impractical; and (4) Due to the distributed and heterogeneous features of grid computing systems, centralized authentication is generally unavailable and multiple-site co-authentication is difficult to implement (thus, the Single-Sign-On [Foster *et al.* (1998)] authentication comes into play). Another example is that grid computing is aimed at providing collaborative services. These services are featured by two important functions: group-oriented communication and information sharing/exchange [Zou *et al.* (2004b)]. As long as communication and information exchange are conducted over the Internet, communication messages should be encrypted with a common key for confidentiality. However, due to the high dynamic nature of grid computing, how to update group key(s) efficiently and effectively becomes a challenging problem. As for resources sharing among different nodes/organizations in the grid, every participating node would like to offer its resources to be used by other nodes. However this sharing must be in a controllable and finely-tuned manner. Thus, security is of great challenges to grid computing, and the solutions for different security problems need to be studied and designed in a comprehensive manner. This chapter is devoted to grid security issues.

In the rest of this chapter, we first overview existing research on grid computing security briefly, then we discuss secure grid communication and resource sharing, and finally we present a dual level key management scheme which can implement secure grid services for grid computing.

6.2   Existing Research on Grid Computing Security

Grid security is a multidimensional problem that should be addressed at multiple levels. It has its own set of security challenges, as users and shared resources can come from separate domains, and either can behave maliciously. The research on grid security has been conducted for about one decade, but the works have been proposed in an isolated and independent manner. We briefly present two exemplary works here.

The early work on grid security was initiated by Ian Foster [Foster *et al.* (1998)]. Their paper first identified some typical characteristics of grid computing environments, and then identified security requirements for grid computing. The identified features include (1) The user population is large and dynamic; (2) The resource pool is large and dynamic; (3) A computation may acquire, start processes on and release resources dynamically; (4) The processes may communicate by using variety of mechanisms such as unicast and multicast; (5) Resource may require different authentication and authorization policies; and (6) A user will be associated with different local name spaces. The identified security requirements for grid computing, besides the standard security functions, such as authentication, authorization, integrity, privacy and non-repudiation, include:

(1) *Single sign-on:* A user should be able to authenticate once and then he can acquire resources, use resources, release resources, and communicate internally, without further authentication of the user.
(2) *Protection of credential:* User credentials must be protected.
(3) *Interoperability with local security solutions:* While grid security solutions may provide inter-domain access mechanism, access to local resources will typically be determined by local security policy that is enforced by local security mechanism.
(4) *Exportability:* The code must be exportable and executable in multi-national test beds.

(5) *Uniform credentials/certification:* Inter-domain access requires, at a minimum, a common way of expressing the identity of the user using the grid resources.

(6) *Secure Group Communication:* A grid computation can comprise a number of processes that will need coordination and communication in a group. The composition of the group would change over the lifetime of the process; therefore, secure communication is needed.

(7) *Support for multiple security implementations:* The security policy should not dictate a specific implementation, but it should support a variety of mechanisms based on technology, platform and legacy.

It is worthy to mention that most of the above requirements are implemented in the Globus security implementation known as Globus Security Infrastructure (GSI).

A grid environment has been defined as a scalable, dynamic, distributed virtual organization (VO) [Foster *et al.* (2001)] containing a collection of diverse and distributed organizations that seek to share and use diverse resources in a coordinated manner. Under this definition, a grid contains different administrative domains, each with autonomous security mechanisms. Effective security architecture must provide protocols and mechanisms to bridge the gaps between them and still give each local site complete control over resources it owns. Many challenges appear as to how to coordinate the secure sharing of diverse resources in a consistent manner. In his paper [Ramakrishnan (2004)], Ramakrishnan identified the following grid-specific security challenges:

(1) *User Identity:* Every organization associates individuals with some form of identity username, password (or combination) or digital certificate. In a grid environment each user must have a grid identity. In a small grid environment, this mapping could be done statically, but for organizations that are large and their association with a VO is complex, this mapping would be most likely assigned dynamically, choosing from a pool of identities that most closely matched the user's role and access permissions. This raises several security issues: it requires users to have local accounts on any machine that is called upon for job execution; it may give the user more access than it is required. It would require the VO administrator to trust the host's access control and accounting mechanisms. It also would require the host to trust the Grid CA (Certificate Authority) to correctly identify the user, and the Grid security service to correctly authenticate them.

(2) *Organizational Diversity:* Organizations participating in a grid usually have significant investment in security mechanisms and infrastructure. Grid security must allow users to use their local identities to authenticate context to access remote sites. Thus, the security fabric must be able to present the authentication context from the local domain in a common representation that other sites can use. A fundamental requirement is to enable VO access to resources that exist within classical organizations and that, from the perspective of those classical organizations, have policies in place that speak only about local users. This VO access must be established via binary relationship a) between local users and their administrative domain and b) between users and VO. Therefore, the Grid security must interoperate with, rather than replace, the already trusted mechanisms in place within an organization platform infrastructure.

Furthermore, while some VOs, such as multiyear scientific collaborations, may be large and long lived, others could be short-lived, created perhaps to support a single task; for example, two users sharing a document as they write a research article. In this case, the overheads involved in creation and operations must be small. In other words, a grid environment should be flexible in supporting operations and tasks of varying scales.

(3) *Dynamic Character:* The grid security is further complicated by the fact that the new services and resources may be deployed and instantiated dynamically over a VO's lifetime. Organizations may join and leave the VO dynamically. New services might be created on the fly, existing resources may be withdrawn from the VO by organizations or even new organizations join the VO. This requires following two key requirements in a grid security model [Cooper and Martin (2006)].

Dynamic creation of services: Users must be able to establish new services (e.g. resources) dynamically, that is, without intervention of the "administrator". These services must coordinate in a secure and reliable manner with other services. Thus we must be able to name these services in an assertive fashion and grant them rights without contradicting the local policies.

Dynamic establishment of trust domains: In order to coordinate resources, VOs must not only create trust among the users and the resources, but also among the VO resources. These resources would span over organization boundaries, as a result the trust domain would span multiple organizations. This trust domain must adapt dynamically as participants join or leave the VO.

(4) *Distributed framework:* An organization might want to regulate the usage of its resource via specific rules. For instance, it might want to restrict the user's access to machines during critical hours of its business, making them more available to the local non grid users. In order to achieve this, the local policy sets must be evaluated when the user's request for a resource comes in. Unlike traditional systems, the grid's service policy evaluation, decisions and enforcement are distributed across the VO's landscape. Trust relations among the VO are another result of it being distributed. If an entity X enters into collaboration with two others who are each other's competitors, they should not come to know about each other's involvement. The context of operation must remain distinct.

(5) *End User Security:* Globus Toolkit (GT), a grid security infrastructure (GSI) has been established for implementing end user security. GSI defines a common credential format based on X.509 identity certificates and protocol based on TLS and SSL. In other words, these are based on Public Key Infrastructure (PKI), a trust hierarchy system that uses previously established trust procedures to authenticate participating member credentials. However, users might find managing their private public keys daunting, especially when there could be many entry points in VO. Online credential Repository- MyProxy [Novotny *et al.* (2001)] has been proposed to store and provide management of user credentials in a grid environment.

(6) *Delegation:* Humphrey and Thompson discuss security issues and challenges from several usage scenarios [Humphrey and Thompson (2002)]. Job execution needing advance scheduling requires delegation of rights to some other service to perform an operation on the user's behalf. Conventionally, it is to grant unlimited delegation to impersonate the user. Clearly, this approach is not valid for computational grid. All delegation in computation grid must be evaluated under the condition under which the delegated rights must be exercised. Delegating too many rights could lead to misuse, and delegating too few could lead to restriction in job completion. Some of the challenges that need to be addressed are: (1) Knowing the minimum set of rights that is required for a job execution, (2) Uniform naming of the rights to help delegation and its identification, and (3) Knowing how many levels of delegation are required. Specifying the delegation extent for a job must be per-

formed to identify how many servers may be called upon to accomplish this task.

(7) *Firewalls and virtual private networks:* Firewalls or VPN between server hosts and user machine or between server hosts pose a serious challenge for Grid security measures. The static managed and centrally controlled nature of Firewall and VPN does not offer much flexibility for Grid security measures that are required to dynamically alter the participating hosts and services. Typically, firewalls open up for specific hosts and to specific ports. Grid security and traditional organizational security measures must align themselves to provide a VO environment for organizations at large at the same time safeguarding existing investment IT infrastructure.

Besides the above examples, many other works have been done or are ongoing for grid security. Typically, they include general grid security architecture [Foster *et al.* (1998)], secure grid services [Welch *et al.* (2003)], visualized grid computing services and their security implications [Humphrey and Thompson (2002)], Globus project and Globus Security Infrastructure [Foster and Kesselman (1997)], Globus Toolkit 4 (GT 4) Authentication Framework [Lang *et al.* (2006)], Grid system security architecture [Li *et al.* (2006)], Scalable Grid Security Architecture [Zhou *et al.* (2005)], and trust based grid security models [Farag and Muthucumaru (2002); Lin *et al.* (2004b,a)]. More recently, web services have provided several security standards that have greatly influenced security in Grid computing. Due to a significant overlap between web services and security requirements, grid services standards are converging with web services. We will not go into detail about these works, instead, we will focus on secure grid communication and controlled resource sharing and data exchange, the two most fundamental functions in grid computing, and propose a practical solution to them.

6.3 Secure Grid Communication and Controlled Resource Sharing in Grid Computing

The real and specific problem that underlies the Grid concept is coordinated resource sharing and problem solving in dynamic, multi-institutional virtual organizations [Foster *et al.* (2001)]. The sharing that we are concerned with is not primarily file exchange but rather direct access to computers, software, data, and other resources. This is required by a range of collaborative problem-solving and resource-brokering strategies emerging in industry and science.

However, there is a significant security challenge on the Grid resource sharing, that is, the data privacy to others outside the group of shared resources. When those resources involved in a task communicate with one another, the task owner may not want other untrusted/unauthorized people to know the communication data. Unfortunately, the Internet contains many malicious factors (such as hackers, viruses), especially for the Grid. One cannot expect everybody in the Internet to be trustworthy. Thus, the information transmitted among remote sites/resources should be encrypted.

Point-to-point cryptographic schemes have been well developed but Grid computing is featured by collaboration among a group of users and their sharing of computational or data resources. Therefore, it is very inefficient to unicast common information one to another, but multicasting shared information among the group is much more efficient. The multicast information needs to be encrypted (by a group key) so that others cannot understand the information, even though they could intercept it. Groups can be dynamic, because users, resources or sites can attend or leave a group at anytime, and groups are organized in real-time according to the availability and workload of various resources. In addition, one member may belong to multiple groups simultaneously. Thus, the follow-up challenges emerge as how to authenticate the group members, how to distribute the group key to the group members, and how to update the group key securely and efficiently when the group members change.

Another important feature of Grid computing is Hierarchical Access Control (HAC). Such a scenario is mainly related to the management in Grid computing. The Grid environment consists of resources and users (the number of users and resources can vary from a few to millions). There are different relations among users and resources. Some special members/nodes have been authorized to monitor the tasks of certain resources or to check the communication among some grid resources, such as system administrators, service/resource providers, Resource Management Systems (RMS) and so on. Hence, they should be able to possess the access keys of the resources under their authority while unable to obtain the keys of others out of their authority. Today, Grid becomes increasingly large and a hierarchical controlling model is widely deployed, i.e. there are different levels of System Administrators, Providers, Users and RMSs. The lower level members/sites/nodes are controlled and monitored by the higher-level ones. This nature needs hierarchical key management.

In summary, one of the prominent features in grid computing is the collaboration of multiple entities to perform collaborative tasks that rely on two fundamental functions: communication and resource sharing. Since the Internet is not security-oriented by design, there exist various attacks, in particular, from malicious internal users. Securing grid communication and controlling access to shared resources in a fine-tuned manner are important issues for grid services. The rest of the chapter proposes an elegant dual-level key management (DLKM) mechanism using an innovative concept/construction of access control polynomial (ACP) and one-way functions. The first level provides a flexible and secure group communication technology, while the second level offers hierarchical access control. Complexity analysis and simulation demonstrate the efficiency and effectiveness of the proposed DLKM in both computational grid and data grid. An example is illustrated.

6.4 Dual-Level Key Management (DLKM)

In HAC problems, nodes in the hierarchy generally represent a set of resources and/or users. Users can join or leave a node dynamically. Resources can be added or removed from a node at any point. This kind of dynamics is different from the hierarchy dynamic operations, such as adding or deleting a node in the access hierarchy (but it will affect the key management somehow). Therefore, there is a need to consider two level dynamics. In this section, we present a dual level key management (DLKM) scheme for dynamic hierarchical access problems [Zou *et al.* (2007)]. DLKM consists of two levels: the first level is to solve the problem of dynamic groups and key distribution; the second level is designed for HAC, which is built upon the first level. We analyze the complexities and security of DLKM and also present some illustrative examples.

6.4.1 *First Level*

It is assumed that every valid user/machine in the system is assigned a permanent Secret key, denoted by SID_i for member U_i (the member here generally represents the user/node/machine in the grid). For example, when a user or an organization registers to the Grid via the Globus Toolkit (www.globus.org/toolkit/), several certificates need to be issued, including the host certificate that authenticates the machine involved in the grid, the service certificate that authenticates the services offered to the grid, and the user certificate that authenticates the users using the grid services. In this registration process, the permanent secret key can be embedded into the certificates issued to the member. Assume p is a large prime which forms a finite field F_p.

Whenever there will be a group of users participating in a grid service, the Key Management Server (KMS) will construct a polynomial $A(x)$ in finite field $F_p[x]$ as:

$$A(x) = \prod_{i \in \psi} (x - f(SID_i, z)) \tag{6.1}$$

where ψ denotes this group under consideration and SID_i are group members' permanent secret keys assigned to the members in ψ. $f(x, y)$ is a public one-way hash function and z is a random integer from F_p. $A(x)$ is called an *Access Control Polynomial* (ACP). As Eq. (6.1), it is apparent that $A(x)$ is equated to 0 when x is substituted with $f(SID_i, z)$ by a valid user with SID_i in ψ ; otherwise, $A(x)$ is a random value.

The KMS selects a random group key K for group ψ and computes the polynomial

$$P(x) = A(x) + K. \tag{6.2}$$

Finally, the KMS publicizes $(z, P(x))$.

From this public information, any group member U_i can get the key by

$$K = P(f(SID_i, z)). \tag{6.3}$$

Here U_i computes $f(SID_i, z)$ first and then substitutes into $P(x)$.

For any other member U_r excluded by ψ, $P(f(SID_r, z))$ yields a random value from which U_r cannot get the hidden key K. This key management mechanism guarantees that only a user whose SID_i is included in $A(x)$ can extract the key from $P(x)$.

With this scheme, dynamic groups can be easily managed to accept and revoke users. If a new user U_t needs to be added, the KMS creates a new SID_t and assigns it to U_t. Then, the KMS includes $(x - f(SID_t, z))$ in the formation of $A(x)$ and gets

$$A'(x) = \prod_{i \in \psi} (x - f(SID_i, z))(x - f(SID_t, z)) \tag{6.4}$$

$A'(x)$ is used to mask key K by computing $P'(x) = A'(x) + K$. Then $(z, P'(x))$ is sent to U_t. After receiving $(z, P'(x))$, U_t can use SID_t to derive the key from Eq. (6.3).

If a current group member U_t needs to be revoked from the group, the KMS just selects a new random z' and recomputes $A'(x)$ by excluding the corresponding $(x - f(SID_t, z'))$. Then, the KMS selects a new group key K', computes $P'(x) = A'(x) + K'$, and multicasts $(z', P'(x))$ Now, the deleted user U_t cannot extract K' from $P'(x)$.

6.4.2 *Second Level*

The Second Level is to solve the HAC problem based on the first level. We will adopt as our second level HAC mechanism the scheme proposed in [Atallah *et al.* (2005)]. The main idea is as follows:

i) for every node v_i, it is assigned a secret key $\hat{k}_i$, a public ID_i, and a private key k_i which is computed by itself as:

$$k_i = f(\hat{k}_i, ID_i) \tag{6.5}$$

ii) for every edge from v_i to v_j, a public edge value $r_{i,j}$ is defined as:

$$r_{i,j} = k_j \oplus f(k_i, ID_j) \tag{6.6}$$

iii) node v_i can compute v_j's key from its own private key k_i and public information ID_j and $r_{i,j}$ as:

$$k_j = r_{i,j} \oplus f(k_i, ID_j) \tag{6.7}$$

iv) most dynamic operations can be performed efficiently by just changing the public information ID_j and $r_{i,j}$.

As for the detail of the scheme, please revisit Section 3.3.5 in Chapter 3.

6.4.3 *Combination of Two Levels*

Now, let's see how the two levels work together. After the two levels are combined, all members in a group represented by vertex v_i share one identical group secret key $\hat{k}_i$ on the second level. Each member U_j has his personal secret key SID_j, as registered at the first level. Every vertex v_i has its own unique group secret key $\hat{k}_i$ and $A_i(x)$. Here $A_i(x)$ is composed out of all SIDs of the members in v_i and used to distribute $\hat{k}_i$ to all v_i 's members via the multicast of $P_i(x)$. Then, all (and only) the members in vertex i can derive the group secret key $\hat{k}_i$. Following that, the group private key k_i can be obtained via Eq. (6.5) by members themselves.

At the first level, when a member U_r leaves a group (vertex v_i), a new group secret key $\hat{k}'_i$ is distributed by computing $A'_i(x)$ without the term $(x - f(SID_r, z'))$ and multicasting $P'_i(x)$. Then, the remaining group members can derive the new group private key k'_i by Eq. (6.5) but U_r cannot. The new $\hat{k}'_i$ and k'_i will result in corresponding changes in the second level. Three types of updates will be performed: (1) all v_i 's parent edge values; (2) all the public IDs (thus, private node keys) in v_i 's sub-tree; and (3) all the edge values in v_i 's sub-tree. These renewing steps can effectively prevent the removed user U_r from extracting the new keys of its former descendant vertices.

The advantage of DLKM is obvious by combining the two levels. At the first level, $A(x)$ and $P(x)$ make key distribution efficient and secure. Also, handling group dynamics is simple by just assigning SID_i and/or adding/deleting corresponding terms in $A(x)$. At the second level, edge values computed from a one-way hash function guarantee the higher level vertex's access control over the lower level vertices. Moreover, updating a node's private key can be done easily by changing the node's ID. As a result, their combination makes sure that the change to one vertex does not have influence on other vertices (e.g. their private node keys).

6.4.4   *Security and Algorithm Analysis*

This section analyzes the complexity, robustness and other measures of the proposed scheme.

6.4.4.1   *Security Analysis*

- Internal Attacks. Internal attack means the users in the same node try to find, individually or by collusion, something they do not know. However, in our scheme, the users in the same node v_i share the same secret key $\hat{k}_i$ and private key k_i. There is nothing except SID_i which one user knows but other users do not know. The only possible attack by an internal individual is that an internal spy attempts to find SID s of other users in the same group from $P(x)$. However, our scheme at the first level defends well against this type of attack in an elegant way: the internal spy can obtain K and then subtract K from $P(x)$ to get $A(x)$. By setting $A(x) = 0$, the internal spy tries to find the root. Even though the internal spy may find a root somehow, the root will be $f(SID, z)$ but not SID. In addition, one cannot get SID from $f(SID, z)$. The only benefit of Knowing $f(SID, z)$ is to get K by plugging it into this very $P(x)$ (For any other $P'(x)$, its z' is different, so does $f(SID, z')$). However, the internal spy had got K already. Thus, the clever utilization of one-way function can prevent the internal individual attack.

As for the collusion of multiple internal users in the sense that w internal spies collude to derive other members' personal secrets using all of their SID_i (i=1,2,3,...,w), our novel idea of $A(x)$ can make such collusion meaningless. This is very different from other polynomial based techniques [Blundo *et al.* (1998a, 1993); Zou *et al.* (2002a)]. In those previous polynomial based schemes, $t + 1$ or more internal users may find the entire polynomial by interpolating their $t + 1$ points (i.e. $(ID_i, h(ID_i))$) (where t is the system security parameter and is the degree of the polynomial in general). However, polynomial interpolation is useless here because the users do not have points but just one value (i.e. SID_i but no $A(SID_i)$) or to say, $f(SID_i, z)$ but $A(f(SID_i, z)) = 0$. Again, $f(SID_{root}, z)$ may be obtained but SID_{root} cannot. In the next activity when the random value z is changed to z', this last $f(SID_{root}, z)$ becomes useless. In summary, this DLKM is perfect against internal collusion of any degrees.

- Attack across Groups. Attacking across groups means the members in different vertices/groups collude to find other group private keys k_i or other users' secret keys SID_i. It may occur in different scenarios, e.g. two users in different child nodes collude to get the key used in their parent node, one user in a sibling node and another user in a child node collude to attack parents.... However, no matter what kinds of combinations they are, their attacks are useless in our DLKM. At the first level, external collusion is meaningless because all the $P(x)$ s, no matter whether they are in different or same vertices, are independent due to the random z which is selected every time. The internal attack has been proven useless as above. Similarly at the second level, the attempt to extract other group's private key k_i has to violate the property of one-way function, thus being impossible.

- Information Glean.
A hacker may attempt to glean many publicized $P(x)$ s, dreaming to break the system by analyzing the relation among $P(x)$ s. As discussed above, this will not work here, since all $P(x)$ s are independent.

In short, the proposed DLKM is perfect in defending against both internal collusions or external attacks, just like the gold in Fort Knox!

6.4.4.2 *Complexity Analysis*

Assume the number of nodes in the hierarchy is n and the maximum possible number of users in a node is m. The one-way hash function is used at both levels. The time complexity of the one-way function is totally determined by the function itself and independent from both n and m. We will ignore its complexity in the following analysis.

- The Analysis at the First Level. At the first level, there are multiple user groups and each is associated with a node in the hierarchy. The CA manages all user groups, but it manages each of them independently. There are three typical operations: initialization, user join, and user leave and three kinds of complexities: storage, computation, and communication. The CA needs to store all the information about the hierarchy, nodes, user groups, and users (personal secrets), thus its space complexity is $O(mn)$. However, since we assume the CA is more powerful than users, this space requirement for the CA is not a problem. For every user, the only thing the user needs to store is his personal secret key SID_i. Thus, the storage requirement at the user end is $O(1)$. Note, this is an important feature which makes the scheme applicable in the devices of limited capability such as PDAs. Let us consider three operations one by one. For initializing a node (i.e. the user group of the node), the CA has to calculate $A(x) = (x - f(SID_1, z)) \cdot (x - f(SID_2, z)) \cdots (x - f(SID_m, z))$ and $P(x) = A(x) + k$ and then multicast $P(x)$ (along with z) to all users in the node. The time complexity for computing $A(x)$ is $O(m^2)$. If $A(x)$ has been computed, the time complexity for computing $P(x)$ is just $O(1)$. Otherwise, the time complexity for $P(x)$ is $O(m^2)$. Multicasting $P(x)$ means multicasting its coefficients. Since $P(x)$ has degree m and $m+1$ coefficients, the message size is $O(m)$. So the communication complexity for initialization is one multicast and $O(m)$ per multicast. Let's consider the complexities for the new user join operation. The CA just computes a new $P(x)$ and only unicasts it (along with z) to this joining user. So, the time complexity is $O(m^2)$ and the communication complexity is one unicast and $O(m)$ per unicast. Note: in the case when a user joins, the user is not allowed to get the previous key for

Table 6.1 Complexities for the first level.

	Space	Computation	Communication
Key storage for each user	$O(1)$		
Key Computation for each user		$O(m^2)$	
Key initial distribution		$O(m^2)$	$O(1)$ multicast, $O(m)$ per multicast
Key update in joining phrase		$O(m^2)$	$O(1)$ unicast, $O(m)$ per unicast
Key update in leaving phrase		$O(m^2)$	$O(1)$ multicast, $O(m)$ per multicast
Key update for multiple joins and leaves simultaneously		$O(m^2)$	$O(1)$ multicast, $O(m)$ per multicast

ensuring backward secrecy, then a new secret key $\hat{k}_i$ needs to be selected and multicast to all users including the joining user in the node. In this case, the communication complexity is one multicast and $O(m)$ per multicast. When a user leaves or is revoked, a new group key must be generated and distributed to all the remaining users in the same node. Similarly, the computation complexity is $O(m^2)$ and the communication complexity is one multicast and $O(m)$ per multicast. Finally, let us consider the computation cost for a user to compute the key k from $P(x)$. Computing k is a simple matter to compute $f(SID_i, z)$ and substitute the result for x in $P(x)$. Since the degree of $P(x)$ is m, the computation complexity is $O(m^2)$. One dynamic scenario is that some users may join and some other users may leave the same group at the same time. The elegance of distributing the key via $P(x)$ is that the CA just includes the $SIDs$ of the new joining users and excludes the $SIDs$ of the leaving users in the formation of new $A(x)$. Thus, multiple joins and leaves can be performed in the same efficiency. Table 6.1 summarizes complexities at the first level.

- The Analysis at the Second Level. One frequent operation for HAC is key derivation, i.e. a node derives the key of its descendant from its own key. This derivation will follow the path from the node to the descendant and use the one-way function iteratively. Obviously, the longer the path, the more complex the key derivation. The worst case is $O(n)$. To decrease the key derivation complexity, some methods proposed in [Atallah *et al.* (2005)] are presented to simplify the second-level computation. The time complexity is relieved by adding some shortcuts. After shortcuts were added, during the process of key derivation, one does not need to follow every edge from the beginning node to the destination node any more. Instead, by using shortcuts,

Table 6.2   Time complexities for the second level.

Dynamic operations	Without shortcuts	With shortcuts
Key derivation	$O(n)$	$O(\log \log n)$
Add a leaf/internal node	$O(F) \ / \ O(F + S)$	$O(n) \ / \ O(n)$
delete a leaf/internal node	$O(1) \ / \ O(n)$	$O(1) \ / \ O(n)$
Add an edge	$O(1)$	$O(n)$
delete an edge	$O(1)$ or $O(n)$	$O(n)$

we can jump from one special node to another special node, covering many edges in between. As a result, for an n node hierarchy with shortcuts, the key derivation time complexity is $O(\log \log n)$ one-way function computations with $O(n)$ public space [Atallah *et al.* (2005)]. The typical dynamic operations at the second level include adding/deleting a node/edge. In addition, the shortcut operation may be combined with each of these operations. Let us analyze them one by one and results are shown in Table 6.2.

When adding a node (it is assumed that the edges between the node and its parents (if any) as well as its children (if any) are also added), the time complexity depends on the position where the new node is added. If the new node is added as a leaf node without any descendants, the time complexity should be constant, because only the edge value between the new node and its parent is created. If it is possible/allowed for a node to have multiple parents, the complexity depends on the number of parents. Assume this number is F, then the complexity is $O(F)$. When the new node is added as a parent of some existing nodes, the edge values between the new node and its children also need to be computed. Suppose the number of children is S. The time complexity is $O(S)$. If shortcuts are used, we have to recompute shortcuts. The computation for shortcuts is in linear time of n. Thus, the total time complexity is $O(n)$ (Shortcuts are created between centroids and the root. When a new node is added or deleted, the position of centroids will move. We have to compute the shortcut again).

Let us consider the operation of deleting a node. When the removed node is a leaf, nothing needs to be done except discarding the parameters related to the node, so the time complexity is constant. However, if the removed node is an internal node, the situation is quite different. The ID_i used in the descendant nodes will be changed. k_i will also be recomputed through $k_i = f(\hat{k}_i, \ ID_i)$. All edge values related to these changed ID and k will be recomputed. Since the extreme case is that all the nodes are the descendants of the deleted node, the worst case time complexity for deleting a node is $O(n)$. In addition, if shortcuts are used, shortcuts will be also recomputed which is also in the linear time of n. Thus, the time complexity is $O(n)$.

Let us consider the time complexity for adding/deleting an edge. For adding an edge, the CA just computes the edge value, which is constant. If shortcuts are used, they need to be recomputed, which is $O(n)$. As for deleting an edge, the CA may just discard the edge value. In case shortcuts are used, there is a need to recompute shortcuts, which is $O(n)$. One issue is that if the deleted edge was the only way for the patent node u of the deleted edge to get to its child node s previously, u should not reach s anymore after deletion. This means that all *ID* values of s and its descendants need to be changed. So all the private keys of these nodes will be recomputed and all the edge values related to these key and *ID* values need to be recomputed. This complexity is $O(n)$.

- The Analysis for Combination of Two Levels.

When a member joins an existing node v_i, what needs to be done is to only distribute the existing $\hat{k}_i$ to this new member with a new $P(x)$. The time complexity will be same as that for the user join operation at the first level. It is $O(m^2)$.

When a member is removed from a node v_i, the situation is more complicated. The CA will not only change $\hat{k}_i$, select a new ID_i and recompute k_i but also select a new ID_j and re-compute k_j for all its descendant nodes v_j. After that, all edges' values in the sub-tree rooted at v_i will be recomputed. These steps are in linear time of n. Then the CA needs to compute $P_i(x)$ by excluding the removed member and distribute $P_i(x)$ to all the remaining members in v_i. This will take $O(m^2)$. Thus, the total time complexity is $O(m^2 + n)$. If shortcuts are used, although no node is deleted and the structure of hierarchy does not change, we also have to recompute the shortcuts because many edge values have been changed. This will contribute another $O(n)$. So, the total time complexity is $O(m^2 + n)$.

From the above description, we can see that when a member moves from one node to another, he was just removed from one node and then joins the other. Thus, the time complexity is the sum of complexities for joining and leaving, being $O(m^2 + n)$ too.

In summary, DLKM has very good performance with efficient support for dynamics.

6.5   Secure Grid Computing by DLKM

DLKM can make grid services secure in data communication and access control. We discuss how to implement DLKM into the grid computing in the section.

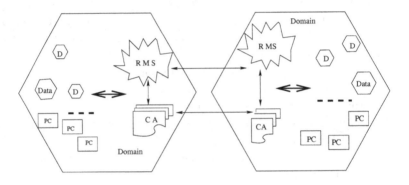

Fig. 6.1   General architecture of grid computing

A general architecture of grid computing is depicted by Figure 6.1. It is not too difficult to merge DKLM with this architecture.

In each domain of the grid system, there is a Central Authenticator (CA) which issues the certificates for hosts, users and services when they are first registered to the grid system. The first step of DLKM to distribute personal secret keys can be combined with the process of issuing the certificates from the CA. Since registration is a point-to-point process between the CA and a member, any two-party public/private key scheme like RSA can be used to encrypt the initial information.

The CA can then act as the KMS to distribute keys using DLKM in an efficient and secure manner. There are two typical types of resource access in grid computing: (1) access Local Resources inside a domain as shown by Figure 6.1; and (2) access Remote Resources of other domains. Securing both cases is described as follows, respectively.

6.5.1 *Access Local Resources*

Based on the above architecture design, accessing local resources can be done as follows (note: the generic process of requesting grid services is also included):

(1) A user submits a request for a certain grid service to the RMS controlling this domain;

(2) The RMS detects a group of available resources (including computational resources and data resources);

(3) The RMS informs the CA. The CA randomly generates a key K_1 and then uses the private key k_i of node v_i to encrypt K_1 where v_i is the vertex these resources belong to;

(4) The CA multicasts the encrypted key to these resources and to the RMS;

(5) The resources with k_i can decrypt K_1. The RMS can derive k_i first. Note: the KMS is usually at the top of the hierarchy and v_i is its descendant. Then, the RMS can also obtain the same K_1 ;

(6) Thus, these resources together with the RMS can use this common key K_1 to communicate. For example, the RMS needs to send jobs/programs to the resources, then the resources need to communicate/access/exchange data, and finally the results need to return to the RMS for composition. All of these communication processes need the common key K_1 to encrypt communication messages for data privacy;

(7) During the process, if certain members (such as system administrators) need to monitor the whole process, they can derive the private key k_i as long as v_i is their descendant, and then decrypt K_1 from the public information generated by the CA. Therefore, they can monitor the process if they want.

In step 3, we assume those resources belong to one group/vertex. However, those available resources may belong to different groups/vertices. The simple way to solve this problem is that the CA encrypts K_1 multiple times corresponding to the multiple groups/vertices involved, and then multicasts. Again, the join/leave/movement of users among groups has already been described in Section 6.4 of this chapter and Section 3.3.5 of Chapter 3.

6.5.2 *Access Remote Resources*

Suppose a user submits a request which needs to use not only the resources in the local domain but also the resources of some other remote domains (controlled by RMS_j, j=1,2,...,J). Each domain has its own CA, so the combined group of local and remote resources can get the key distributed as follows:

(1) A user submits a request for a certain grid service to the local RMS;

(2) The local RMS finds that besides some local resources, the request needs to use remote resources from other domains;

(3) The local CA picks up a random K_1 and distributes K_1 to those local resources and the local RMS (following the same procedure as above);

(4) The local CA talks with other CAs of those remote domains and distributes K_1 to those CAs, as depicted by Fig. 6.1. There are different ways to do it. One way is via the RSA system as follows: a) Each CA has a public key; b) the local CA uses the public key of the corresponding CA to encrypt K_1 by the RSA algorithm; c) Each remote CA can decrypt K_1 using its own private key;

(5) Each remote CA uses its own hierarchy and the DLKM mechanism to distribute K_1 to related resources;

(6) Then, the group is formed and the group members can communicate with one another securely knowing the common Key K_1. The corresponding hierarchical monitoring or data access is also allowed.

6.5.3 *Data Grid*

The above schemes are suitable for the computational grid services in which the computing resources are allocated to share the workload. The data communication in this case is mostly generated from the computational task. However, there is another type of grid services, called as the Data Grid, whose purpose is mainly data access. Many data sources are offered as resources for other grid nodes/members to access. For example, some bioinformatics problems were solved by the data grid via mining different public databases through the Internet, see e.g. [Dai *et al.* (2006)].

Nevertheless, some data sources may contain sensitive data and do not allow unauthorized members or machines to access. This condition is very important for further development of data grids. However, the current grid computing schemes make a data source unable to deny some data requests during the grid service, because these requests are issued by other nodes that are assigned by the RMS. Moreover, the data source does not know in advance who requests such types of service, because the service request also goes to the RMS from users. In this case, many sensitive data sources dare not dedicate themselves into the data grid due to the dearth/loss of access control on their own data. The proposed DLKM can solve this concern.

The above described procedure for computational grids can be easily adjusted to the data grid for access control. The steps of distributing the common key K_1 are similar. Moreover, for a certain sensitive data source which needs to confine its data access only to trusted users or machines, the data source should not use the common shared key K_1 to encrypt the data. Rather, it uses its own group private key k_i (suppose it belongs to vertex/group v_i). Then, only those users who are its ancestors and allowed/trusted to read the data can derive k_i via the hierarchical relation (as Figure 6.2). The following protocol should be abided by:

(1) Sensitive data sent from a data source should be encrypted by its group private key k_i ;

(2) When a trusted machine receives the encrypted data, it can derive k_i ;

(3) On the other hand, if a machine is not a trusted one, it cannot get the correct key k_i. In this case, it will report to the RMS and then the RMS will reassign the job to another machine (computational resource) that is trusted by the data source according to the publicized hierarchy of groups.

(4) Then, once a machine obtains k_i, it can decrypt the data, and then operates on the data. If the results out of the sensitive data are also sensitive, then the machine encrypts the results with k_i again before sending back. The encrypted results are sent to the member/user who requested this grid service either directly or through the RMS;

(5) When the user obtains the encrypted sensitive results, he can use his own group private key to derive k_i and then decrypts the results. If he has no right (i.e. neither an ancestor nor in a same group of the sensitive data source), the results are indecipherable to him without deriving the correct key k_i.

By this DLKM mechanism, data sources can also control access to their data using keys and encryption without violating the advantages of the grid computing (large-scale resource sharing). Only those trusted members or sites can derive the key and understand the data, whereas other unauthorized users are unable to understand the encrypted message even though they may be recruited in the grid task and know the common Key K_1. Apparently, the hierarchical design that defines the relations of trust/accessibility is very important. If certain data sources are not satisfied with the CA's hierarchical design, they can suggest the CA to modify or select to quit if the CA cannot accept their requirements. Such strategy between the CA and members is bi-directed via our DLKM scheme, which is flexible and fair to both parties who consent on the publicized hierarchy for maintaining appropriate security levels.

6.5.4 *Non-Monitored Grid Service*

For certain special users (such as the Governments), they have the right to select non-monitored option for requesting some special grid services. This means they do not want other people (such as an administrator) to monitor their requested services/results. This requirement is easy to solve by our DLKM along the following steps:

(1) The special request arrives at the RMS and the RMS assigns the available resources to finish the service while notifying the CA with the non-monitored requirement.

(2) The CA randomly generates a key K_1, and then uses the first-level mechanism (rather than the second-level) in our DLKM to hide and distribute K_1 directly. That is, the CA computes $P(x) = \prod_{i \in \psi}(x - f(SID_i, z)) + K_1$ and publicizes $(z, P(x))$ where ψ is the set of involved resources and SID_i are the first-level secrets of those resources.

(3) Then, the involved resources can derive K_1 whereas others, including those ancestors in the hierarchy, cannot obtain K_1.

Thus, the non-monitored grid services can also be offered by our DLKM. Note that not everybody is allowed to request such service. Only those special users who need to be strictly authenticated can request such type of non-monitored services. Without monitoring, some malicious users are easy to abuse the power of grid computing for their evil purposes.

6.5.5 *An Illustrative Example*

The proposed DKLM has been implemented in a study of the grid computing case in our TEGO (Trusted Electronics and Grid Obfuscation) center (tego.iupui.edu). To help readers understand better, this case study contains two parts: one is an illustration of a simplified example to show the key generation/publication/derivation processes; while the other is the practical implementation in a real case. Suppose the prime is $P = 13$ and the one way function is $f(x, y) = 2^{x \oplus y} \bmod P$.

6.5.5.1 *Initialization*

Suppose the hierarchy at the second-level is designed as Figure 6.2. Suppose there are m users in the group represented by the middle vertex 6. For illustration, we use a simplified example with $m = 2$ users. User 1 has personal secret $SID_1 = 7$ and User 2 has $SID_2 = 9$. Then, the group secret key needs to be distributed to both users (suppose $\hat{k}_6 = 11$ and $z = 5$). By Eq. (1-2), the following polynomial is generated:

$$P(x)\%13 = \{A(x) + K\}\%13 = \{(x - 2^{7 \oplus 5})(x - 2^{9 \oplus 5}) + 11\}\%13$$
$$= x^2 - 5x + 2 \tag{6.8}$$

Then, the coefficients of Polynomial (6.8) are publicized in an array as $\{ 1,-5,2 \}$. User 1 computes $f(SID_1, z) = 2^{7 \oplus 5} = 4$ and substitutes 4 for x into Eq. (6.8) to obtain -2%13=11. User 2 obtains 11 too. Thus, both of them get $\hat{k}_6 = 11$. Suppose another user not in this group with $SID_3 = 6$ to substitute his $f(SID_3, z)$ (=8) into Eq. (6.8), then he derives 26%13=0 which is not the key.

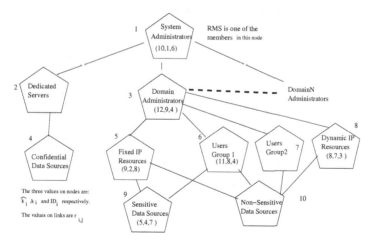

Fig. 6.2   A part of the sample hierarchy for grid computing.

The above is just an illustrative example. In our real case study, the system prime P is not as small as 13, but a number with 128 bits. The number m of users in a group should also be much more than 2, and the degrees of polynomials are much higher than 3. In addition, a strong secure one-way hash function other than the one above can be used.

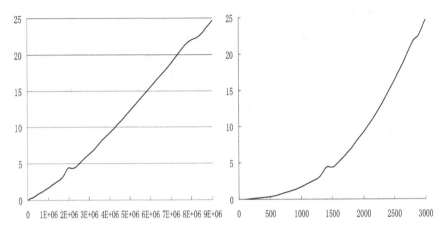

Fig. 6.3   Performance for generating polynomials to numbers of group members: (left) running time *vs.* group members *(m)*; (right) time is linear to m^2

Generating polynomials is one of the most time-consuming operations. Its performance (running time) for different group sizes from 5 to 3000 is depicted by Figure 6.3. The left figure shows the efficiency of the algorithm. Usually, the number of group members will not be as high as 3000. Otherwise, the group members can be divided into multiple sub groups. The right figure validates that the complexity of this algorithm is $O(m^2)$.

As another example to illustrate the second level's key creation and derivation, we will show how users compute private group keys with the received secret information (i.e. secret group keys), and how users use their private keys and public information to derive the private group key of a descendant vertex. Suppose ID_6 was selected as 4 and $\hat{k}_6$ as 11. Vertex 9 has $ID_9 = 7$ and secret key $\hat{k}_9 = 5$. After the secret keys were distributed to users in two vertices respectively, the private key used in group 6 can be computed by two users as $k_6 = f(\hat{k}_6, ID_6) = 2^{11 \oplus 4} \% 13 = 8$. Similarly, every user in group 9 can compute private key $k_9 = f(\hat{k}_9, ID_9) = 2^{5 \oplus 7} \% 13 = 4$. Furthermore, the KMS computes and publicizes the edge value from vertex 6 to vertex 9, that is, $r_{6,9} = k_9 \oplus f(k_6, ID_9) = 4 \oplus 2^{8 \oplus 7} \% 13 = 12$. When any user in vertex 6 wants to visit resources in vertex 9, he just needs to plug k_6, ID_9, and $r_{6,9}$ in $k_j = r_{i,j} \oplus f(k_i, ID_j)$ to compute $k_9 = r_{6,9} \oplus f(k_6, ID_9) = 12 \oplus 2^{8\oplus7}\%13 = 4$. Once this group key is obtained, all resources in vertex 9 are available.

6.5.5.2 *Illustration of DLKM for a Grid Service*

We give a concrete example to illustrate the usage of DLKM to a grid service. Let us review the Figure 6.2. Now, suppose user 1 in vertex 6 requests a grid service that needs to use sensitive data sources in vertex 9. The available resources assigned by the RMS belong to both vertex 5 and vertex 8. The private and public information on both vertices and links of those involved elements are marked in Fig. 6.2.

As shown in the part of Data Grid in section 2.3, suppose a common key used by all four groups (and their ancestors) is randomly selected as $K_1 = 3$ by the CA. Along the hierarchy, the CA should encrypt K_1 with the key of group 8 ($k_8 = 7$) once and with the key of group 9 ($k_9 = 4$) another time. Then, the CA multicasts the encrypted key to group 8 with the former one, and to groups 1,3,5,6,9 with the latter one. Groups 8 and 9 can directly decrypt $K_1 = 3$. If a member in group 1 (such as the RMS) needs to get K_1, it can find a path from group 1 to group 9 and then derive the keys of those intermediate vertices one by another along the public information of links and nodes. For instance, the RMS can get $k_3 = r_{1,3} \oplus f(k_1, ID_3) = 7 \oplus 2^{1\oplus4}\%13 = 9$, then $k_5 = 11 \oplus 2^{9\oplus8}\%13 = 2$, and finally $k_9 = 4 \oplus 2^{2\oplus7}\%13 = 4$. Thus, the RMS can decrypt K_1 using k_9 from the multicast message it received. Similar procedures are applicable to other groups. Then, common data can be securely exchanged among them with $K_1 = 3$.

On the other hand, the sensitive data from a data source in group 9 will be communicated with $k_9 = 4$ (not K_1). Thus, the sensitive data can be protected from unauthorized resources/users such as the dynamic IP resources in group 8 though they know the common key $K_1 = 3$. For instance, the computational resources in group 5 access the sensitive data from a database in group 9. The sensitive data is encrypted by $k_9 = 4$ that can be derived by group 5. Then, these computational resources compute the results from the decrypted data, encrypt the results with k_9, and send the results to the RMS in group 1. After composing all results, the RMS returns the final results to the user in group 6 who requested for this service. The insensitive results in the final results are encrypted by $K_1 = 3$ whereas sensitive results are encrypted by $k_9 = 4$. Thus, the authorized users can derive both keys and know the entire results. In case some malicious resources in group 8, holding $K_1 = 3$, attempt to access the sensitive data, or some resources are accidentally assigned by the RMS for operating on the sensitive data, those malicious attempts from unauthorized users cannot understand the data without the correct key ($k_9 = 4$). Moreover the accidentally assigned resources can report to the RMS to reassign other authorized resources to continue the jobs. As a result, a data source can also control its data privacy through the above process rather than makes itself known by all involved or assigned resources/users.

As it is well recognized, grid computing intensively involves collaborative tasks, which multiple entities work together to complete via interactions, data exchange and resource sharing. Thus, secure group communication and hierarchical access control would be necessary in the grid security architecture. Our proposed Dual level key management solution is the first to integrate SGC and HAC systematically for secure grid computing services. In addition, the prior schemes pose certain assumptions which are difficult to implement in reality and/or have some problems. For example, most schemes require that group members be organized/ordered as a tree (called as member serialization) which exposes group members and their positions. They also require multiple encryptions and/or multiple round broadcasts for key updating. In contrast, our ACP based key distribution solution has no serialization issue, can hide membership, and is able to perform rekeying with just one polynomial multicast, no matter how many members join or leave.

6.6   Conclusion

In this chapter, we discussed security issues in grid computing. We also proposed a Dual Level Key Management scheme and analyzed its security and performance. The scheme is highly secure and efficient and is able to support highly dynamic operations at both user level and group level. We also showed how the scheme can be used for securing different Grid-based services. The illustrative example showed the efficiency of the proposed DLKM and validated its correctness. It also helped the readers clearly understand the proposed DLKM and know how to implement it in real grid computing services.

Chapter 7

Trusted and Seamless Medical Information Systems

7.1 Overview of Trusted and Seamless Medical Information Systems

The medical information system (MIS) is a typical collaborative computing application in which people such as physicians, nurses, professors, researchers, health insurance personnel, etc. share patient information (including text, images, multimedia data) and collaboratively conduct critical tasks via the networked system. In April 2004, President Bush outlined a plan to have electronic health records (EHR) for most Americans within ten years. This is a clear indication of the importance of MIS to medical practice and health care services. Medical/health data is extremely important; it can help physicians to diagnose patient's diseases, cure patient's illness, recover people's health, and save people's lives. On the other hand, medical/health data is most sensitive and if used or disclosed inappropriately, it could jeopardize people's privacy and endanger people's lives. The greatest concern people have with MIS is the security, privacy, and confidentiality of their personal health information [Goldschmidt (2005)]. People would be willing to step into the digitized health information age only when individuals' privacy and integrity can be protected and guaranteed within the MIS systems. Accessing patient data must be monitored, controlled, confined, and granted only to authorized users. As a result, security of the MIS is very critical for those digitized health services. From the administrative/managerial point of view, governments in different countries have stipulated regulations about medical data. For example, the U.S. Department of Health and Human Services passed The Health Insurance Portability and Accountability Act (HIPAA) on August 21, 1996 [HIPAA (1996)]. The HIPAA privacy regulations require that access to patient information be limited to only those authorized, that only the information necessary for a task be available to them, and finally that personal health information be protected and kept confidential. However, from the technical point of view, how to enforce the security of MIS is a challenging question. This chapter aims to answer this question and provides a practical solution to it.

Dependability is also very important for MIS. For example, it could be potentially fatal if a patient's records fail to be loaded due to system failures and are unavailable in the event of life-threatening emergency. Therefore, the MIS has very high requirements for reliability. The newly developed grid computing technology is applied to MISs and proves to be of great reliability without sacrificing performance.

In summary, the MIS needs very high levels of dependability and security. We have implemented our dependability and security mechanisms into a real MIS, in collaboration with VA (Veterans Affairs) Hospitals and DoD (Department of Defense) in the U.S. [Schneider (2006)]. The key management services and security modules are integrated into this real MIS system without modifying the existing system components including the client GUI interface, the MIS application server, and MIS databases. Via this seamless integration, the new MIS is able to guarantee patient (data) privacy and integrity and would improve people's health and lives. Moreover, the holistic feature of our mechanism allows different MIS systems from different organizations to be integrated together to provide comprehensive clinic practice, health care services, and medical research. For example, doctors, professors, and researchers can collaborate to conduct health and medical research via the integrated MIS system. They can retrieve patient data from different databases, exchange and share data among them, mine information, perform statistics, analysis and decision-making, and obtain new discoveries.

Another very important collaborative service offered by the MIS is tele-medicine via a way of video conferencing and virtual reality. In this scenario, doctors, specialists, surgeons, nurses, etc. from different places can conduct consulting, diagnosis, and surgery through the Internet, just as they would gather together to have a face-to-face meeting to discuss or diagnose patients. The primary issue for this kind of tele-medicine is the transmission and processing of different types of signals such as images, video, audio, multimedia, text, documents, etc. Clearly, the security of these confidential signals, activities and services is critical. The new MIS, after integration with our new security and reliability mechanisms, guarantees various security needs and provides secure and reliable tele-medicine service.

The remainder of the chapter is organized as follows. Section 7.2 introduces the background of the Medical Information System; Section 7.3 describes the middleware architecture for key management services that are used in the MIS; Section 7.4 presents how to improve the MIS reliability by integrating the Grid computing technology; and Section 7.5 concludes this chapter.

7.2   Health Information Technology and Medical Information System

Information technologies have been widely used in every field of modern society including health care. However, its adoption to healthcare industry lags behind other industries by as much as ten to fifteen years [Missing-Author (2003); Goldschmidt (2005)]. Medical Information System (MIS) / Health Information Technology (HIT), defined as "the application of information processing involving both computer hardware and software that deals with the storage, retrieval, sharing, and use of health care information, data, and knowledge for communication and decision making" [Thompson and Brailer (2004)], was initially used for financial accounting of medical transactions [Goldschmidt (2005)]. The first electronic health records (EHRs) were designed and deployed in the late 1960s and early 1970s. HIT/MIS tends to help reduce costs, to liberate resources to satisfy unmet needs, and to restore competitiveness [Goldschmidt (2005)]. In particular, when combined with the Internet, "HIT is expected to foster patient-focused care, to promote transparency in prices and performance, and to enable consumers to drive the transformation of the health care system." [Goldschmidt (2005)]. There are at least two desires which motivate the adoption of HIT/MIS: (1) increasing productivity achieved in other industries that have extensively adopted Information Technology (IT), and (2) reducing the incidence of medical errors and improving quality by relating patient outcomes to care processes, along with an increased ability to measure and pay providers for performance [Goldschmidt (2005)]. The primary benefits associated with the adoption of HIT/MIS are reduced cost and improved quality of health care. Many challenges are also associated with HIT/MIS, including Complexity of the health care enterprise; Magnitude of the investment and who should make it; the absence of standards; a lack of interoperability; and the danger that acceleration of using inadequate products may increase the total investment and discourage providers [Goldschmidt (2005)]. Many obstacles exist along with the way in developing and deploying HIT/MIS: (1) enormous amounts of money may need to be expended or even be wasted, (2) vast expenditures must be invested in the short-term, while most benefits can only be gained in the long-term, and (3) widespread utilization of HIT/MIS can doubtlessly improve the quality of health care in the long run. However, improvements in patient outcomes may be less than expected in the short run. In addition, the introduction of new technology increases the potential for error at its initial (and unstable) stage [Goldschmidt (2005)]. All these factors can affect people's trust and confidence in MIS. Even though there are a number of challenges and difficulties, the broad applications of HIT/MIS would not be blocked. These challenges are not the main obstacles in adopting HIT/MIS. Instead, what people are concerned about most and affects people's willingness to step into the HIT/MIS age is "the security, privacy, and confidentiality of their personal health information." [Goldschmidt (2005)]. We, in collaboration with the VA hospitals and Indiana University School of Medicine, are putting our effort in this direction and embedding our innovative security and dependability technologies into the existing MISs to create the new generation MIS system.

Like many information systems in other fields, the MIS basically consists of three components (tiers): client/user interface, database, and application servers. (Note: the author in [Goldschmidt (2005)] classifies the MIS applications (Modules) as: Electronic health record, Personal health record (controlled by a consumer in contrast to a provider), Decision-support tools, and Tele-medicine.) For example, in the VISTA system (Veterans Health Information System and Technology Architecture) of the U.S. Department of Veterans Affairs, the three components are CPRS client (Computerized Patient Record System), VISTA application server, and Database (See: http://worldvista.sourceforge.net/vista/history/index.html). We implemented and integrated our security modules into the VISTA system to transform the VISTA into a secure MIS system [Schneider (2006)]. Apart from the provided security services such as confidentiality, integrity, authentication, fine-tuned access control, and detection of stealing and masquerading attacks, one prominent feature of our new technology is the seamless and transparent integration in the sense that the security modules are integrated without modification of any existing components and users can continue to use the system in the same way as before.

Legacy MIS systems are generally isolated ones in the sense that each is located in and used by only one organization/hospital. Moreover, different MIS systems in different organizations (even different hospitals belonging to the same organization) are quite heterogeneous, often with incompatible technologies, databases, languages, user interfaces, etc. It is becoming more important and imperative that different MIS systems from different organizations (even nation-wide and internationally) be integrated (e.g. via the Internet) so patient data can be shared and exchanged across organizations and collaborative diagnosis, and research can be conducted to provide better and comprehensive services to patients. There are two primary technical challenges here: (1) how to integrate and what is the architecture of the integration? (2) how to ensure secure and fine-controlled data exchange/access/sharing across organizations in a flexible and efficient way? Some projects are going on in this integration effort, for example, the Regional Health Information Organization (RHIO) initiative, but these projects have not provided promising results. One big issue is related to Master Patient Index (MPI). Fortunately, our innovative technology is not only good at implementing various security functions, but also suited well for integration of heterogeneous MIS systems without requirement for MPI.

7.3   Architecture of the Proposed Secure MIS

As discussed above, dependability and security are very important and imperative for new generation MIS systems. We have invented advanced security and dependability technologies, such as the Access Control Polynomial (ACP) based key management mechanism and grid-computing based reliability services. These technologies are well suited for MIS systems. Due to the power of our new ACP mechanism (see Section 6.4.1), different functions/services required in the MIS can be implemented efficiently and flexibly. We have implemented our ACP mechanism into a real MIS. The result has been recently featured by the news [Schneider (2006)]. We present the result and describe the architecture of the implemented secure MIS system here. Some parameters and data we have cited are either normalized or shifted so as to maintain the patients' data privacy as put forth in the agreement with the VA and DoD Sponsors, but we still retain sufficient context and clear examples for the purpose of illustration. Moreover, besides securing MIS systems, the ACP mechanism can be applied to various other collaborative computing applications that require all those security needs, such as financial systems, information forensics, government systems, distributed signal processing, etc.

The organization of this section is as follows. We will first present the system architecture of the ACP based MIS system. Then we will show that all the security functions, i.e. Secure Group Communication (SGC)/Secure Dynamic Conferencing (SDC), Differential Access Control (DIF-AC), Hierarchical Access Control (HAC), prevail in the MIS and are supported by our ACP mechanism. Finally, we will discuss some prominent features resulting from the integration of our ACP mechanism with MIS.

7.3.1 *System Architecture*

Figure 7.1 shows the architecture of the ACP based secure MIS system. Three main security components are added into the existing MIS system: ACP Key Management Server (KMS), Secure Server (SS), and User Application (UA). The UA module is integrated in the existing client application, the SS is configured to stand at the front of each existing database/application server and the KMS offers comprehensive key management services (It is worthy to note that the integration did not change anything in the existing systems). The three components work together to provide comprehensive security services involved in MISs. Let us begin the simple case that a user (e.g., a doctor) accesses a patient data and how access control and confidentiality are enforced, and then dig into more interesting but complicated functions and how the ACP mechanism supports them based on various security needs.

When a doctor accesses a patient's data (assume that the doctor has logged in and been authenticated) (Step 1,3 in Figure 7.1), the request with the patient's basic information is sent to the SS (Step 2) which is standing in front of the database server. The SS passes the request to the database server and obtains the patient's record, including patient ID (PID) and other required fields (Step 4). The SS then passes the user's UID and the patient's PID to the KMS (Step 5). The KMS then checks the access control hierarchy against the UID and PID. Because the hierarchy specifies which groups of users can access which groups of patient records in which granularity, the KMS can validate whether and how the user can access the patient (Step 9). If yes, the KMS generates a random key and the ACP polynomial $A(x)$ according to the hierarchy and hides the key in $P(x)$ (Step 10) and sends $(z, P(x))$ back to the SS (Step 11, See Eq.(6.1) and Eq.(6.2) in Section 6.4.1 for the definition and formula of $A(x)$ and $P(x)$). The SS then derives the key from $P(x)$ (Step 12) and encrypts the data (Step 13)

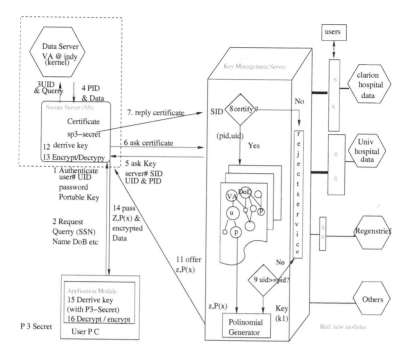

Fig. 7.1   ACP based Secure Medical Information System.

and sends the data along with $(z, P(x))$ to the user (Step 14). The user can derive the key from $P(x)$ (Step 15) and the decrypts the data (Step 16). Note, the SS is treated as a (super)user and belongs to the highest node of one organization's hierarchy, thus the SS can derive the key also under the HAC design. It is worthy to note that the ACP mechanism does not constrain data types. Patient data could be in the form of text, images, video, audio, multimedia, etc. Our security scheme can seamlessly encrypt all of them and guarantee their confidentiality and integrity.

7.3.2   Security Functions Supported by ACP

The central component in the MIS system is hierarchical access relation between users (e.g., doctors, nurses, hospital clerks, insurance personnel, etc.) and patients. This is a typical HAC scenario which has been correctly implemented and enforced by our ACP mechanism (See Section 6.4.1). For example, in Figure 7.2, suppose a physician p_2 in node P_2 wants to access patient data d_8 in node P_8. The KMS will generate a random key K. The patient data will be encrypted using K before the data is sent back to the physician. The K will be hidden in the polynomial $P(x) = A(x) + K$ where $A(x) = (x - f(CID_8, z))(x - f(CID_4, z))(x - f(CID_5, z))(x - f(CID_2, z))$ and CID_i is the secret node ID for node i and it is only known to the users of node i. Thus, physician p_2 can obtain K first and then decrypt the patient data and use it.

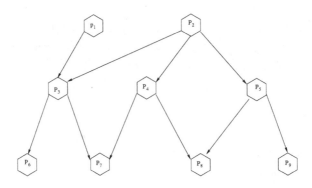

Fig. 7.2   A physician and patient access hierarchy.

The Differential Access Control (DIF-AC) also appears in MIS. One basic format of DIF-AC is that one patient has multiple doctors, such as his family physician and multiple specialists, and these doctors share the patient' information; on the other hand, a family physician can have multiple patients. Another format of DIF-AC is the following many-to-many relation: for any patient belonging to a node, his data can be accessed by all the users belonging to this node and the ancestral nodes; correspondingly, a user belonging to a node can access the patient data of his node as well as all his descendant nodes. Yet, some other DIF-AC format is that a doctor transmits some notifications to his patients or a hospital announces some events to certain patients. No matter which kind of DIF-AC, our ACP scheme can support and enforce it correctly.

Sscure Group Communication (SGC) and Secure Dynamic Conferencing (SDC) scenarios occur often in MIS. One case is that a patient's data is located in several databases. The data need to be collected from all these databases. The data need to then be encrypted for transmission. Thus, the SSs in front of these databases form a temporary conference and the KMS generates a key for this transmission and hides the key in the $P(x)$ which is formed from these SSs. Another typical scenario for SGC/SDC is tele-medicine. Our ACP based SGC scheme will enable tele-medicine to be highly secure with great power.

7.3.3   Tele-medicine Service

Tele-medicine is the utmost goal of MIS systems. In Tele-medicine, physicians and specialists from geographically distant locations in the U.S., even worldwide, collaborate to investigate some common diseases, such as SARS, diagnose a patient illness, and participate in or instruct a tough surgery. Most of them need to share the real-time image signals/streams and audio/video information. The size of data transmitted through the Internet could be huge (such as images). Therefore, the communication channels will be unstable due to the long distance. The above ACP based security mechanism is generic and independent from data content, formats, or volumes; therefore, it can be applied to secure tele-medicine. As for reliability of tele-medicine, we will introduce our new grid-computing based reliability mechanism which can provide comprehensive reliability services for MIS in Section 7.4. Here we propose using an effective technology to improve the reliability for data transmission: checkpoint. After the data is encrypted, the transmission begins. During the transmission, checkpoints are set up. At each checkpoint, the sender and receiver exchange signals to make sure the data that have been received before this point are correct. The signal sent by the receiver can include the check information, such as the length of received data and a section of codes for parity check. The sender will compare the signal from the receiver with the real values. If they are matched, it means the information before the checkpoint has been correctly received without loss or errors. Thus, the data being transmitted between two checkpoints is temporarily cached in the memory. In the case that the confirmation signal is wrong at the checkpoint, it means some errors occur during the communication, and the cached information between the two checkpoints will be resent. When it passes the check, the temporary cached data can be deleted and the cache storage can be used for the next section of data. Thus, the extra memory reserved for the checkpoint scheme will be no more than the data between two checkpoints. As a result, this scheme can reach a very high reliability for data transmission and is very efficient compared to the prior scheme, which includes resending the large file again when the receiver cannot read it (perhaps just due to the loss/error of a small section of information). In addition, the overhead of this scheme is small (<1%) in time.

Apart from the security and reliability guaranty for tele-medicine, we propose to enhance the Tele-medicine service including the following functions: remote diagnosis involving multiple doctors' collaboration, real-time and mobile communication and data sharing as dynamic conferencing, and faster, smoother multimedia stream (e.g. visualization) by the Grid Computing and P2P technology.

7.3.4 *Additional Features Resulting from the ACP Mechanism*

Apart from its supports to SGC/SDC, DIF-AC, and HAC, the ACP mechanism also provides several important advantages for MIS, such as seamless integration of different data sources, fine-tuned access control in flexible granularity, and portable login and accessing to patient data from anywhere. As it can be seen from the above description, the ACP mechanism supports random HAC structures, including multiple roots. This makes data sharing and integration of different data sources/systems easier. Looking at Figure 7.1, there are two roots: one for VA and the other for DoD. Through appropriate connection among the nodes in the VA access hierarchy and the DoD access hierarchy, the correct sharing (and control) between VA data sources and DoD data sources can be effectively implemented.

The ACP scheme is so powerful that it can support the fine-tuned granularity access control in the sense that not only the record level access is enforced but also the field level access is implemented. For example, common patient data, such as name and date of birth, are accessible to any valid users, including nurses and health insurance personnel, the sensitive information and disease information can only be accessible to certain doctors, and some historical information, such as allergies, can be accessible to all doctors. Due to the "on the fly" property of the ACP mechanism, the different fields of a patient record can be encrypted by different keys which are hidden in different polynomials $P(x)$s. These polynomials, due to its specific construction, can control who can derive which keys and then decrypt which fields.

One other advantage is that since each user is assigned his own Permanent Personal Secret, the secret can be saved in some portable storage device, such as a USB card. Thus, the user can take the portable media and log in to the MIS system from anywhere. This Permanent Personal Secret also strengthens the implemented MIS system by dual authentications: *what you know* (i.e., user name and password) and *what you have* (i.e., the portable storage media). Thus, stealing either the password or the

Permanent Personal Secret will be detected. One last advantage of our ACP based MIS system is that the three components are quite independent from the existing systems and can be integrated into the existing MIS systems without much modification of the existing systems/databases and without affecting the existing security functions.

In summary, the new proposed ACP mechanism has been validated to be powerful and practical by being implemented and integrated into a real MIS system. The ACP based MIS system has the following properties: 1) support all security functions required by the MIS in a uniform manner; 2) support the seamless integration of different data sources/systems without the need for centralized master patient index (MPI); 3) provide fine-tuned access control in terms of users, user groups, data domains, data records, and record fields; 4) provide portability; and 5) support secure tele-medicine.

7.4 Dependable MIS based on Grid Computing Technology

Reliability is extremely important for information systems, including MIS. Traditional techniques of using duplication can enhance the capability of fault-tolerance and thus, reliability, but can potentially affect the performance. Tai et al. [Tai *et al.* (1993)] mentioned that there exists tradeoff between performance and reliability. When more components are duplicated for completing the same subtask in order to reach a high reliability, the performance can be decreased due to the lack of full load sharing. On the contrary, if a task is fully divided into disjoint subtasks shared by the resources without duplication, any single failure can cause the incompletion of the task. Grid computing [Foster and Kesselman (2003)] is a newly developed technology for complex systems with large-scale resource sharing, wide-area communication, and multi-institutional collaboration etc, see e.g. [Berman *et al.* (2003); Das *et al.* (2001); Foster *et al.* (2002, 2001); Kumar (2000)]. Many experts believe that grid technologies will offer a second chance to fulfill the promises of the Internet. A novel Grid computing architecture proposed in [Dai *et al.* (2007)] offers a new reliability technique, instead of the prior duplication, and thus performance and reliability do not negatively affect each other, but both are improved.

The new services based on grid computing technology include the caching and coherence service, backup and recovery service, fault-tolerant service, and self-healing service [Dai *et al.* (2007)]. We briefly describe each of them below.

- Caching and coherence service. By building a caching module using a portion of disk in the client machine to temporarily store the recently requested results, one can in fact retrieve most of the data directly from its cache on the local disk when the user requests the data again. By this means, the caching service can alleviate the bottleneck of network transmission and achieve high performance. One problem with caching is data consistency, which means that the data in one's local cache may be out-of-date and inconsistent with the data in the server or other caches. Coherence service with update request buffer will solve this problem [Dai *et al.* (2007)].

- Backup and recovery service. Traditionally, the backup of a database was to duplicate at least one redundant databases. This will double the cost. The new grid based backup service can significantly save money while maintaining the same availability as the duplicated database backup scheme. The idea is as follows. During subscription to the Resource Management Service (RMS), a data source will be asked to reserve a portion of its disk space for the RMS to use, and as a return, same portion of space for backing up its data will be free of charge. Then the data sources can mutually backup each other's data. (Note: in order to prevent the data of one data source A from the access of data source B when it is backed up in B, encryption and key management mechanisms can be applied.) This way, once a data source was damaged totally, its data can be completely recovered from the backups in other data sources.

- Fault-tolerant service. Fault-tolerance means that a user can successfully get the requested data even though some faults or failures may occur when he requests the service. The grid-based information system can provide a strong capability to tolerate faults without additional cost or hardware through the following steps: fetch from one's own local cache, visit to its data source, go to backup data source, search other local caches, and resort to self-healing.

- Self-healing service. The self-healing mechanism will make use of the computation resources in the Grid system (such as the idle machines). The following three services, when integrated together, realize the intelligent self-healing service: Fault-Detection service, Diagnosis service, and Curing service. Fault-detection service will be automatically run in the grid system and detect any system fault or failure. Once faults or failures are detected, the diagnosis service is triggered. It will monitor (specific) regions and nodes and analyze the causes for the combination of symptoms, such as the over-used memory, the over-slow CPU, the virus infections, the network traffic jams, etc. After diagnosis, the curing service is activated. It will match some possible prescriptions based on the diagnosed results and assign actuators to heal the problem according to the prescriptions.

The MIS system is very sensitive to reliability. An unreliable or faulty MIS system could be a disaster and may damage people's lives. Fortunately, the MIS system we are designing includes the reliability model and modules as its coherent components. In particular, the above described highly robust reliability services based on grid computing technology, when integrated into the MIS system, will greatly increase the dependability of the MIS system.

7.5 Conclusion

The secure and dependable medical information system will benefit everyone. Security and reliability come as two important and safety-critical concerns in developing any mission-critical information systems like medical information system. We, collaborating with the Veterans Affairs hospitals (VA) and Indiana University Medical School, have implemented a preliminary secure medical information system [Goldschmidt (2005)]. The security and reliability model and the seamless integration capability of the model have been proven via this system. We are planning to extend it into the larger scope of MIS systems, such as Regional Health Information Organization (RHIO) and finally the nation-wide health information system.

This chapter presented the core concepts and techniques of security and reliability for MIS system. Along with further development of the MIS systems, new modules and methods will be designed and presented.

Bibliography

Abdalla, M., Shavitt, Y. and Wool, A. (2000). Key management for restricted multicast using broadcast encryption, *IEEE/ACM Transactions on Networking(TON)* , pp. 443–454.

Abraham, A. and Jain, R. (2004). Soft computing models for network intrusion detection systems, *http://falklands.globat.com/ softcomputing.net/saman2.pdf* .

Abramson, D., Buyya, R. and Giddy, J. (2002). A computational economy for grid computing and its implementation in the nimrod-g resource broker, *Future Generation Computer Systems* **18**, 28, pp. 1061–1074.

Adusumili, P. and Zou, X. (2005). KTDCKM-SDC: A distributed conference key management scheme for secure dynamic conferencing, *Proceedings of THE TENTH IEEE SYMPOSIUM ON COMPUTERS AND COMMUNICATIONS (ISCC)* , pp. 476–481.

Adusumilli, P., Zou, X. and Ramamurthy, B. (2005). DGKD: Distributed group key distribution with authentication capability, *Proceedings of 2005 IEEE Workshop on Information Assurance and Security, West Point, NY, USA*, pp. 476–481.

Agrawal, M., Kayal, N. and Saxena, N. (2002). A deterministic poly-time primality testing algorithm, *IIT Kanpur, India, available at http://www.cse.iitk.ac.in/users/manindra/primality.ps, accessed in June 2004* .

Akl, S. G. and Taylor, P. D. (1983). Cryptographic solution to a problem of access control in a hierarchy, *ACM Transactions on Computer Systems* **1**, 3, pp. 239–247.

Al-Duwairi, B. and Govindarasu, M. (2006). Novel hybrid schemes employing packet marking and logging for ip traceback, *IEEE Transactions on Parallel and Distributed Systems* **17**, 5, pp. 403–418.

Al-Kahtani, M. A. and Sandhu, R. (2004). Rule-based RBAC with negative authorization, *20th Annual Computer Security Applications Conference (ACSAC'04)* , pp. 405–415.

Alert, I. S. S. S. (2000). Trinity v3 distributed denial of service tool, *http://xforce.iss.net/xforce/alerts/id/advise59* .

Asaka, M., Taguchi, A. and Goto, S. (1999). The implementation of IDA: An intrusion detection agent system, *Proceedings of the 11th Annual FIRST Conference on Computer Security Incident Handling and Response* , pp. 2–11.

Asokan, N. and Ginzboorg, P. (2000). Key agreement in ad-hoc networks, in *Computer Communications*, Vol. 23, pp. 1627–1637.

Atallah, M. J., Blanton, M. and Frikken, K. B. (2006). Key management for non-tree access hierarchies, *ACM SACMAT'06* , pp. 11–18.

Atallah, M. J., Frikken, K. B. and Blanton, M. (2005). Dynamic and efficient key management for access hierarchies, *ACM CCS'05* , pp. 190–202.

Ayres, P. E., Sun, H., Chao, H. J. and Lau, W. C. (2006). Alpi: A ddos defense system for high-speed networks, *IEEE Journal on Selected Areas in Communications* **24**, 10, pp. 1864–1876.

Bakkardie, A. (1996). Scalable multicast key distribution, *RFC 1949* .

Balachandran, R., Ramamurthy, B., Zou, X. and Vinodchandran, N. (2005). CRTDH: An efficient key agreement scheme for secure group communications in wireless ad hoc networks, *Proceedings of IEEE ICC 2005* .

Balasubramaniyan, J. S., Garcia-Fernandez, J. O., Isacoff, D., Spafford, E. and Zamboni, D. (1998). An architecture for intrusion detection using autonomous agents, *14th Annual Computer Security Applications Conference*, pp. 13–20.

Bar-Haim, P. (2001). The NDS guide to conditional access, *http://www.broadcastpapers.com/satellite/NDSGuide CondAccess103.htm, accessed in May 2005* .

Barlow, J. and Thrower, W. (2000). TFN2K– an analysis, *http://www.securiteam.com/securitynews/5YP0G000FS.html* .

Basagni, S., Herrin, K., Rosti, E. and Bruschi, D. (2001). Secure pebblenets, in *In Proc. of ACM International Symposium on Mobile Ad-Hoc Networking and Computing (MobiHoc).*

Becker, C. and Wille, U. (1998). Communication complexity of group key distribution, in *In Proc. of 5th ACM Conference on Computer and Communication Security.*

Bell, D. and LaPadula, L. (1973). Secure computer systems: Mathematical foundations, *Technical Report, MTR2547, MITRE Corporation* .

Bellovin, S. M. (2000). ICMP traceback messages, *Internet Draft, IETF, draft-bellovin-itrace-05.txt* .

Bencsath, B. and Vajda, I. (2004). Protection against ddos attacks based on traffic level measurements, *Western Simulation MultiConference, CA. USA* .

Berman, F., Wolski, R., Casanova, H., Cirne, W., Dail, H., Faerman, M., Figueira, S., Hayes, J., Obertelli, G., Schopf, J., Shao, G., Smallen, S., Spring, N., Su, A. and Zagorodnov, D. (2003). Adaptive computing on the grid using apples, *IEEE Transactions on Parallel and Distributed Systems* **14**, 14, pp. 369–382.

Bishop, M. (2003). *Computer Security: Art and Science* (Second Edition, Addison Wesley), ISBN 0-201-44099-7.

Blundo, C., D'Arco, P., Santis, A. D. and Listo, M. (2004). Design of self-healing key distribution schemes, *Des. Codes Cryptography* **32**, 1-3, pp. 15–44, doi: http://dx.doi.org/10.1023/B:DESI.0000029210.20690.3f.

Blundo, C., Mattos, L. A. F. and Stinson, D. R. (1998a). Generalied beimel-chor scheme for broadcast encryption and interactive key distribution, *Theoretical Computer Science* **200**, pp. 313–334.

Blundo, C., Mattos, L. A. F. and Stinson, D. R. (1998b). Generalized Beimel-Chor scheme for broadcast encryption and interactive key distribution, *Theoretical Computer Science* **200**, 1-2, pp. 313–334.

Blundo, C., Santis, A. D., Herzberg, A., Kutten, S., Vaccaro, U. and Yung, M. (1993). Perfect secure key distribution for dynamic conferences, *Advances in Cryptology - CRYPTO'92, LNCS, Springer, Berlin* **740**, pp. 471–486.

Bolzoni, D., Etalle, S., Hartel, P. and Zambon, E. (2006). POSEIDON: a 2-tier anomaly-based network intrusion detection system, *Fourth IEEE International Workshop on Information Assurance* , pp. 144–156.

Bresson, E., Chevassut, O. and Pointcheval, D. (2001). Provably authenticated group diffie-hellman key exchange - the dynamic case, *ASIACRYPT '01: Proceedings of the 7th International Conference on the Theory and Application of Cryptology and Information Security* .

Briscoe, B. (1999). MARKS: Multicast key management using arbitrarily revealed key sequences, *Proceedings of 1st International Workshop on Networked Group Communication* .

Burmester, M. and Desmedt, Y. (1994). A secure and efficient conference key distribution system, in *In Advances in Cryptology - EUROCRYPT*.

Canetti, R., Garay, J., Itkis, G., Micciancio, D., Naor, M. and Pinkas, B. (1999a). Multicast security: a taxonomy and some efficient constructions, *Proceedings of INFOCOM'99: Conference on Computer Communications* **2**, pp. 708–716.

Canetti, R., Malkin, T. and Nissim, K. (1999b). Efficient communication-storage tradeoffs for multicast encryption, *Lecture Notes in Computer Science (Advances in Cryptology-EUROCRYPT'99)* **1592**, pp. 459–470.

Cao, J., Jarvis, S. A., Saini, S., Kerbyson, D. J. and Nudd, G. R. (2002). An agent-based resource management system for grid computing, *Scientific Programming* **2**, 10, pp. 135–148.

Caronni, G., Waldvogel, K., Sun, D. and Plattner, B. (1998). Efficient security for large and dynamic multicast groups, *Proceedings of the Seventh IEEE International Workshop on Enabling Technologies: Infrastructure for Collaborative Enterprises (WETICE '98) (Cat. No.98TB100253)* , pp. 376–383.

Chang, C. and Buehrer, D. (1993). Access control in a hierarchy using a one-way trapdoor function, *Computers and Mathematics with Applications* **26**, 5, pp. 71–76.

Chang, C.-C., Lin, I.-C., Tsai, H.-M. and Wang, H.-H. (2004). A key assignment scheme for controlling access in partially ordered user hierarchies, in *AINA (2)*, pp. 376–379.

Chen, D. J., Chen, R. S. and Huang, T. H. (1997). A heuristic approach to generating file spanning trees for reliability analysis of distributed computing systems, *Computers and Mathematics with Application* , pp. 225–131.

Chen, D. J. and Huang, T. H. (1992). Reliability analysis of distributed systems based on a fast reliability algorithm, *IEEE Transactions on Parallel and Distributed Systems*, pp. 139–154.

Chen, T. and Chung, Y. (2002). Hierarchical access control based on chinese remainder theorem and symmetric algorithm, *Computers and Security* **21**, 6, pp. 565–570.

Chen, T.-S., Chung, Y.-F. and Tian, C.-S. (2004). A novel key management scheme for dynamic access control in a user hierarchy, in *COMPSAC*, pp. 396–397.

Chick, G. C. and Tavares, S. E. (1989). Flexible access control with master keys, *Proceedings on Advances in Cryptology: CRYPTO '89, LNCS* **435**, pp. 316–322.

Chien, H. (2004). An efficient time-bound hierarchical key assignment scheme, *IEEE Transactions on Knowledge and Data Engineering* **16**, 10, pp. 1301–1304.

Chien, H. and Jan, J. (2003). New hierarchical assignment without public key cryptography, *Computers and Security* **22**, 6, pp. 523–526.

Chiou, G. H. and W.T.Chen (1989). Secure broadcasting using the Secure Lock, *IEEE Transactions on Software Engineering* **15**, 8, pp. 929–934.

Chou, J., Lin, C. and Lee, T. (2004). A novel hierarchical key management scheme based on quadratic residues, *Internation Symposium on Parallel and Distributed Processing and Applications (ISPA04)* , pp. 858–865.

Chou, S. T., Stayrou, A., Ioannidis, J. and Keromytis, A. D. (2005). GORE: Routing-assisted defense against ddos attacks, *Proceedings of International Supercomputer Conference* , pp. 179–193.

Cooper, A. and Martin, A. (2006). Towards a secure, tamper-proof grid platform, *Proceedings of the Sixth IEEE International Symposium on Cluster Computing and the Grid* , pp. 373–380.

Costa-Requena, J. (2001). Recent development in ddos research, *http://www.tml.tkk.fi/Studies/T-110.501/2001/papers/jose.requena.pdf* .

Crampton, J. (2003). On permissions, inheritance and role hierarchies, *ACM CCS'03* , pp. 85–92.

Dai, Y., Zou, X. and Guo, Y. (2007). Novel grid services for data access with high performance, fault tolerance and self-healing, *International Journal of High Performance Computing and Networking* **In Press**.

Dai, Y. S., Palakal, M., Hartanto, S., Wang, X. and Guo, Y. (2006). A grid-based pseudo-cache solution for misd biomedical problems with high confidentiality and efficiency, *International Journal of Bioinformatics Research and Applications* **2**, 3, pp. 259–281.

Dai, Y. S., Xie, M. and Poh, K. L. (2002). Analysis of grid computing systems, *IEEE Pacific Rim International Symposium on Dependable Computing (PRDC2002)* , pp. 97–104.

Das, M. L., Saxena, A., Gulati, V. P. and Phatak, D. B. (2005). Hierarchical key management scheme using polynomial interpolation, *SIGOPS Operating Systems Review* **39**, 1, pp. 40–47.

Das, S. K., Harvey, D. J. and Biswas, R. (2001). Parallel processing of adaptive meshes with load balancing, *IEEE Transactions on Parallel and Distributed Systems* **12**, 12, pp. 1269–1280.

Denning, D. E. (1976). A lattice model of secure information flow, *Communications of the ACM* **19**, 5, pp. 236–243.

Denning, D. E. (1987). An intrusion detection model, *IEEE Transaction on Software Engineering* **13**, 2, pp. 222–232.

Desmedt, Y. and Viswanathan, V. (1998). Unconditionally secure dynamic conference key distribution, *Proceedings of the IEEE International Symposium on Information Theory* , pp. 383–383.

Dietrich, S., Long, N. and Dittrich, D. (2000). An analysis of the shaft distributed denial of service tool, *http://www.adelphi.edu/ spock/shaft_analysis.txt* .

Diffie, W. and Hellman, M. E. (1976). Multiuser cryptographic techniques, *AFIPS conference proceedings* **45**, pp. 109–112.

Ding, Q., Chen, G. L. and Gu, J. (2002). A unified resource mapping strategy in computational grid environments, *Journal of Software* **13**, 7, pp. 1303–1308.

Dittrich, D. (1999a). The dos project's trinoo: distributed denial of service attack tool, *http://staff.washington.edu/dittrich/misc/trinoo.analysis.txt* .

Dittrich, D. (1999b). The stacheldraht distributed denial of service attack tool, *http://staff.washington.edu/dittrich/misc/stacheldraht.analysis.txt* .

Dittrich, D. (1999c). The tribe flood network distributed denial of service attack tool, *http://staff.washington.edu/dittrich/misc/tfn.analysis.txt* .

Dittrich, D., Weaver, G., Dietrich, S. and Long, N. (2000). The mstream distributed denial of service attack tool, *http://staff.washington.edu/ dittrich/misc/mstream.analysis.txt* .

Dondeti, L. R., Mukherjee, S. and Samal, A. (1999). A dual encryption protocol for scalable secure multicasting, *In Fourth IEEE Symposium on Computers and Communications* , pp. 2–8.

Dondeti, L. R., Mukherjee, S. and Samal, A. (2000). DISEC: a distributed framework for scalable secure many-to-many communication, *In Proceedings of Fifth IEEE Symposium on Computers and Communications (ISCC 2000)* , pp. 693–698.

ElGamal, T. (1985). A public key cryptosystem and a signature scheme based on discrete logarithms, *IEEE Transactions on Information Theory* **31**, pp. 469–471.

Farag, A. and Muthucumaru, M. (2002). Evolving and managing trust in grid computing systems, *Proceedings of the 2002 IEEE Canadian Conference on Electrical Computer Engineering* **3**, pp. 1424–1429.

Ferraiolo, D. F., Sandhu, R., Gavrila, S., Kuhn, D. R. and Chandramouli, R. (2001). Proposed nist standard for role-based access control, *ACM Transactions on Information and System Security (TISSEC)* **4**, 3, pp. 224–274.

Forrest, S., Hofmeyr, S. A., Somayaji, A. and Longstaff, T. A. (1996). A sense of self for Unix Processes, *IEEE Symposium on Security and Privacy* , pp. 0120–0126.

Foster, I., Kessekan, C., Tsudik, G. and Tueckel, S. (1998). A security architecture for computational grid, *Proceedings of ACM Conference on Computer and Communication Security (CCS)* , pp. 83–92.

Foster, I. and Kesselman, C. (1997). Globus: A metacomputing infrastructure toolkit, *International Journal of Supercomputer Applications* **11**, 2, pp. 115–128.

Foster, I. and Kesselman, C. (2003). The grid 2: Blueprint for a new computing infrastructure, *Morgan-Kaufmann* .

Foster, I., Kesselman, C., Nick, J. M. and Tuecke, S. (2002). Grid services for distributed system integration, *Computer* **35**, 6, pp. 37–46.

Foster, I., Kesselman, C., Nick, J. M. and Tuecke, S. (2005). The physiology of the grid: An open grid services architecture for distributed systems integration, *Open Grid Service Infrastructure WG, Global Grid Forum* .

Foster, I., Kesselman, C. and Tuecke, S. (2001). The anatomy of the grid: Enabling scalable virtual organizations, *International Journal of High Performance Computing Applications* **15**, 2, pp. 200–222.

Geng, X. J. and Whinston, A. B. (2000). Defeating distributed denial of service attacks, *IT Professional* **2**, 4, pp. 36–42.

Goldschmidt, P. G. (2005). HIT and MIS: implications of health information technology and medical information systems, *Communications of ACM* **48**, 10, pp. 68–74.

Gong, L., Hui, R., Zulkernine, M. and Abolmaesumi, P. (2005). A software implementation of a genetic algorithm based approach to network intrusion detection, *Proceedings of the Sixth International Conference on Software Engineering, Artificial Intelligence, Networking and Parallel/Distributed Computing* .

Gouda, M. G., Huang, C.-T. and Elnozahy, E. N. (2002a). Key trees and the security of interval multicast, *Proceedings 22nd International Conference on Distributed Computing Systems* , pp. 467–468.

Gouda, M. G., Huang, C.-T. and Elnozahy, E. N. (2002b). Key trees and the security of interval multicast, *Technical Report TR-02-18, Department of Computer Sciences, The University of Texas at Austin, Austin, Texas* .

Grassi, V., Donatiello, L. and Iazeolla, G. (1980). Performability evaluation of multicomponent fault tolerant systems, *IEEE Transactions on Reliability* **37**, 2, pp. 225–131.

Group, L. T. I. (2004). Phatbot trojan analysis, *http://www.lurhq.com/phatbot.html* .

Guangchun, L., Xianliang, L., Jiong, L. and Jun, Z. (2003). MADIDS: a novel distributed ids based on mobile agent, *ACM SIGOPS Operating Systems Review Vol. 37* , pp. 46–53.

Hamey, H. and Muckenhim, C. (1997a). Group Key Management Protocol (GKMP) Architecture and Specification, *RCF 2093 and 2094* .

Hamey, H. and Muckenhim, C. (1997b). Group Key Management Protocol (GKMP) Specification, *RCF 2093* .

Harn, L. and Lin, H. Y. (1990). A cryptographic key generation scheme for multilevel data security, *Computers and Security* **9**, 6, pp. 539–546.

Harrison, M., Ruzzoand, W. and Ullman, J. (1976). Protection in operating systems, *Communications of the ACM* **19**, 8, pp. 461–471.

Hassan, H. M., Mahmoud, M. and El-Kassas, S. (2006). Securing the aodv protocol using specification-based intrusion detection, *Proceedings of the 2nd ACM international workshop on Quality of service and security for wireless and mobile networks* , pp. 33–36.

He, M., Fan, P., Kaderali, F. and Yuan, D. (2003). Access key distribution scheme for level-based hierarchy, *International Conference on Parallel and Distributed Computing, Applications and Technologies (PDCAT03)* , pp. 942–945.

Heberlein, L. T., Dias, G. V., Levitt, K. N., Mukherjee, B., Wood, J. and Wolber, D. (1990). A network security monitor, *Proceedings of IEEE Computer Society Symposium on Research in Security and Privacy* , pp. 296–304.

Hietalahti, M. (2001). *Efficient Key Agreement for Ad-hoc Networks*, Master's thesis, Helsinki University of Technology.

HIPAA (1996). Health insurance portability and accountability act of 1996 (hipaa), *U.S. Department of Health and Human Services* .

Hofmeyr, S. A. and Forrest, S. (1999). Immunity by design: An artificial immune system, in *Proceedings of the Genetic and Evolutionary Computation Conference*, Vol. 2, pp. 1289–1296, URL `citeseer.ist.psu.edu/hofmeyr99immunity.html`.

Hsu, C. L. and Wu, T. S. (2003). Cryptanalyses and improvements of two cryptographic key assignment schemes for dynamic access control in a user hierarchy, *Computers and Security* **22**, 5, pp. 453–456.

Huang, Y.-L., Shieh, S.-P. W. and Wang, J.-C. (2000). Practical key distribution schemes for channel protection, *Proceedings of the Twenty-Fourth Annual International Computer Software and Applications Conference (COMPSAC'00)* , pp. 569–575.

Humphrey, M. and Thompson, M. R. (2002). Security implications of typical grid computing usage scenarios, *Cluster Computing* **5**, 3, pp. 257–264.

Hwang, M. (1999). An improvement of novel cryptographic key assignment scheme for dynamic access control in a hierarchy, *IEICE Trans. Fundamentals* **E82A**, 2, pp. 548–550.

Hwang, M. and Yang, W. (2003). Controlling access in large partially ordered hierarchies using cryptographic keys, *Journal of Systems and Software* **67**, 2, pp. 99–107.

Ilgun, K. (1993). USTAT: A real-time intrusion detection system for UNIX, *Proceedings of the IEEE Symp. Research in Security and Privacy* , pp. 16–28.

Ingemarsson, I., Tang, D. and Wong, C. (1982). A conference key distribution system, *IEEE Transactions on Information Theory* **28**, 5, pp. 714–720.

Institute, S. (2000). Help defeat distributed denial of service attacks: Step-by-step, *http://www.sans.org/dosstep/* .

Ioannidis, J. and Bellovin, S. (2002). Implementing pushback: Router-based defense against ddos attacks, *NDSS Conference Proceedings* , pp. 6–8.

Jin, C., Wang, H. and Shin, K. (2003a). Hop-count filtering: An effective defense against spoofed DDoS traffic, in *Proceedings of the 10th ACM International*

Conference on Computer and Communications Security (CCS), pp. 30–41,
URL citeseer.ist.psu.edu/jin03hopcount.html.

Jin, C., Wang, H. and Shin, K. G. (2003b). Hop-count filtering: an effective
defense against spoofed ddos traffic, *In Proceedings of the 10th ACM conference on Computer and communication security(CCS)* , pp. 30–41.

Jin, X., Zhang, Y., Pan, Y. and Zhou, Y. (2006). ZSBT: A novel algorithm for
tracing dos attackers in manets, *EURASIP Journal on Wireless Communications and Networking* **Vol. 2006**, pp. 1–9.

Kannadiga, P. and Zulkernine, M. (2005). DIDMA: A distributed intrusion detec-
tion system using mobile agents, *The Proceedings of the Sixth International
Conference on Software Engineering, Artificial Intelligence, Networking and
Parallel/Distributed Computing and First ACIS International Workshop on
Self-Assembling Wireless Networks* , pp. 238– 245.

Karandikar, Y., Zou, X. and Dai, Y. (2006). An effective key management approach to differential access control in dynamic environments, *Journal of
Computer Science* **2**, 6, pp. 542–549.

Katz, J. and Yung, M. (2003). Sclable protocols for authenticated group key
exchange, in *Crypto 2003*, pp. 110–125.

Kaufman, C., Perlman, R. and Speciner, M. (2002). *Network security: private
communication in a public world* (Prentice Hall, Upper Saddle River, NJ,
USA), ISBN 0-13-046019-2.

Kenney, M. (1996). Ping of death, *http://insecure.org/sploits/ping-o-death.html* .

Keromytis, A. D., Misra, V. and Rubenstein, D. (2004). SOS: An architecture for
mitigating ddos attacks, *IEEE Journal on Selected Areas in Communications (JSAC), special issue on Recent Advances in Service Overlay Networks*
22, 1, pp. 176–188.

Khattab, S. M., Sangpachatanaruk, C., Mosse, D., Melhem, R. and Znati, T.
(2004). Roaming honeypots for mitigating service-level denial-of-service attacks, *Proceedings of ICDCS* , pp. 328–337.

Kim, H., Li, S. and Lee, D. (2004a). Sclable protocols for authenticated group
key exchange, in *Asiacrypt 2004*.

Kim, Y. and Helmy, A. (2006). Attacker traceback with cross-layer monitoring in
wireless multi-hop networks, in *SASN '06: Proceedings of the fourth ACM
workshop on Security of ad hoc and sensor networks* (ACM Press, New
York, NY, USA), ISBN 1-59593-554-1, pp. 123–134, doi:http://doi.acm.
org/10.1145/1180345.1180361.

Kim, Y., Lau, W. C., Chua, M. C. and Chao, H. J. (2004b). Packetscore:
Statistics-based overload control against distributed denial-of-service attacks, *IEEE INFOCOM* .

Kim, Y., Perrig, A. and Tsudik, G. (2000a). Simple and fault-tolerant key agreement for dynamic collaborative groups, *In Proceedings of the 7th ACM
Conference on Computer and Communications Security (ACM CCS 2000)*,
pp. 235–244.

Kim, Y., Perrig, A. and Tsudik, G. (2000b). Simple and fault-tolerant key agreement for dynamic collaborative groups, in *In Proc. of the 7th ACM Conference on Computer and Communication Security*, pp. 235–244.

Kim, Y., Perrig, A. and Tsudik, G. (2004c). Tree-based group key agreement, *ACM Transactions on Information Systems Security* **7**, 1, pp. 60–96.

Ko, C., Fink, G. and Levitt, K. (1994). Automated detection of vulnerabilities in privileged programs by execution monitoring, *Proceedings of 10th Annual Computer Security Applications Conference* , pp. 134–144.

Koblitz, N. (1994). *A Course in Number Theory and Cryptography* (Springer, Verlag, NY, USA), ISBN 3-540-94293-9.

Kogan, N., Shavitt, Y. and Wool, A. (2003). A practical revocation scheme for broadcast encryption using smart cards, *Proceedings of the 2003 IEEE Symposium on Security and Privacy (SP03)* , pp. 225–235.

Korty, A. (2000). mstream forensics analysis, *http://itso.iu.edu/staff/ajk/mstream/* .

Koutepas, G., Stamatelopoulos, F. and Maglaris, B. (2004). Distributed management architecture for cooperative detection and reaction to ddos attacks, *Journal of Network and Systems Management Vol. 12* , pp. 73–94.

Krauter, K., Buyya, R. and Maheswaran, M. (2002). A taxonomy and survey of grid resource management systems for distributed computing, *Software - Practice and Experience* **32**, 2, pp. 135–164.

Krawetz, N. (2004). Anti-honeypot technology, *IEEE Security and Privacy Magazine* **2**, 1, pp. 76–79.

Kumar, A. (2000). An efficient supergrid protocol for high availability and load balancing, *IEEE Transactions on Computers* **49**, 10, pp. 1126–1133.

Kumar, S. and Spafford, E. (1994). A pattern matching model for misuse intrusion detection, *Proceedings of 17th Nat'l Computer Security Conference* , pp. 11–21.

Kumar, V. K. P., Hariri, S. and Ragavendra, C. S. (1986). Distributed program reliability analysis, *IEEE Transactions on Software Engineering* , pp. 42–50.

Lampson, B. (1974). Protection (computer system access), *Operating Systems Review* **8**, 1, pp. 18–24.

Lang, B., Foster, I., Siebenlist, F., Ananthakrishnan, R. and Freeman, T. (2006). A multipolicy authorization framework for grid security, *Proceedings of the Fifth IEEE International Symposium on Network Computing and Applications* , pp. 269–272.

Lee, H. C., Thing, V. L., Xu, Y. and Ma, M. (2003). Icmp traceback with cumulative path, an efficient solution for ip traceback, *Lecture Notes in Computer Science* **2836**, pp. 124–135.

Lee, P., Lui, J. and Yau, D. (2002). Distributed collaborative key agreement protocols for dynamic peer groups, *Proc. IEEE Int'l Conf. Network Protocols (ICNP)* , pp. 322–333.

Lee, S. C. and Shields, C. (2001). Tracing the source of network attack: A technical, legal and societal problem, *Proceedings of the 2001 IEEE Workshop on Information Assurance and Security* , pp. 239–246.

Lee, W., Stolfo, S. J. and Mok, K. W. (1999). A data mining framework for building intrusion detection models, *1999 IEEE Symposium on Security and Privacy* , pp. 120–129.

Leu, F.-Y., Li, M.-C. and Lin, J.-C. (2006). Intrusion detection based on grid, *In the Proceedings of the International Multi-Conference on Computing in the Global Information Technology* . .

Levitin, G. (ed.) (2003). *Universal generating function in reliability analysis and optimization* (Morgan-Kaufmann, San Fransisco, CA).

Li, J. and Cordes, D. (2005). A scalable authorization approach for the globus grid system, *Future Generation Computer Systems* **21**, 2, pp. 291–301.

Li, M., Cui, Y., Tian, Y., Wang, D. and Yan, S. (2006). A new architecture of grid security system construction, *Proceedings of the 2006 International Conference on Parallel Processing Workshops* , pp. 1–6.

Li, X., Wang, Y. and Frieder, O. (2002). Efficient hybrid key agreement protocol for wireless ad-hoc networks, in *IEEE 11th International Conference on Computer, Communication and Networks*, pp. 404–409.

Li, X., Yang, Y., Gouda, M. and Lam, S. (2001). Batch rekeying for secure group communications, *Proc. 10th Int'l WWW Conf.* , pp. 525–534.

Lidl, R. and Niederreiter, H. (1986). *Introduction to finite fields and their applications* (Cambridge University Press, New York, NY, USA), ISBN 0-521-30706-6.

Lin, C. (2001). Hierarchical key assignment without public-key cryptography, *Computers and Security* **20**, 7, pp. 612–619.

Lin, C., Varadharajan, V., Wang, Y. and Pruthi, V. (2004a). Enhancing grid security with trust management, *Proceedings. 2004 IEEE International Conference on Service Computing* , pp. 303–310.

Lin, C., Vardhrajan, V. and Wang, Y. (2004b). Enhancing grid security with trust management, *Proceedings of the IEEE International Conference on Services Computing* , pp. 303–310.

Lin, C. H. (1997). Dynamic key management schemes for access control in a hierarchy, *Computer Communications* **20**, pp. 1381–1385.

Lin, M. S., Chen, M. S., Chen, D. J. and Ku, K. L. (1997). The distributed program reliability analysis on ring-type topologies, *Computers and Operations Research* , pp. 225–131.

Liu, D., Ning, P. and Sun, K. (2003). Efficient self-healing group key distribution with revocation capability, in *CCS '03: Proceedings of the 10th ACM conference on Computer and communications security* (ACM Press, New York, NY, USA), ISBN 1-58113-738-9, pp. 231–240, doi:http://doi.acm.org/10.1145/948109.948141.

Livny, M. and Raman, R. (1998). High-throughput resource management, in the grid: Blueprint for a new computing infrastructure, *Morgan-Kaufmann* , pp. 311–338.

Mackinnon, S. T., Taylor, P. D., Meijer, H. and Akl, S. G. (1985). An optimal algorithm for assigning cryptographic keys to control access in a hierarchy, *IEEE Transactions on Computers* **34**, 9, pp. 797–802.

Mahajan, R., Bellovin, S. M., Floyd, S., Ioannidis, J., Paxson, V. and Shenker, S. (2001). Aggregate-based congestion control, URL citeseer.ist.psu.edu/530614.html.

Menezes, A., Ooschot, P. V. and Vanstone, S. (eds.) (1996). *Handbook of applied cryptography* (CRC Press, Inc., Boca Raton, Florida, USA), ISBN 0-262-22030-X.

Meyer, J. (1997). On evaluating the performability of degradable computing systems, *IEEE Transactions on Computers* , pp. 225–131.

Mirkovic, J., Dietrich, S., Dittrich, D. and Reiher, P. (2004). *Internet Denial of Service: Attack and Defense Mechanisms* (Prentice Hall, Upper Saddle River, NJ, USA), ISBN 0131475738.

Mirkovic, J. and Reiher, P. (2005). D-WARD: a source-end defense against flooding denial-of-service attacks, *IEEE Transactions on Dependable and Secure Computing* **2**, 3, pp. 216–232.

Mirkovic, J., Robinson, M., Reiher, P. and Kuenning, G. (2003). Alliance formation for ddos defense, *Proceedings of the New Security Paradigms Workshop*, pp. 11–18.

Missing-Author (2003). Is it the cure? *Economist* .

Mittra, S. (1997a). Iolus: A framework for scalable secure multicasting, *Journal of Computer Communication Reviews* **27**, 4, pp. 277–288.

Mittra, S. (1997b). Iolus a framework for scalable secure multicasting, in *Journal of Computer Communication Reviews*, Vol. 27, pp. 277–288.

More, S. M., Malkin, M., Staddon, J. and Balfanz, D. (2003). Sliding-window self-healing key distribution, in *SSRS '03: Proceedings of the workshop on Survivable and self-regenerative systems in ACM CCS 2003* (ACM Press, New York, NY, USA), ISBN 1-58113-784-2, pp. 82–90, doi:http://doi.acm.org/10.1145/1036921.1036930.

Moyer, M. J. and Ahamad, M. (2001). Generalized role-based access control, *The IEEE 21st International Conference on Distributed Computing Systems* , pp. 0391–0396.

Mutz, D., Valeur, F. and Vigna, G. (2006). Anomalous system call detection, *ACM Transactions on Information and System Security* **9**, 1, pp. 61–93.

Nabrzyski, J., Schopf, J. M. and Weglarz, J. (eds.) (2003). *The Grid Resource Management* (Kluwer Publishing).

Ng, W. H. D., Howarth, M., Sun, Z. and Cruickshank, H. (2007). Dynamic balanced key tree management for secure multicast communications, *IEEE Transactions on Computers* **56**, 5, pp. 577–589.

Noubir, G. (1998). Multicast security, *European Space Agency, Project: Performance Optimization of Internet Protocol Via Satellite* .

Novotny, J., Tuecke, S. and Welch, V. (2001). An online credential repository for the grid: Myproxy, *Proceedings of the Tenth IEEE International Symposium on High performance Distributed Computing (HPDC-10)* , p. 0104.

Park, J. S. and Hwang, J. (2003). RBAC for collaborative environments: Role-based access control for collaborative enterprise in peer-to-peer computing environments, *Proceedings of the eighth ACM symposium on Access control models and technologies* , pp. 93–99.

Patrikakis, C., Masikos, M. and Zouraraki, O. (2004). Distributed denial of service attacks, *The Internet Protocol Journal* **7**, 4, pp. 1–10.

Paxson, V. (1999). Bro: A system for detecting network intruders in real-time, *Computer Networks* **31**, 23-24, pp. 2435–2463.

Pegueroles, J. and Rico-Novella, F. (2003). Balanced batch lkh: New proposal, implementation and performance evalution, *Proc. IEEE Symp. Computers and Comm. (ISCC)* , pp. 815–820.

Pez, R., Satizbal, C. and Forn, J. (2006). Cooperative itinerant agents (cia): Security scheme for intrusion detection systems, *International Conference on Internet Surveillance and Protection* , pp. 26–31.

Pfleeger, C. and Pfleeger, S. L. (eds.) (2003). *Security in Computing* (Third Ed. Prentice Hall, Upper Saddle River, NJ), ISBN 0-13-035548-8.

Pham, H. (ed.) (2000). *Software Reliability* (Springer-Verlag, Singapore).

Pietro, R., Mancini, L. and Jajodia, S. (2002). Efficient and secure keys management for wireless mobile communications, in *Proceedings of the second ACM international workshop on Principles of mobile computing*, pp. 66–73, iSBN: 1-58113-511-4.

Power, D., Politou, E., Slaymaker, M. and Simpson, A. (2006). Securing web services for deployment in health grids, *Future Generation Computer Systems* **22**, 5, pp. 547–570.

Rafaeli, S. and Hutchison, D. (2002). Hydra: A decentralized group key management, *Proceedings of 11th IEEE International WETICE: Enterprise Security Workshop* .

Ramakrishnan, L. (2004). Securing next-generation grids, *IEEE IT Professional* **6**, 2, pp. 34–39.

Ray, I., Ray, I. and Narasimhamurthi, N. (2002a). A cryptographic solution to implement access control in a hierarchy and more, in *SACMAT '02: Proceedings of the seventh ACM symposium on Access control models and technologies* (ACM Press), ISBN 1-58113-496-7, pp. 65–73.

Ray, I., Ray, I. and Narasimhamurthi, N. (2002b). cryptographic solution to implement access control in a hierarchy and more, *ACM Symposium on Access Control Models and Technologies* , pp. 199–205.

Rodeh, O., Birman, K. and Dolev, D. (2000). Optimized group re-key for group communication systems, *In Network and Distributed System Security, CA, USA* .

Sandhu, R. S. (1988). Cryptographic implementation of a tree hierarchy for access control, *Information Processing Letters* **27**, pp. 95–98.

Sandhu, R. S. (1993). Lattice-based access control model, *IEEE Computer* **26**, 11, pp. 9–19.

Sandhu, R. S., Coyne, E. J., Feinstein, H. L. and Youman, C. E. (1994). Role-based access control: a multi-dimensional view, *Proceedings of 10th Annual Security Application Conference. Orlando, Florida* , pp. 54–62.

Sandhu, R. S., Coyne, E. J., Feinstein, H. L. and Youman, C. E. (1996). Role-based access control models, *IEEE Computer* **29**, 2, pp. 38–47.

Sandhu, R. S. and Samarati, P. (1994). Access control: principle and practice, *IEEE Communications Magazine* **32**, 9, pp. 40–48.

Santis, A. D., Ferrara, A. and Masucci, B. (2004). Cryptographic key assignment schemes for any access control policy, *Information Processing Letters* **92**, 4, pp. 199–205.

Savage, S., Wetherall, D., Karlin, A. and Anderson, T. (2000). Practical network support for IP traceback, in *SIGCOMM '00: Proceedings of the conference on Applications, Technologies, Architectures, and Protocols for Computer Communication* (ACM Press, New York, NY, USA), ISBN 1-58113-223-9, pp. 295–306, doi:http://doi.acm.org/10.1145/347059.347560.

Schneider, R. (2006). IUPUI computer scientists develop revolutionary medical information system, *http://www.iupui.edu/news/releases/060222_med_info_system.htm* .

Sekar, R., Gupta, A., Frullo, J., Shanbhag, T., Tiwari, A., Yang, H. and Zhou, S. (2002). Specification-based anomaly detection: a new approach for detecting network intrusions, in *CCS '02: Proceedings of the 9th ACM conference on Computer and communications security* (ACM Press, New York, NY, USA), ISBN 1-58113-612-9, pp. 265–274, doi:http://doi.acm.org/10.1145/586110.586146.

Setia, S., Koussih, S. and Jajodia, S. (2000). Kronos: A scalable group re-keying approach for secure multicast, *Proceedings of IEEE Symposium on Security and Privacy* .

Shamir, A. (1979a). How to share a secret, *Communication of ACM* **22**, pp. 612–613.

Shamir, A. (1979b). How to share a secret, *Communications of ACM* **22**, pp. 612–613.

Shen, V. R. L. and Chen, T.-S. (2002). A novel key management scheme based on discrete logarithms and polynomial interpolations, *Computers and Security* **21**, 2, pp. 164–171.

Sherman, A. T. and McGrew, D. A. (2003). Key establishment in large dynamic groups using one-way function trees, *IEEE transactions on Software Engineering* **29**, 5, pp. 444–458.

Silberschatz, A., Galvin, P. B. and Gagne, G. (2001). *Operating System Concepts, Sixth Ed.* (John Wiley & Sons, Inc., Indianapolis, IN), ISBN 0-471-41743-2.

Snapp, S. R., Brentano, J., Dias, G. V., Goan, T. L., Heberlein, L. T., lin Ho, C., Levitt, K. N., Mukherjee, B., Smaha, S. E., Grance, T., Teal, D. M. and Mansur, D. (1991). DIDS (distributed intrusion detection system) - motivation, architecture, and an early prototype, in *Proceedings of the 14th National Computer Security Conference* (Washington, DC), pp. 167–176, URL citeseer.ist.psu.edu/snapp91dids.html.

Snoeren, A. C. (2001). Hash-based ip traceback, in *SIGCOMM '01: Proceedings of the 2001 conference on Applications, technologies, architectures, and protocols for computer communications* (ACM Press, New York, NY, USA), ISBN 1-58113-411-8, pp. 3–14, doi:http://doi.acm.org/10.1145/383059.383060.

Specht, S. M. and Lee, R. B. (2004). Distributed denial of service: Taxonomies of attacks, tools and countermeasures, *Proceedings of the 17th International Conference on Parallel and Distributed Computing Systems and International Workshop on Security in Parallel and Distributed Systems* , pp. 543–550.

Spitzner, L. (2003). The honeynet project: trapping the hackers, *IEEE Security and Privacy Magazine* **1**, 2, pp. 15–23.

Staddon, J., Miner, S., Franklin, M., Balfanz, D., Malkin, M. and Dean, D. (2002). Self-healing key distribution with revocation capability, in *SP '02: Proceedings of the 2002 IEEE Symposium on Security and Privacy* (IEEE Computer Society, Washington, DC, USA), ISBN 0-7695-1543-6, p. 241.

Stayrou, A., Cook, D. L., Morein, W. D., Keromytis, A. D., Misra, V. and Rubenstein, D. (2005). WebSOS: an overlay-based system for protecting web servers from denial of service attacks, *Computer Networks* **48**, 5, pp. 781–807.

Stillerman, M., Marceau, C. and Stillman, M. (1999). Intrusion detection for distributed applications, *Communications of the ACM Vol. 42* , pp. 62–69.

Stinson, D. R. (ed.) (1995). *Cryptography: Theory and Practice* (CRC Press, Inc., Boca Raton, Florida, USA), ISBN 0-262-22030-X.

Strayer, W. T., Jones, C. E., Tchakountio, F. and Hain, R. R. (2004). SPIE-IPv6: Single IPv6 packet traceback, *Proceedings of 29th Annual IEEE International Conference on Local Computer Networks* , pp. 118–125.

Sun, B., Wu, K. and Pooch, U. W. (2003). Alert aggregation in mobile ad hoc networks, *Proceedings of the 2003 ACM workshop on Wireless security* , pp. 69–78.

Sun, Y. and Liu, K. J. R. (2004). Scalable hierarchical access control in secure group communications, *proceedings of IEEE INFOCOM* **2**, pp. 1296–1306.

Sung, M. and Xu, J. (2003). Ip traceback-based intelligent packet filtering: A novel technique for defending against internet ddos attacks, *Proc. IEEE Trans. Parallel and Distributed Systems* **14**, 9, pp. 861–872.

Sy, D. and Bao, L. (2006). Captra: coordinated packet traceback, in *IPSN '06: Proceedings of the fifth international conference on Information processing in sensor networks* (ACM Press, New York, NY, USA), ISBN 1-59593-334-4, pp. 152–159, doi:http://doi.acm.org/10.1145/1127777.1127803.

Tai, A., Meyer, J. and Avizienis, A. (1980). Performability enhancement of fault-tolerant software, *IEEE Transactions on Reliability* **42**, 2, pp. 227–237.

Tai, A., Meyer, J. and Avizienis, A. (1993). Performability enhancement of fault-tolerant software, *IEEE Transactions on Reliability* **42**, 2, pp. 227–237.

Tanachaiwiwat, S. and Hwang, K. (2003). Differential packet filtering against ddos flood attacks, *ACM Conference on Computer and Communications Security (CCS)* .

Thomas, R., Zhu, H., Huck, T. and Johnson, T. (2003). Netbouncer: Client-legitimacy-based high-performance ddos filtering, *Proceedings of DARPA Information Survivability Conference and Exposition* **2**, pp. 111–121.

Thompson, T. and Brailer, D. (2004). Health it strategic framework, *DHHS, Washington, DC* .

Tolone, W., Ahn, G.-J., Pai, T. and Hong, S. (2005). Access control in collaborative systems, *ACM Computing Surveys* **37**, 1, pp. 29–41.

Tripunitara, M. V. and Li, N. (2004). Access control: Comparing the expressive power of access control models, *Proceedings of the 11th ACM conference on Computer and communications security* , pp. 62–71.

Tzeng, W. (2002). A time-bound cryptographic key assignment scheme for access control in a hierarchy, *IEEE Transactions on Knowledge and Data Engineering* **14**, 1, pp. 182–188.

Uppuluri, P. and Sekar, R. (2001). Experiences with specification-based intrusion detection, *Proceedings of 4th International Symposium on Recent Advances in Intrusion Detection (RAID)* , pp. 172–180.

Wagner, D. and Soto, P. (2002). Mimicry attacks on host-based intrusion detection systems, *Proceedings of the 9th ACM conference on Computer and communications security* , pp. 255–264.

Walfish, M., Vutukuru, M., Balakrishnan, H., Karger, D. and Shenker, S. (2006). Ddos defense by offense, *SIGCOMM* , pp. 303–314.

Wallner, D., Harder, E. and Agee, R. (1998). Key management for multicast: Issues and architectures, *Internet Draft (work in progress), draft-wallner-key-arch-01.txt, Internet Eng. Task Force* .

Wang, H., Zhang, D. and Shin, K. G. (2002). Detecting SYN flooding attacks, *Proceedings of IEEE INFOCOM* **3**, pp. 1530–1539.

Wang, S. Y. and Laih, C. S. (2005). Cryptanalyses of two key assignment schemes based on polynomial interpolations, *Computers and Security* **24**, pp. 134–138.

WebSite (2006). The team cymru bogon reference page, *http:// www.cymru.com/Bogons/* .

Welch, V., Siebenlist, F., Foster, I., Bresnahan, J., Czajkowski, K., Gawor, J., Kesselman, C., Meder, S., Pearlman, L. and Tuecke, S. (2003). Security for grid services, *Proceedings of 12th IEEE International Symposium on High Performance Distributed Computing* , pp. 48–57.

Wong, C. K., Gouda, M. and Lam, S. S. (1998). Secure group communications using key graphs, *SIGCOMM '98, Also University of Texas at Austin, Computer Science Technical report TR 97-23* , pp. 68–79.

Wong, C. K., Gouda, M. and Lam, S. S. (2000). Secure group communications using key graphs, *IEEE/ACM Transactions on Networks* **8**, 1, pp. 16–30.

Wool, A. (2000). Key management for encrypted broadcast, *ACM Transactions on Information and System Security* **3**, 2, pp. 107–134.

Wu, T. C. and Chang, C. C. (2001). Cryptographic key assignment scheme for hierarchical access control, *International Journal of Computer Systems Science and Engineering* **1**, 1, pp. 25–28.

Xie, M. (ed.) (1991). *Software Reliability Modeling* (World Scientific Publishing Company).

Xie, M., Dai, Y. S. and Poh, K. L. (eds.) (2004). *Computing Systems Reliability: Models and Analysis* (Kluwer Academic Publishers, New York, NY, U.S.A).

Yaar, A., Perrig, A. and Song, D. (2003). Pi: A path identification mechanism to defend against ddos attacks, *IEEE Symposium on Security and Privacy*, pp. 93–107.

Yaar, A., Perrig, A. and Song, D. (2004). Siff: A stateless internet flow filter to mitigate ddos flooding attacks, *IEEE Symposium on Security and Privacy*, pp. 130–143.

Yaar, A., Perrig, A. and Song, D. (2006). StackPi: New packet marking and filtering mechanisms for ddos and ip spoofing defense, *IEEE Journal on Selected Areas in Communications* **24**, 10, pp. 1853–1863.

Ye, N. (2000). A markov chain model of temporal behavior for anomaly detection, *IEEE Workshop on Information Assurance and Security* , pp. 171–174.

Yi, X. (2005). Security of chien's efficient time-bound hierarchical key assignment scheme, *IEEE Transactions on Knowledge and Data Engineering* **17**, 9, pp. 1298–1299.

Yi, X. and Ye, Y. (2003). Security of tzeng's time-bound key assignment scheme for access control in a hierarchy, *IEEE Transactions on Knowledge and Data Engineering* **15**, 4, pp. 1054–1055.

Zhang, S. and Dasgupta, P. (2003). Denying denial-of service attacks: a router based solution, *International Conference on Internet Computing* .

Zhang, X. B., Lam, S. S., Lee, D.-Y. and Yang, Y. R. (2001). Protocol design for scalable and reliable group rekeying, *Proceedings SPIE Conference on Scalability and Traffic Control in IP Networks* , pp. 87–108.

Zhang, Y., Lee, W. and Huang, Y. (2003). Intrusion detection techniques for mobile wireless networks, *Wireless Networks Vol. 9* , pp. 545–556.

Zhicai, S., Zhenzhou, J. and Mingzeng, H. (2004). A novel distributed intrusion detection model based on mobile agent, *InfoSecu '04: Proceedings of the 3rd international conference on Information security* , pp. 155–159.

Zhong, S. (2002). A practical key management scheme for access control in a user hierarchy, *Computers and Security* **21**, 8, pp. 750–759.

Zhou, Q., Yang, G., Shen, J. and Rong, C. (2005). A scalable security architecture for grid, *Proceedings of the Sixth International Conference on Parallel and Distributed Computing Applications and Technologies* , pp. 89–93.

Zhu, S., Setia, S. and Jajodia, S. (2003). Adding reliable and self-healing key distribution to the subset difference group rekeying method, *Lecture Notes in Computer Science (LNCS), Springer-Verlag* **2816**, pp. 107–118.

Zou, X., Dai, Y. and Ran, X. (2007). Dual-level key management for secure grid communication in dynamic and hierarchical groups, *Future Generation of Computer Systems (in press)* .

Zou, X., Magliveras, S. and Ramamurthy, B. (2002a). A dynamic conference scheme extension with efficient burst operation, *Congressus Numerantium* **158**, pp. 83–92.

Zou, X., Magliveras, S. and Ramamurthy, B. (2004a). Key tree based scalable secure dynamic conferencing schemes, *Proceedings of International Conference on Parallel and Distributed Computing and Systems (PDCS 2004), MIT Cambridge, MA, USA, November 9-11* , pp. 61–66.

Zou, X., Ramamurthy, B. and Magliveras, S. (2001). Chinese Remainder Theorem based hierarchical access control for secure group communications, *Lecture Notes in Computer Science (LNCS), Springer-Verlag (International Conference on Information and Communication Security)* **2229**, pp. 381–385.

Zou, X., Ramamurthy, B. and Magliveras, S. (2002b). Efficient key management for secure group communication with bursty behavior, *Proceedings of International Conference on Communication, Internet, and Information Technology (CIIT)* , pp. 148–153.

Zou, X., Ramamurthy, B. and Magliveras, S. S. (eds.) (2004b). *Secure Group Communications over Data Networks* (Springer, Norwell, MA), ISBN 978-0-387-22970-6.

Index

(Probabilistic) IP Packet Marking,
122

dual level key management, 175

Access Control Polynomial, 197
access control polynomial, 175
Access Polynomial, 79
access polynomial, 71
ACP, 175, 197
Aggregate Operation, 18
Anomaly modeling, 95, 100–102
AP, 79
Asymmetric Cryptosystem, 6
Attempted break-in, 96
Attempted break-ins, 95

backward secrecy, 181
Bijection, 6
Bogon Filtering, 129
Botnet, 111
Bulk Operation, 18
Bursty Operation, 18

CAPTCHA, 135
CHAC, 63, 71
Chargen Attack, 109
Ciphertext, 7
Ciphertext Space, 7
Collision Resistant, 4
Communicant, 8
Completely Automated Public Turing

test to Tell Computers and
Humans Apart, 135
Complexity, 5
Space Complexity, 5
Time Complexity, 5
Computational Security, 4
Computationally Infeasible, 7
Computationally Secure, 4
Congruence, 6
CRT, 3, 6
Cryptographic Hash Function, 3, 4
Cryptography based Hierarchical
Access Control, 63, 71
Cyclic Multiplicative Group, 5

D-Ward, 130
Data Mining Modeling, 103
DDoS, 110
Botnet, 111
Zombie, 110
DDoS Tool
Mstream, 114
Phatbot, 115
Shaft, 114
Stracheldraht German, 114
TFN, 113
TFN2K, 114
Tribe Flood Network, 113
Tribe Flood Network 2000, 114
Trinity, 115
Trino, 113
Decryption Rule, 8

Virus, 97

WinNuke, 109

Zombie, 110